POLICING CYBER HATE, CYBER THREATS AND CYBER TERRORISM

T0299841

This work is dedicated to Sobia, Hiba, Shereen, Tasvir, and Liz, our beloved family members, who have supported us so well and forgiven us for the time we missed with our families whilst editing this text.
Imran and Brian

Policing Cyber Hate, Cyber Threats and Cyber Terrorism

Edited By
IMRAN AWAN AND BRIAN BLAKEMORE
University of Glamorgan, UK

Routledge
Taylor & Francis Group

LONDON AND NEW YORK

First published 2012 by Ashgate Publishing

Published 2016 by Routledge
2 Park Square, Milton Park, Abingdon, Oxfordshire OX14 4RN
711 Third Avenue, New York, NY 10017, USA

First issued in paperback 2016

Routledge is an imprint of the Taylor & Francis Group, an informa business

British Library Cataloguing in Publication Data
Policing cyber hate, cyber threats and cyber terrorism.
  1. Cyberterrorism. 2. Cyberterrorism – Prevention.
  I. Awan, Imran. II. Blakemore, Brian.
  363.3'25-dc23

Library of Congress Cataloging-in-Publication Data
Policing cyber hate, cyber threats and cyber terrorism / edited by Imran
Awan and Brian Blakemore.
    p. cm.
  Includes bibliographical references and index.
  ISBN 978-1-4094-3816-8 (hbk. : alk. paper)
  1. Cyberterrorism. 2. Computer crimes. 3. Hate crimes. I. Awan, Imran.
  II Blakemore, Brian.
  HV6773.15.C97P65 2011
  363.3250285'4678—dc23

                                                              2011048770

ISBN 13: 978-1-138-25458-9 (pbk)
ISBN 13: 978-1-4094-3816-8 (hbk)

Contents

List of Figures

List of Tables

Notes on Contributors

Mr Imran Awan is a senior lecturer at the Centre for Police Sciences at the University of Glamorgan. He has taught on a variety of awards and modules such as International Police Duties and Law, Criminal Law and Criminal Justice, Terrorism, Law and Policy, and Violent Extremism and Terrorism. He has written numerous articles in the area of counter-terrorism, human rights and police powers and is the author of 'Terror in the Eye of the Beholder: The 'Spy Cam' Saga in Birmingham: Counter-Terrorism or Counter-productive?' published in *The Howard Journal of Criminal Justice*. In 2010, he was invited as a keynote speaker in the 'Combating Cyber terrorism, Online Crime and Law' series, by the School of Law at the University of Derby, [Available at: http://www.derby.ac.uk/news/combating-cyber-terrorism-and-online-crime; http://www.derby.ac.uk/news/laying-down-the-law] where he discussed counter-terrorism policy in relation to cyber terrorism. In March 2010 he was invited by the Office for Security and Counter-Terrorism to a Prevent Seminar held in London to discuss government policy on how to prevent violent extremism. He is currently involved in a research project that examines the impact of counter-terrorism legislation upon Muslim families in Cardiff. His areas of expertise include the study of extremism and radicalisation over the Internet, policing minority communities, the impact of counter-terrorist legislation upon Muslim families, policing in Pakistan and policing Pakistani gangs and culture. He is also a Fellow of the Higher Education Academy.

Mr Brian Blakemore is Head of the Police Sciences Division at the University of Glamorgan. Brian had previous experience on a wide range of academic awards with several academic management positions during his previous 26 years within this institution. Brian teaches on modules such as Science for Law Enforcement, Crime Investigation, Researching Police Practice and Researching Contemporary Issues. He has published on cognitive processes in investigation, Higher Education for police officers and professionalising the police force, the human rights aspects and investigative effectiveness of the national DNA database, and has co-edited three texts with Dr Colin Rogers on community and partnership working. Brian has also taught on several postgraduate programmes, often distance programmes, with the universities of Bradford, Bristol and Bath and also with Bristol Management centre. He is a vice chair of the Higher Education Forum for Learning and Development in Policing and represents this forum on the NPIA HE framework Steering Group.

Mr Geoff Coliandris is a former South Wales Police inspector, having served for 29 years in a range of posts including operational response, community safety and training. His police service included three periods of secondment to national police training bodies as well as project head/team leader roles at force level. He joined the university in 2006 as a part-time lecturer and has taught several modules on the Police Sciences degree award, including Police Duties and Law and Strategic Management in the Police Service. He has also taught on Foundation Studies Practical Skills for Police Officers and Foundation Degree (Leadership) modules. He has published (with Dr Colin Rogers) on police culture and leadership, partnerships and counter-terrorism and, most recently, police reform. He is also the author of a postgraduate diploma module on 'extremism' offered by the university as part of its Master's degree programme in Community and Partnerships.

Mr James Gravelle has previously worked for the University of Glamorgan as a consultant and research assistant (RA), and has carried out research on behalf of South Wales and Gwent Police Service. Research for the police included work on Tasking Demand Management Units (TDMUs), community intelligence, the use of volunteers and knowledge management. More recently, James now works within the division of Police Sciences as an associate lecturer and research officer. As an Associate of the Higher Education Academy, James has been involved in planning, writing and development of material within higher education on such areas as 'policing in the big society', 'knowledge management', 'policing in the financial crisis' 'the use of intelligence' and 'the impact of terrorism on policing'. As a Welsh-speaker, James also designs and delivers modules and material through the medium of Welsh. James has published many articles, papers and chapters in books over recent years aimed at both national and international audiences. James has given several radio and television interviews in relation to high profile police events and commenting on policing procedures and the impact of the economic situation of the delivery of policing services both in English and in Welsh. Being a member of many societies and groups such as the British Society of Criminology, and the European Society of Criminology, James also regularly attends and presents at national and European conferences on policing.

Dr Jane Prince is a Chartered Psychologist and Principal Lecturer in the School of Psychology at the University of Glamorgan where she is course tutor for two MSc awards; she has a particular research interest in identity, social identity and the ways in which individuals respond to threats and challenges to their identity positions. She has published on identity threats across the lifespan, identity issues in migration and social identity. Dr Prince's PhD research was on the challenges to identity experienced by policewomen; she has studied in Cardiff, London and Bordeaux and has worked in the UK, France and the Netherlands.

Mr Tim Read joined the University of Glamorgan in December 2007 and is now award leader for the Master's degree in Community and Partnerships. Previously he was Senior Research Consultant for Evidence-Led Solutions, a research consultancy working in the community safety field. Between 2001 and the end of 2005 he was a Senior Lecturer and Programme Leader for the Community Safety and Crime Prevention Master's degree course at the University of the West of England, Bristol. Prior to taking up the post at UWE he worked for the Research and Statistics Directorate of the Home Office for over 8 years, starting as a Research Officer, ending as a Principal Research Officer. He has extensive research and evaluation experience with the police and other criminal justice agencies and has published widely. He has just co-authored a book entitled *Policing and Young People* with Dr Colin Rogers.

Dr Colin Rogers is a former police inspector with South Wales Police with 30 years' service and joined the university full time in 2004, having taught as a part-time lecturer in criminology since 1997. His areas of expertise include community safety partnerships, situational crime prevention, problem oriented partnerships and also police governance and accountability. He is responsible for Research Study in the Division and is also responsible for developing postgraduate courses. The author of numerous articles on policing, he is also the author of four books, namely *Crime Reduction Partnerships* (2006), *Introduction to Police Work* (with Rhobert Lewis) (2007), *Leadership Skills in Policing* (2008), *Police Work: Principles and Practice*, (2011), (with Rob Lewis, Tim Read and Tim John) and has co-authored a series of three books with Brian Blakemore entitled *Problem Oriented Partnerships:* A Reader; (2009) *Crime Analysis and Evaluation:* A Reader; (2009) and *Community Safety: A Reader* (2009). He has just co-authored a book entitled *Policing and Young People with Tim Read*. Dr Rogers was awarded the title of Reader in Police Sciences in June 2010 in recognition for his research and scholarly activities.

Introduction

This text aims to bring together a diverse range of multidisciplinary ideas to explore the extent of cyber hate, cyber threat and cyber terrorism: studying its development, the present situation and look to the future of the forms and ability to police cyber hate, cyber threat and cyber terrorism. This text is designed to be a 'one stop shop' for all these aspects of cyber threat, cyber hate and cyber terrorism. The text will look at the psychology of potential cyber terrorists, the journey into cyber terrorism, the use of cyberspace by terrorists, the formation of cyber terrorist groups, the definitions of cyber terrorism will also be analysed and discussed, national legislation and international treaties and legislation will be critiqued in terms of effectiveness to combat the problems posed by cyber terrorism, the use of knowledge within the police and security services and how this may be marshalled to prevent and counter cyber terrorism. Also intelligence-led policing will be examined, the national strategies proposed by UK and other governments will be reviewed and their effectiveness examined. A final chapter will draw on all the preceding work to speculate on the future of policing cyber hate, cyber threats, and cyber terrorism. This is not an encyclopaedia but is more than an introduction and references and further reading are provided for the reader.

The text includes a study of the behaviour and motivations of cyber terrorists. The legal frameworks and legislation regarding cyber terrorism and its limitations in an international setting will be analysed. The public perceptions and understanding of cyber terrorism is also explored as is the policing and the threat of overreaction and working with communities to prevent development into terrorism. The main aim is to give a full understanding of the range of activities that form the spectrum of cyber threat, cyber hate to cyber terrorism; how such activity forms in our communities and what can be done to try to prevent individuals from becoming cyber terrorists.

There has been very little literature in this area as many academics have been trying to tackle what is cyber espionage and cyber attacks by state-sponsored governments so this book will provide a key insight into what the government regards as the main threat to UK security by making a contribution to this area of work. The text is multi-faceted as it covers the origins of cyber terrorism, how far it dates back and why we have missed a great opportunity in dealing with the problem. The book will give a policing rationale alongside specific e-crime units yet providing key details for policy readers as well as academics and students of this area.

The text may be considered to have two sections: the early chapters look at the background areas such as the concept of cyberspace and how it provides a platform for cyber hate, cyber threat and cyber terrorism, definitions of these terms and analysis of the type of person likely to be recruited into activist groups and the methods used to recruit such individuals. Global networks of cyber criminals and cyber terrorists are creating new challenges for attorneys, judges, law enforcement agents, forensic examiners and corporate security professionals (Casey 2004:1) who are trying to find 'the balance between the need to maintain order online and the need to enforce the law' (Wakefield and Fleming 2009: 77). Sheldon and Wright state 'that cyber-security has become a national security issue' (2010: 10) that needs to be addressed. Ball and Webster (2003) argue that following the 9/11 attacks a massive expansion of security-surveillance capacities around the globe ensued. There was also an accompanying set of legislative powers such as the 'Patriot Act' in the USA which Roy (2004) describes as ushering in an automatic systematic of surveillance with the government using the powers to monitor phones, emails and computer use in general. While technology can aid prevention and detection of cyber crime, there have been notable design flaws, and aspects such as privacy and human rights issues need to be addressed. It can be appreciated that one piece of technology cannot be expected to be the 'silver bullet' of any specific form of cyber crime or cyber terrorism, and technology is double-edged enabling the criminal or terrorist as well as having a role in policing such activities. No security system can be considered impregnable to terrorist attacks such as a terrorist groups obtaining access to computers and hiding malicious software within them that then allows the computers to be controlled remotely (zombie computers). The necessary addresses to access such a set of zombie computers is called a botnet and again malicious software can be used to create such a botnet. The psychology relating to hate, terrorism and cyber hate and cyber terrorism is explored as well as an examination of the wider theories that relate to cyber crimes, such as social identity theory, social influence, the social identity model of de-individuation effects (side) and selective moral disengagement. The recruitment of individuals who are likely to become deployable agents ready to commit atrocities for the cause follows well-established patterns and processes and the use of the Internet enables activists to magnify the propaganda effect of their argument and to phish for suitable individuals. The amplification of the propaganda effect online is analysed using the terror management theory. Cyber hate is a phenomenon exhibiting multiple dimensions with hate-groups achieving their goals in four main ways: promoting ideology, promoting hatred of other racial or religious groups, exerting control over others and targeting opponents. The paradox of connectivity in relation to cyber hate is discussed.

The second section is concerned with policing this cyber activity and looks at the processes used to effectively combine data of many forms, from conversations on the street or networking sites, to police records of crime and criminals and biometric databases. The ability and desire to share of data and knowledge amongst the many agencies that need to work in partnership to prevent and catch cyber terrorists is examined. The level of need for more international cooperation and legislation to combat a global network of activists is explored. Finally we consider the overall position in relation to policing these cyber activities. However, there are many questions on the best way to tackle cyber terrorism and ultimately whose responsibility it is to tackle it. The 'sheer volume of material generated, the global scope of the problem and the difficulty in applying laws to criminal activities across geographical boundaries' (Jewkes and Yar 2003:592), became apparent and an understanding surfaced that the 'scope, scale and structure of the Internet outstrips the capacity of any single enforcement or regulatory body' (Wall 2007:167). In response the UK government decided to restructure its cyber policing and formulate 'E-crime Strategy' in 2008, that aimed to coordinate local and international responses to cyber crimes through coordinated strategies and proactive responses. National and international strategies to deal with cyber terrorism need to be strengthened. Lenk (1997) comments that jurisdictional issues surrounding cyber crime go far beyond 'legal loopholes exposed within countries' (Slevin 2000:214), such as, 'double criminality', where a 'cyber criminal' cannot be extradited or charged for a crime committed in another country 'unless it constitutes a crime according to the laws of both the requesting and the requested states' (Shearer 1971:137). The scale and complexity of cyber crimes has compelled 'police partnerships with banks, telecommunication providers' (Broadhurst 2006:416) and with private security industries (PSIs) in order to tackle cyber crimes in an economic way. One possible model is the creation of private–public partnerships where private organisations would fund the monitoring of the Internet and breakdown 'raw' cyber crime data, and the public would pay for the arrest and prosecution of 'cyber criminals by their existing police service'. Even if strategies are agreed, implementation may fail if businesses or organisations are relied upon to implement them, if they are overwhelmed by costs or if it results in loss of convenience and reliability for the product, as noted by Burns and Weir (cited Jahankhani et al. 2008).Young (2009) suggests that 'the cost to industry and individuals of electronically assisted crime may have already far outstretched that of physical crime' (Eurim 2002:5) and as such the police must solely 'bear the brunt' of any cyber crime response because private organisations and ordinary citizens simply do not have the resources, time or money.

References

Ball, K. and Webster, F. (eds). 2003. *The Intensification of Surveillance: Crime, Warfare and Terrorism in the Information Age*. London: Pluto Press.

Broadhurst, R. 2006. 'Developments in the global law enforcement of cyber crime policing', *International Journal of Police Strategies and Management*, 29 (3), 408–33.

Jahankhani, H., Revett, R. and Palmer-Brown, D., 2008. *Global e-security: 4th International Conference, ICGeS 2008*. [e-book]. Germany: Springer. [Online]. Available at: http://books.google.co.uk/books?id=oeaTCy1Qaq4C&pg=PA 40&dq=uk+card+fraud+capital+of+europe#v=onepage&q=uk%20card%20 fraud%20capital %20of %20europe&f=false [accessed: 25 October 2010].

Casey, E. 2004. *Digital Evidence and Computer Crime: Forensic Science, Computers and the Internet*. San Diego: Academic Press.

EURIM. 2002. The European Information Society Group. *E-crime – A new opportunity of partnership briefing paper*, France: EURIM.

Jewkes, Y. and Yar, M. 2003. 'Policing Cybercrime: Emerging Trends and Future Challenges', in *Handbook of Policing*, edited by Newburn, T. Cullompton: Willan.

Lenk, K. 1997. 'The Challenge of Cyber Spatial Forms of Human Interaction to Territorial Governance and Policing', in *The Governance of Cyberspace: Politics, Technology and Global Restructuring*, edited by Loader, B. London: Routledge, 126–35.

Roy, A. 2004. *An Ordinary Person's Guide to Empire*. Cambridge MA: South End Press.

Shearer, I. 1971. *Extradition in International Law*. Manchester: Manchester University Press.

Sheldon, B. and Wright, P. 2010. *Policing and Technology*. Exeter: Learning Matters.

Slevin, J. 2000. *The Internet and Society*. London: Routledge.

Wakefield, A. and Fleming, J. 2009. *The Sage Dictionary of Policing*. London: Sage.

Wall, D. 2007. *Cybercrime*. Cambridge: Polity.

Young, T. 2009. *Foiling a Thoroughly Modern Bank Heist*. [Online]. Available at: http://news.cnet.com/8301–1009_3–10152246–83.htm [accessed: 17 October 2010].

Chapter 1
Cyberspace, Cyber Crime and Cyber Terrorism

Brian Blakemore

The terminology and concepts of cyberspace, cyber hate, cyber threats, cyber terrorism and policing need to be carefully defined. This chapter will examine how Cyberspace in particular lends itself to all these activities and assemble analogies from the wider field of cyber crime about which there is more information in the public domain. Initially the phrase cyber terrorism will be used in its broadest sense, recognising that it is the least well-defined of these terms. A full discussion of what cyber terrorism is and whether an activity is cyber hate, cyber threat or cyber terrorism is developed in Chapter 2 which will also include a more detailed analysis of cyber activities recognising that the computer can be both a weapon to be used and also the subject of a potential attack with examples such as possible attacks on critical national infrastructures such as gas, water, electricity and the use of digital steganography.

Cyberspace

Cyberspace may be considered as:

> a metaphor for describing the non-physical terrain created by computer systems. Online systems, for example, create a cyberspace within which people can communicate with one another (via e-mail), do research, or simply window shop. Like physical space, cyberspace contains objects (files, mail messages, graphics, etc.) and different modes of transportation and delivery. Unlike real space, though, exploring cyberspace does not require any physical movement other than pressing keys on a keyboard or moving a mouse … Some programs, particularly computer games, are designed to create a special cyberspace, one that resembles physical reality in some ways but defies it in others. In its extreme form, called virtual reality, users are presented with visual, auditory, and even tactile feedback that makes cyberspace feel real. (Webopedia nd)

Cyber refers to concepts of an organised movement and use of electronic data, and of control which is derived from manipulating such data. Space refers to the virtual place where two or more human activities interact. Cyberspace can be used to describe simply the World Wide Web, the Internet as a whole and also to include all global media and communication channels. Sterling (1992) credits Barlow (1990) as the first to use the phrase cyberspace to refer to 'the present-day nexus of computer and telecommunications networks'.

This convergence of different media creates a world where all modes of communication and information are continually changing, not just the Information and Communication Technology (ICT) product used for communication but fundamentally 'changing the way we create, consume, learn and interact with each other' (Jenkins 2006). Current systems may be only at the 'end of the beginning' of this fundamental change as virtually all aspects of life, be they institutional activities such as business, government, art, journalism, health and education or recreational and social activities, are all increasingly being carried out in cyberspace across an ever-expanding and evolving network of information and converging communication technology devices. ICT is defined by Schuchart (2003:np) as:

> an umbrella term that includes any communication device or application, encompassing: radio, television, cellular phones, computer and network hardware and software, satellite systems and so on, as well as the various services and applications associated with them, such as videoconferencing and distance learning.

The Internet forms the backbone of cyberspace and is a global network of individual computer systems owned by businesses, governments and other public bodies and even individuals. The World Wide Web, which was launched in late 1990, operates within the Internet and is a network of linked multimedia information (web pages) available to all (universality). The technical standards are open and royalty-free and allow anyone to create applications without requiring formal permission or sanction. This is accomplished using common naming (address) and production protocols (URL (uniform resource locator) and HTTP (hypertext transfer protocol)).

The pace of technological change is rapid and accelerating. 'On the 15th June 2009, 20 hours of new content were posted on YouTube every minute, 494 exabytes [a billion gigabytes] of information were transferred seamlessly across the globe, over 2.6 billion mobile phone minutes were exchanged across Europe and millions of enquiries were made using a Google algorithm' (Lord Carter, cited in Sheldon and Wright 2010:165). This convergence coupled with the ubiquitous low cost and ease of operation of future ICT systems, suggests that cyberspace will become the place where all our senses coincide with all possibilities of thought and action. Weiser (1991) coined the term 'ubiquitous computing' in 1988 referring to a future time when devices and systems would be so numerous and integrated into our lives that technology becomes the media through which people live. This time is nearly upon us and that the final boundary between online life and real life is already ill-defined.

Burns and Weir (cited in Jahankhani et al. 2008:45) propose that 'Security is a balance between confidentiality, authentication and integrity versus convenience, cost and reliability'. Such factors must be taken into account in the development of new anti cyber crime interventions and especially for technology to support such interventions. This view is supported by Everett (2006) who stated that '... perfect security is not economically viable even if practically achievable'. Security systems within cyberspace require continuous innovation in order to match the rapid pace of general technological advancement in cyberspace and the new potential cyber crime opportunities such development produces. It has been asserted that '... design flaws and errors are normally the main cause of security holes that are explored by attackers' (Khan and Mustafa 2009:10). Generally technological developments are far from perfect; for example, Chip and PIN has not eliminated all plastic card fraud. If there are loopholes, cyber criminals and cyber terrorists will seek these and exploit them to their advantage. Even when advances are made, the length of time taken to roll them out across the world may allow for cyber criminals and cyber terrorists to continue operating and initiate ways of countering these advances as they become widespread. With the government and mass media raising awareness of new breakthroughs, cyber criminals and cyber terrorists receive prior warning of the need to develop new ways to penetrate and attack the new technology.

There are a number of crucial factors affecting any new ICT or online security systems success; for example, do they depend upon implementation by another organisation? Kovacich (2007:156) stated, 'We should never consider any high technology device, any controls, or any portion of any anti fraud program to be able to stop 100 per cent of all fraud threat agents or to thwart all fraud schemes, all we can ever expect is the levels of risk to be made as low as possible'. In support of this statement, Levi and Handley (2002:16) announced, 'Unless a completely secure payment system is devised, then there will inevitably be some risk, and greater use will normally provide more opportunities for fraud' and 'With sophisticated technical systems, the weakest link is often human error' (ibid:20). Both authors are critical of the expectations often associated with new technology. Many ICT users' understanding of security issues is lagging behind technological developments; for example according to one study, 56 per cent of Internet users did not understand what a 'cookie' was and how it held useable information about the Internet user's activities (Pew Internet and American Life project 2000:3). However, if all the stakeholders work together cyber crime can be reduced. The UK Card association report a 17 per cent reduction in reported crime involving credit cards during 2010. This is attributed to a combination of efforts amongst the card industry, banks and consumers (UKCA 2011) and Financial Fraud Action UK (2011:1) report reduced levels of some cyber crime in 2010: 'Online banking fraud losses totalled £46.7 million in 2010 – a 29% fall from the 2009 figure', demonstrating that using existing security measures can reduce the rate of these crimes but not prevent them. If this is also the case for cyber terrorism then such terrorist acts will continue so long as there is a political, religious or ideological will to commit such activities.

There is a technological arms race between cyber criminals and those policing cyberspace; the race is one of technological leapfrog with each side trying to make an advantage and capitalise on it during a brief period of technological supremacy. The time frame during which harmful activities can occur in cyberspace is much shorter than in a non-ICT system but the scope for gain or damage is significantly greater. Wall (2007) describes the current situation as the third generation of cyber crimes utilising networked technologies that are converging with other technologies.

One example of such technological leapfrogging is the discovery of a tailored computer attack in a process control system. Generally, malicious software programs that attack systems or steals information from systems are known as worms that spread across networks by finding and using security flaws or viruses that inhabit static files and require the user to unwittingly assist with their spread. Specifically the 'Stuxnet' worm was discovered in Sieman's propriety software systems that are used to control and monitor the performance of industrial processes. The worm rewrote the computer controllers in the system, and concealed these changes. Stuxnet is estimated to have infected 100,000 host computers and although this worm has been found worldwide, 60 per cent of the infections have been linked to Sieman's systems in Iran (TCE 2010a), suggesting a focused cyber state-sponsored attack that is undoubtedly designed to slow the development of Iran's nuclear capability: this may be an example of a cyber threat or even cyber warfare. These issues are discussed in greater depth in Chapter 2. Iran has confirmed that the worm caused problems at its enrichment plant in Natanz (TCE 2010b). The infection spread from five industrial domains that have operations in Iran and that were linked to the Natanz uranium production facility to impede this site's operation (TCE 2011). A spokesperson from the security firm Kaspersky described Stuxnet as 'a working and fearsome prototype of a cyber-weapon that will lead to the creation of a new arms race' (BBC News 2010b).

Other cyber attacks include the following: in 2007, Estonia was the subject of a series of cyber attacks which crippled the Internet across the country; Operation Aurora attacks on Google in China in January 2010 penetrating this ICT company's protective software, targeting information on human rights activists; and the 'Night Dragon', a series of ongoing attacks which are coordinated attempts to penetrate at least a dozen multinational oil, gas and energy companies that began in November 2009. These attacks exploited Microsoft's operating systems despite the security systems installed by these organisations (TCE 2011). The National Security Review (HM Government 2010) rated cyber attacks as a tier one risk to the UK's security – the highest possible level of threat. There is no completely secure Internet system (TCE 2011) which raises the risk of successful cyber attacks following the introduction of increasingly complex Internet-based systems such as Cloud Computing.

Cloud computing replaces the storing of bought software on individual computers with the rental of such software on servers and accessing the software via the Internet. Organisations can expand processing power by adding more servers. There are already both public and private clouds systems in operation (Greenaway 2010). Cloud computing had a market worth $47 billion in 2008 and will be ubiquitous within 3 years according to Microsoft, with 20 per cent of email using cloud computing by 2012 (Payton 2010). This will allow organisations to save money on internal ICT services and to spread costs of new software over a longer period via rental rather than purchasing licence agreements. However, this will fundamentally shift the onus for security to the Internet-based provider. The advocates of cloud computing argue that such providers will have the resources, that is, finance and technical expertise, to provide more enhanced security than the present system which depends very much upon individual organisations perceptions of risks, technical ability, expertise and outlook. The breaching of Sony's PC games site (Goodin 2011) demonstrates that very large organisations that have invested considerable resources into their network security cannot be considered 100 per cent secure and that the personal details of its 77 million customers may have been accessed. Certainly Facebook, a cloud-based system, has become a part of daily life for many people in modern society. The US, Japanese and UK governments are all launching cloud applications (Greenaway 2010) and need to come to terms with some processing of their data taking place outside their national boundaries. Governments will be concerned with access to sensitive data and will use encryption, access and storage security measures within their risk assessments to decide precisely what can be located on a cloud application (Greenaway 2010).

Encryption technology, such as the digital certificates used to secure payment transactions using Paypal, allows users to protect their files from being opened by others but this tool can be employed by cyber criminals and cyber terrorists to keep their own material secure from police and security monitoring activities. Oliver Drage was imprisoned for 4 months for refusing to reveal his 50-character encryption key to Lancashire police who were investigating child exploitation. Seventeen months after seizing his computer they had still not cracked his code (Radenedge 2010). With the emails sent by Rajib Karim, a convicted terrorist, it took a team of code-breakers nine months to crack the codes he used (Twomey 2011). Encryption can use several layers of data and can include more than keyboard characters by using graphics and photographs to compose the key or code (Radenedge 2010). Further discussion of encryption and digital steganography follows in Chapter 2. Government legislation such as in the USA has required providers to design and provide a 'backdoor' into encrypted programmes so that law enforcement agencies can more easily read messages but this also allows for the possibility of hackers or terrorists finding and accessing this 'backdoor'. The legislative approaches to dealing with cyber terrorism are discussed more fully in Chapter 6.

Artificial intelligence (AI) is an ICT development that can be used by businesses and security/ law enforcement agencies to protect themselves from cyber attacks. Many organisations ranging from Amazon to banks, credit card companies and Yahoo use AI and this includes the use of AI in their security systems (Chillingworth 2011). According to Sabarirajan (in Chillingworth 2011) AI is the preferred method of fraud detection in the financial sector. However, the use of AI is limited at present as using AI to analyse language is complicated because of the numerous rules and even more numerous exceptions to those rules (Norvig in Chillingworth 2011). Another limitation in intercepting communications is the limitation of speech recognition programs, and although the company Nuance has stored millions of speech samples and can use these to train speech-recognition applications rapidly, it is not yet able to accurately transcribe a phone call. However, it can be used to recognise single words or phrases as used in word command applications in automatic customer service answer phone algorithms for many organisations (Pogue 2010).

An application to scan the contents of a packet of information while it was being transmitted by an Internet service provider (ISP) was developed by Phorm, a private company in 2008. Specifically it could determine the URL that any user was browsing and create a user profile to facilitate targeted marketing to that user (Berners-Lee 2010). This application could also be used by security services to seek those accessing terrorist-hosted sites or by cyber terrorists to find those more likely to be supportive of their cause. The Federal Bureau of Investigation's (FBI) 'Carnivore ' application can check millions of email messages 'sniffing' for cues as does the international 'Echelon' intelligence-gathering system that monitors telephone, telex, fax and email messages. The 'Echelon' system is based in the USA but has listening apparatus further afield, for example Menwith Hill in the UK (Lyon 2007). These surveillance systems can gather dispersed personal data on suspected individuals, some of which the individuals may not even be aware of. Such files have been referred to as 'Digital Personas' by Clarke (1994) who argues that they can have the potential for active control resulting in exclusion, not just passive monitoring and so are socially dangerous. There is a trend to try to create such specific personas from the aggregate data stored on organisations' servers, and Millward (2007) claims that the US Homeland Security Service is keen to access all types of consumer data for this purpose from organisations such as businesses, schools, airlines and from organisations owned and operating outside the USA. Lyon (2007:180) uses the phrase 'increasingly porous institutional boundaries' and he states that attention must be focused upon this classification and profiling process to prevent incorrect, negative discrimination and the erosion of social coherence.

The personality profiles of who are likely to become cyber terrorists is discussed in Chapter 3 but no single profile fits all cases: cyber criminals have been described as ranging from state-sponsored mercenaries, organised gangs to teenagers sitting in their bedrooms (BBC News 2011). It is likely that terrorists will borrow techniques from criminal and activist groups, for example the Distributed

Denial of Service (DDoS) attacks carried out by the group calling themselves Anonymous. This attack was focused on Amazon, Mastercard, Visa and PayPal in retaliation for those firms hampering Wikileaks' ability to raise funds. The websites were overloaded with demand and data so that the system could no longer function (BBC News 2010b). Furthermore, terrorists may be able to hire cyber attackers '... in cyberspace, the criminals could be used as mercenaries and proxies to fulfil the tasks others have told them to do' (BBC News 2010a). The nature of terrorist organisations, cults and cells is discussed more fully in Chapters 3 and 4.

The Level of Cyber Crime Activity

'Cyber crime has become part of everyday business for organised crime' (Verizon Business 2009:2), and now cyber terrorism is part of everyday activity for terrorists. 'Cyber Crime is a whole new ball game' (Rogers and Lewis 2007:141) that ranges from the most minor to the most serious of crimes and from affecting one individual to affecting large populations. The issue of cyber hate crime is examined in Chapter 5.

Police-recorded statistics of crime are generally considered to be a poor indication of the actual level and trends. Many cyber deceptions go unreported to the police: 'The scale of cyber crime is very difficult to measure' (Rogers and Lewis 2007:142), and there are 'difficulties involved in gathering accurate data' (ACPO 2009:2), either because the victims have not discovered that they are the subject of a criminal act, or the victims report the offence to a providing company rather than the police, while the companies tend not to disclose their levels of loss or attack to avoid loss of reputation and custom. This lack of a clear reporting process has been noted: 'no one has a clue whom they should report e-crimes to' (Mitchell 2008:3). For example, instead of reporting Internet fraud to the police 'victims are now told to talk to their bank. However the banks are not obliged to pass on the crime reports to the police' (Mitchell 2008:4). Similarly the security forces have limited resources and may not be able to investigate all their lists of suspects and the lists are only likely to include some terrorists and some of those individuals undergoing radicalisation. This makes it hard to distinguish the true extent of the problem, but gives an indication that the level of such activity is probably underestimated. It is likely that the scope of the problem of cyber terrorism is extensive. The challenge is exacerbated by the combination of global communication systems and individual terrorist cells scales in which cyber terrorism occurs. Cyber terrorism operates on all tiers, namely local, regional, national and international so that finding a cyber terrorist cell is similar to looking for a needle in a haystack. The use of intelligence-led policing may be the answer to this challenge and this approach is examined in Chapter 8.

Fafinski and Minassian (2009:3) identified that '3.6 million criminal acts were committed online in 2008', and the commissioner of the Metropolitan Police Service stated that 'in 2007, online fraud generated £53 billion worldwide and that there is a major under reporting of all types of cyber crime' (Police professional 2010:12). However, these statistics 'represent only the tip of the iceberg' (Fafinski and Minassian 2009:23) and different researchers give widely different estimates of the scale of activity with Mills (2009:1) claiming that 'The global cost of cyber crime is currently estimated to be one trillion dollars a year'. Cyber crime has been estimated to cost the UK economy £27bn a year according to a joint study by The Office of Cyber Security and Information Assurance in the Cabinet Office and the information intelligence firm Detica (BBC News 2011). The report also suggests that there are too many companies which do not know enough about how their systems function and so cannot begin to anticipate attacks and protect against them.

The public's opinions of cyberspace are 'easily swayed by contradictory messages' (Wakefield and Fleming 2009:75) and the media has created a reassurance gap with the public's level of fear being far greater than the actual level of physical threat: this has left some people believing that cyberspace is used by terrorists to recruit new members using uncensored propaganda: 'youngsters are groomed by paedophiles and upstanding citizens are robbed of their identity and savings' (ibid:75) and a general perception 'that the Internet was a lawless wild west' (House of Lords 2007:3). The British Security Minister Baroness Neville-Jones indicated that the government was committed to working in partnership with the private sector to tackle this issue. 'It is both a national security and commercial priority and both sides need to work together to strengthen our existing resilience' (PS 2011).

Policing Cyber Crime

General Noble, head of Interpol's information security, stated that cyber crime may be one of the most dangerous criminal threats ever (Police professional 2010). The UK government has realised that science and technology has been exploited by terrorists and that it must use the same tools to counter terrorism, to counter terrorist propaganda and to frustrate the development of new terrorist activity. 'While technology has provided new tools, techniques and tactics in support of the terrorist agenda, it is also key element in our response. Success in delivering relevant science, innovation and technology is vital' (Home Office 2009:9).

Due to the number of countries, organisations and politics involved, it is difficult to create an agreed overall strategy or new technological scheme that will be able to work effectively on a global scale. National and international strategies to deal with cyber terrorism are discussed in Chapter 9. It should be a fundamental priority for not only governments and Internet providers, but for the legitimate cyber users themselves to take action individually and in concert against cyber crime especially cyber terrorism.

Some jurisdictional difficulties, both between agencies within a national boundary and between different nations, have hindered cyber crime investigations due to parochial thinking, 'letting foreign police tread a square meter of their soil in hard pursuit of criminals is still anathema to ... national governments' (Lenk 1997:129). Glick (2001) states that the removal of jurisdictional boundaries and cooperation between states is essential but in reality this will be difficult to achieve as 'investigations can be held up for months while law enforcement agents from different countries struggle to find compatible modus operandi' (Jewkes and Yar 2003:583). Such constraints equally apply to policing cyber terrorism. This aspect is explored in detail in Chapters 9 and 10.

One possible approach that might be utilised is private–public partnerships where private organisations would fund the monitoring of the Internet and analysis of primary cyber crime data, and the public would fund the arrest and prosecution of cyber criminals and cyber terrorists. Young (2009) comments that if private organisations assisted or took over cyber crime investigations there could arise a serious conflict of interest between revenue streams and policing effort: cyber policing makes use of technologies that follow real movements in physical space such as CCTV, facial recognition and automatic number-plate-recognition that can be coupled with digital personal data and monitored messages to automatically evaluate the individual's possible intentions and classify their moral worthiness as they are tracked in real time moving through physical space (Norris and Armstrong 1999).

The policing of cyber crime needs a flexible framework but there must be a framework in place, according to Deleuze (1995). The surveillance assemblage has grown not as a hierarchical structure but as a rhizome, the way the roots of some plants grow outwards in a haphazard manner and in turn form additional nodes from which other roots spread. The application of knowledge management within law enforcement agencies and partner organisations is essential to effectively tackle cyber terrorism and this issue is explored in Chapter 7.

Informal Social Control in Cyberspace

Formal social control is achieved using legislation and public agencies such as the police to enforce these rules, regulations and protocols. Informal social control depends upon the culture, norms or mores of a society that creates an atmosphere of acceptable and unacceptable attitudes and behaviour. The sanctions that build such culture are acceptance or rejection by society, ridicule and reward by that society.

Stollard (1991) argues that in the real world informal social control that occurs as a result of natural surveillance is increasingly effective when those who perform the task of observation are familiar with those observed, or they share the same territorial space. Newman (1972) concurs, stating that surveillance by observers is most effective if the area is thought to be part of 'their own area'. Similarly according to Routine Activity Theory (Felson 1994) crime will be lower in an area 'guarded' merely by the presence of many individuals who may be seen by the criminal as potential onlookers and subsequent witnesses. However, the opposite view has also been expressed: 'criminals were increasingly operating online where the chances of being detected were much smaller' (BBC News 2011). Could informal social control be exerted in cyberspace and could online social networking play a part in it? According to Putnam (2000), social capital such as belonging to a social network increases the capability of a community to cooperate towards common goals, and it makes an individual more inclined to assist another member of that social network. Putnam (ibid.) claimed that social capital is declining, and held that the growth of television and other indoor activities are partly responsible for dwindling social networks and a lack of connections between people. Will social networking in cyberspace redress this balance or enhance existing trends?

It is questionable as to how aware the public are of the various forms and scale of cyber crime and cyber terrorism and whether if they were better informed they would do more to assist in its prevention. This argument is reinforced by the media; for example, relying 'on individuals to take responsibility for their own security' will simply not work because 'they will always be out-foxed' (BBC 2007:1).

Everett (2009) concluded that 'people-based-governance' needed to be established, with everyone at all levels of society taking individual and collective responsibility for helping to police the Internet. One of the problems of such an approach, also labelled as 'responsibilisation' (Lyon 2007:116), is that if the policing is solely looking out for suspicious individuals, events and Internet activities then the distrust engendered will undoubtedly threaten society cohesion.

Informal social control of animal abuse as via cyberspace has been demonstrated in the UK in 2010: a woman who spontaneously placed a cat in a wheelie bin was filmed on an individual's home CCTV and the images were broadcast on the Internet and the culprit was identified. A similar incident of a man filmed kicking the dog he was walking was also broadcast on the Internet and also resulted in his identification and ensuing prosecution. Such a citizen-based surveillance approach might prove a low-cost and effective policing strategy. A further example is the recent call to boycott a restaurant posted on Facebook after one of its waiters allegedly sent a customer an obscene photograph (Varmer 2011).

A combination of blogs and mobile phones were used in 2005 by rioters in Paris to protest against perceived police discrimination towards North African minorities (Lyon 2007). Morozov (2011) used the term 'Twitter Revolution' at the time of the protests in Moldova in April 2009 to describe the active social networking used to support the organisation, implementation and galvanisation against the regime that took place:

> It was hard not to be infected by a sense of optimism and excitement about the freedom agenda that was around at that time. I genuinely thought it was making a difference. Democracy appeared to be advancing and marching, and the web 2.0 seemed to be part of it, bringing people on to the streets. (Pilkington 2011:1)

The 'Arab Spring' of 2011 has also followed this trend of being a social media-based series of organised demonstrations, protests and uprisings attributed to the ordinary people demanding democracy rather than existing political, religious or terrorist organisations pursuing ongoing agendas. Forsyth (2011) suggests that the Internet and mobile phone had facilitated younger Arabs to access the world beyond their national boundaries and ask why they did not have freedom and other privileges: this questioning led to discontentment which sparked these uprisings.

There is a liberal view amongst many of those who created and developed the Internet that any form of government control is oppressive and to be avoided, as demonstrated by Google's refusal to assist police in tracing an alleged criminal photographed by a Google street view camera (Jeeves 2011:36). Berners-Lee (2010), the inventor of the World Wide Web, is a staunch defender of an open web that allows anyone to create a web page and publish what they want on that page. He argues that the web is a public resource and is a crucial support of free speech. Berners-Lee argues against ownership and control of the web by companies breaking the web into 'fragmented lands' and or centralised control by governments. Morozov (2011) terms this belief in the ability of the Internet to give power to the people as 'cyber-utopianism'. Lessig (1999) argues that cyberspace is regulated by code; that is, the way applications, programmes and systems are designed and operated forms the regulation in the system and he claims the basic failing is to believe that cyberspace is unregulated; rather, the regulators are anyone who can contribute to the codes in use. Lyon (2007) describes cyberspace as a place of virtual struggle and argues that codes can be positive and democratic as well as threatening and offering totalitarian control.

The police are using online social networks to engage with their communities; for example, neighbourhood officers in the UK are currently using Twitter. The messages need to have a relevance to the people living in that neighbourhood or who may have a connection to the area or belong to that social network (physically or online). According to Amandacomms (2011) using Twitter only as an extension to the police's public relations strategy will not work as the community may be cynical. However, giving details that will change public behaviour or giving the social network actions they can participate in is more beneficial. This may be about making people aware of extremism taking place in their area, or it could be asking them to undertake cyber surveillance to be cyber guardians. This use of Twitter by law-enforcement agencies can have a direct impact on people's lives affecting their level of fear of both physical and cyber crime or encouraging them to help tackle both physical and cyber crime. For those in the geographical area or social network they can be more vigilant and protect themselves as well as report anything noteworthy they encounter. It is a way of more fully understanding what is going on in their neighbourhood or cyber network. Jackson and Gray (2010) have found that a quarter of the population who are anxious about crime, exhibit a functional fear of crime. This group use problem-solving approaches to take precautions to prevent crime and so feel safer and as a consequence of both their attitude and these activities: consequently they did not appear to have a reduced quality of life despite having this fear of crime. If a functional fear of cyber terrorism can be instilled in a greater proportion of the population then not only will the risk of cyber terrorism reduce but the population's quality of life may benefit. Furthermore, if this positive approach can be supported by government and social policy the maintenance of social control without reducing community cohesion will be possible as Jackson and Gray (ibid.) state that worry about crime is stimulated by weak informal provision of social control.

Conclusion

Cyberspace is developing rapidly and fundamentally changing the way we live, think, interact and view the world and its reality. Cyber terrorism has become more of a threat as it becomes more interwoven in the World Wide Web of our lives, becoming more real as we inevitably become more virtual. Arguably the old military notion of a front line of troops or the thin blue line of police protecting us from criminality is now outdated and the motto should be that 'online is the new front line' and that the war on terror is to be fought in the home not on the beaches. This fight requires cyber tools and the development of a positive attitude (functional fear) in the population and as such applications such as True Vision, a new system for reporting hate crime and online local crime mapping are just the beginning of cyber front-line developments for creating a safer world using social networks to affect social control.

Further Reading

Andress, J. and Winterfield, S. 2011. *Cyber Warefare: Techniques, Tactics and Tools for Security Practitioners*. Waltham, USA: Syngress.
The Computer Security Institute online at GoCSI.com.
The Cloud Security Alliance online at: http://www.cloudsecurityalliance.org/ topthreats the CSA provides best practices for providing security assurance within Cloud Computing, and provides education services on the uses of Cloud Computing to help secure all other forms of computing.
The Register [Online]. Available at: http://www.theregister.co.uk/security/ is an excellent site reporting on various cyber crimes [accessed: 2 March 2011].

References

ACPO. 2009. *E-crime Strategy Version 1.0*. London: ACPO.

Amandacomms. 2011. 10 Tips for Twitter in a Hyperlocal Way. [Online]. Available at: http://amandacomms1.wordpress.com/2011/02/13/10-tips-for-twitter-in-a-hyperlocal-way/posted on February 13 [accessed: 24 February 2011].

Andress, J. and Winterfield, S. 2011. *Cyber Warefare: Techniques, Tactics and Tools for Security Practitioners*. Waltham, USA: Syngress.

Barlow, J.P. 1990. Crime and Puzzlement: in advance of the law on the electronic frontier. Whole Earth Review. [Online]. Fall: 44–57. Available at: http://w2.eff.org/Net_culture/Cyberpunk/cyber_net.biblio [accessed: 17 May 2011].

BBC News. 2007. Government 'Must Act On e-Crime'. [Online]. Available at: http://news.bbc.co.uk/1/hi/technology/6938796.stm [accessed: 17 October 2010].

BBC News. 2010a. Cyber-war a Growing Threat Warn Experts. [Online]. Available at: http://www.bbc.co.uk/news/10339543 [accessed: 25 February 2011].

BBC News. 2010b. Cyber-Sabotage and Espionage Top 2011 Security Fears. [Online]. Available at: http://www.bbc.co.uk/news/technology-12056594 [accessed: 24 February 2011].

BBC News. 2011. UK Cyber Crime Costs £27bn a Year – Government Report. [Online]. Available at: http://www.bbc.co.uk/news/uk-politics-12492309 posted 17/02/11 2011 [accessed: 24 February 2011].

Berners-Lee, T. 2010. Long live the web. *Scientific American*, December, 56–61.

Cabinet Office. 2009. *Cyber Security of the United Kingdom*: *Safety, Security and Resilience in Cyber Space*. Norwich: The Stationery Office.

Chillingworth, M. 2011. The rise of the machines. *Financial Management*. January/February, 32–4, CiMA.

Clarke, R. 1994. The digital persona and its application to the data surveillance. *The Information Society*, 10(2), 77–92.

Deleuze, G. 1995. *Negotiations 1972–1990*. New York: Columbia University Press.

Everett, D., 2006. Chip and PIN Security. [Online]. Available at: http://www.smartcard.co.uk/Chip%20and%20PIN%20Security.pdf [accessed: 24 October 2009].

Everett, C., 2009. Who is responsible for policing the Internet? *Computer Fraud and Security*. (5) 5–6, [Online]. Available at: http://www.sciencedirect.com. ergo.glam.ac.uk/science?_ob=ArticleURL&_udi=B6VNT-4WGKC34–6&_user=477543&_coverDate=05%2F31%2F2009&_alid=1062816337&_rdoc=7&_fmt=high&_orig=search&_cdi=6187&_st=13&_docanchor=&_ct=30&_acct=C000022838&_version=1&_urlVersion=0&_userid=477543&md5=323311eb55969fa42f0 cc7c68394ab36 [accessed: 24 October 2009].

Fafinski, S. and Minassian, N. 2009. *UK Cyber-Crime Report 2009*. Richmond: Garlik UK.

Felson, M. 1994. *Crime and Everyday Life: Insight and Implications for Society.* Thousand Oaks, CA: Pine Forge Press.

Financial Fraud Action UK. 2011. [Online]. Available at: http://www. attorneygeneral.gov.uk/nfa/WhatAreWeSaying/Pages/fraud-news-mar11-fraud-losses-on-cards-drop.aspx. [accessed: 17 March 2011].

Forsyth, F. 2011. Internet gives youth a vision of real freedom. *Daily Express,* 25 February, 13.

Glick, B. 2001. *Cyber Criminals Mock Arcane Legal Boundaries.* [Online]. Available at: http://www.computing.co.uk/ctg/analysis/1831154/cyber-criminals-mock-arcane-legal-boundaries. [accessed: 5 May 2011].

Goodin, D. 2011. Sony Closes PC Games Site Over Security 'Concern'. [Online, 2 May]. Available at: http://www.theregister.co.uk/2011/05/02/sony_online_ entertainment_closed/ [accessed: 5 May 2011].

Greenaway, A. 2010. Get your head in the clouds. *Public Servant,* 29. [Online]. Available at: www.publicservant.co.uk. [accessed:18 January 2011].

HM Government. 2010. *Securing Britain in an Age of Uncertainty: The Strategic Defence and Security Review.* Norwich: TSO.

Home Office. 2009. *Cyber Security Strategy of the United Kingdom: Safety, Security and Resilience in Cyber Space.* London: The Stationery Office.

House of Lords. 2007. *Personal Internet Security Report, Volume 1.* London: The Stationery Office.

Jackson, J. and Gray, E. 2010. Functional fear and public insecurities about crime. *British Journal of Criminology,*50, 1–22.

Jahankhani, H., Revett, R., and Palmer-Brown, D. 2008. *Global e-security: 4th International Conference, ICGeS 2008.* [e-book]. Germany: Springer. [Online]. Available at: http://books.google.co.uk/books?id=oeaTCy1Qaq4C&pg=PA 40&dq=uk+card+fraud+capital+of+europe#v=onepage&q=uk%20card%20 fraud%20capital%20of%20europe&f=false [accessed: 25 October 2010].

Jeeves, P. 2011. Google snubs helping catch thief it filmed. *Daily Express,* 7 January, 36.

Jenkins, H. 2006. *Convergence Culture.* New York: New York University Press.

Jewkes, Y. and Yar, M. 2003. 'Policing Cybercrime: Emerging Trends and Future Challenges', in *Handbook of Policing,* edited by Newburn, T. Cullompton: Willan.

Khan, R.A. and Mustafa, K. 2009. From threat to security indexing: a causal chain. *Computer Fraud and Security,* (5) 9–12. [Online]. Available at: http://www. sciencedirect.com/science?_ob=ArticleURL&_udi=B6VNT-4WGKC34–8&_ user=477543&_coverDate=05%2F31%2F2009&_alid=1062816337&_ rdoc=17&_fmt=high&_orig=search&_cdi=6187&_st=13&_docanchor=&_ ct=30&_acct=C000022838&_version=1&_urlVersion=0&_userid=477543& md5=dff3f3c12c2ece6b9f6ba3384bf30cd2 [accessed: 26 October 2010].

Kovacich, G. 2007. *Fighting Fraud: How to Establish and Manage an Anti-Fraud Program.* [e-book]. London: Elsevier Academic Press. [Online]. Available at: http://books.google.co.uk/books?id=TcwadnS2zyAC&pg=PA153&dq=gove

rnment+explains+anti+fraud+technology+for+public#v=onepage&q=&f=fal
se [accessed: 23 October 2010].

Lenk, K. 1997. 'The Challenge of Cyber Spatial Forms of Human Interaction
to Territorial Governance and Policing', in *The Governance of Cyberspace:
Politics, Technology and Global Restructuring*, edited by Loader, B. London:
Routledge, 126–35.

Lessig, L 1999. *Code and Other Laws of Cyberspace*. New York: Basic Books.

Levi, M., and Handley, J. 2002. *Criminal Justice and Payment of Future Card
Fraud*. [e-book]. London: IPPR. [Online]. Available at: http://books.google.
co.uk/books?id=zjup1vr8rsC&pg=PA22&dq=problem+of+plastic+card+fr
aud#v=onepage&q=problem%20of%20plastic%20card%20fraud&f=false
[accessed: 27 October 2010].

Lyon, D. 2007. *Surveillance Studies: An Overview*. Cambridge, UK: Polity.

Mills, E. 2009. 'Cyber-Crime Cost Firms $1 Trillion Globally', in *Policing and
Technology*, edited by Sheldon, B. and Wright, P. Exeter: Learning Matters, 29.

Millward, D. 2007. US Licence to snoop on British air travellers. *Daily Telegraph*,
2 January, 7.

Mitchell, S. 2008. The E-crime Epidemic. [Online]. Available at: http://www.
pcpro.co.uk/features/164145/the-e-crime-epdidemic [accessed: 17 October
2010].

Newman, O. 1972. *Defensible Space: Crime Prevention through Urban Design*.
London: MacMillan.

Norris, C. and Armstrong, G. 1999. *The Maximum Surveillance Society: The Rise
of CCTV*. Oxford and New York: Berg.

Morozov, E. 2011. *The Net Delusion*. New York: Allen Lane.

Payton, S. 2010. Fluffy Logic. *Financial Management*, November, p.22–5, CiMA.

Pew Internet and American Life Project. 2000. *Trust and Privacy Online: Why
Americans Want to Rewrite the Rules*. [Online, 20 August]. Available at: www.
pewInternet.org/pdfs/PIP-Trust-Privacy-Report.pdf [accessed: 7 January
2011].

Pilkington, E. 2011. Evgeny Morozov: how democracy slipped through the net.
Guardian. [Online]. Available at http://www.guardian.co.uk/technology/2011/
jan/13/evgeny-morozov-the-net-delusion [accessed: 15 February 2011].

Pogue, D. 2010. Talk to the machine. *Scientific American*, December, 18.

Police professional. 2010. E-specialists as important as frontline officers. *Police
professional*. [Online]. Available at: www.policeprofessional.com [accessed: 8
January 2011].

Public Service. 2011. Cyber crime costs UK £27bn each year. *Public Service*.
[Online]. Available at: http://www.publicservice.co.uk/news_story.
asp?id=15539 [accessed: 25 February 2011].

Putnam, R. 2000. *Bowling Alone: The Collapse and Revival of American
Community*. New York: Simon and Schuster: 288–90.

Radenedge, A. 2010. Jailed for refusing to reveal password. *Metro*, 6 October, 1.

Rogers, C. and Lewis, R. 2007. *Introduction to Police Work*. Cullumpton: Willan.

Roy, A. 2004. *An Ordinary Person's Guide to Empire*. Cambridge MA: South End Press.

Schuchart, W. 2003. ict (information and communications technology – or technologies.) [Online]. Available at: http://searchciomidmarket.techtarget. com/definition/ICT [accessed: 25 May 2011].

Sheldon, B. and Wright, P. 2010. *Policing and Technology*. Exeter: Learning Matters.

Sterling, B. 1992. *The Hacker Crackdown: Law and Disorder on the Electronic Frontier*. New York: Spectra Books.

Stollard, P. 1991. *Design against Crime*. London: Design Council.

Taylor, P. 2003. 'Maestros or misogynists ? Gender and the social construction', in *Dot. Coms: Crime, Deviance and Identity on the Internet*, edited by Jewkes, Y. Collompton: Willan, 124–46.

TCE. 2010a. Bugs in the system: tailored virus threatens process control. *The Chemical Engineer*, November, 7.

TCE. 2010b. Stuxnet targets uranium enrichment plants. *Chemical Engineer*, December, 10.

TCE. 2011. Snatching secrets by stealth. *Chemical Engineer*. December, 5.

Twomey, J. 2011. Jailed for 30 years BA engineer who plotted second 9/11. *Daily Express*, 19 March, 31.

UKCA. 2011. Plastic fraud in Decline. *Daily Express*, 9 March, 26.

Varmer, A. 2011. Call to boycott obscene pic balti. *Birmingham Mail*, 16 February, 9.

Verizon Business. 2009. Data Breach Investigations Report. [Online]. Available at: www.verzonbussiness.com/resources/security/reports/2009_databreach_ rp.pdf [accessed: 17 October 2010].

Wakefield, A., and Fleming, J. 2009. *The Sage Dictionary of Policing*. London: Sage.

Wall, D. 2007. *Cybercrime*. Cambridge: Polity.

Webopedia. nd. [Online]. Available at: http://www.webopedia.com/TERM/C/ cyberspace.html. [accessed: 4 November 2010].

Weiser, M. 1991. The Computer for the twenty-first century. *Scientific American*, September, 94–104.

Young, T. 2009. Foiling a Thoroughly Modern Bank Heist. [Online]. Available at: http://news.cnet.com/8301–1009_3–10152246–83.htm [accessed: 17 October 2010].

Chapter 2

Cyber Threats and Cyber Terrorism: The Internet as a tool for Extremism

Imran Awan

The British Strategic Defence and Security Review in 2010 warned that the UK is facing a serious threat of a cyber terrorist attack in the future. This threat has intensified since the death of Osama bin Laden as Al-Qaeda begin to plot the next major terrorist attack, possibly through simply the use of a computer and with nothing more than the click of a mouse. The fear is that terrorists may be able to play the role of hostile actors that are willing to die to avenge the death of their spiritual leader with a cyber terrorist attack a possible way of getting their point across (Denning 2010). Indeed, the British Home Secretary Theresa May has acknowledged in a speech to the Royal United Services Institute in 2011 that Al-Qaeda is increasingly using online technology, such as Google Earth and Street View as well as popular social networking sites such as Facebook and Twitter to indoctrinate and recruit would-be extremists for terrorist purposes. Moreover, she argued that since the 'Arab Spring' and the death of Osama bin Laden the cyber threat from Al-Qaeda was increased because of the risk associated with Al-Qaeda led splinter groups that are based in different countries across the world who are all willing to take part in what she describes as 'cyber jihad'. She stated that: 'Since the death of Osama bin Laden, al-Qa'ida has explicitly called not only for acts of lone or individual terrorism, but also for cyber-jihad' (May 2011).

However, this sense of fear is pervaded with an anxiety within many Muslim communities who feel they may now be labelled as cyber terrorists or extremists that are using cyberspace for terrorist purposes (Awan 2011a).

Indeed, the British Prime Minister, David Cameron argued that:

> Over the last decade the threat to national security and prosperity from cyber attacks has increased exponentially. Over the decades ahead this trend is likely to continue to increase in scale and sophistication, with enormous implications for the nature of modern conflict. (Cabinet Office 2010:4)

UK Government policy in this area has been quick to anticipate this threat with an established programme management office within the Office of Cyber Security and Information Assurance to oversee, prioritise and regulate the National Cyber Security Programme, and thus create a new Infrastructure: the Security and Resilience Advisory Council, which it is hoped will enhance cooperation between both the public and private sector. Cyber threats and cyber hate are not easily defined but both terms are mainly concerned with threats from individuals that utilise computers to cause psychological injury or offence. The broader literature in this area suggests that hate crimes committed against Muslim communities are increasing and includes the role of cyber hate (Githens-Mazer and Lambert 2010). This chapter will explore the debate around the terms cyber threats and cyber terrorism.

Cyber Threats

The cyber threat to Britain has intensified since recent cyber attacks from the 'Stuxnet' virus through to attacks from groups of hackers (such as Lulzsec and Anonymous) who have all aimed to disrupt computer systems, and target high profile institutions, namely Sony, the US Senate and various law-enforcement agencies (Stuart 2011). Most of these cyber threats relate to criminal gangs, terrorists, hackers and hostile governments that are willing to cause cyber attacks against critical infrastructure and attack Internet systems. With 'globalisation' in an age of network systems there is a real sense of vulnerability of critical infrastructures. Moreover, this issue of cyber threats was raised and debated in 2010 by the House of Lords in Britain. Lord Reid at the time suggested that cyber threats are increasingly playing an important role as technological advances are made. His perception was that the UK, like many other foreign countries, faces a realisation that cyber attacks will target critical infrastructure that have a capacity to cripple security systems (including the public and private sectors). He states that 'It is to be expected in a House like this, for all our wisdom, that we might not be as au fait with technological advances as the younger generation. However, we ignore this at our peril' (Reid 2010). This view was reinforced by Lord Browne who in the same parliamentary debate argued that cyber threats had become more sophisticated as cyber enthusiasts begin to develop their online ambitions. He states that 'the nature and character of weaponry, is changing' (Browne 2010).

Indeed, this level of threat was further heightened by the head of the Government Communications Head Quarters (GCHQ is responsible for combating cyber threats in Britain) Iain Lobban who argues that the UK is facing multifaceted cyber threats which are coming from a wide range of sources. These include worms that could disrupt governmental electronic systems. For example a hacker could interrupt runway lights or the wider electronic control at an airport by shutting down computer systems with a worm or virus. Other threats include malicious emails sent to government networks; cyber techniques used by countries to target different nations; the use of online theft; the threat from hackers; and finally the generic risks attached with the growth of the Internet.

According to Iain Lobban, this threat has now manifested itself to a more complex and uncertain level of terrorist threat. In a speech to the International Institute for Strategic Studies, he stated that 'Terror cyber attacks pose a real threat that goes to the heart of our economic well-being and national interest' (Lobban 2010). His assertion seems to suggest a need for a wider debate on cyber threats and also cyber terrorism (Chapter 5 defines and discusses cyber hate in detail).

What is Cyber Terrorism?

In the UK a terrorist is defined under s40 (1) of the Terrorism Act 2000, as a person who:(a) has committed an offence under any of sections 11, 12, 15 to 18, 54 and 56 to 63, *or* (b) is or has been concerned in the commission, preparation or instigation of acts of terrorism (The Terrorism Act 2000).

However, the term cyber terrorism has not been clearly defined with law enforcement agencies such as the FBI in the US and the Centre for the Protection of National Infrastructure in the UK who have all attempted to define it. Academics are also attempting to examine the potential threat of cyber terrorism: Dorothy Denning argued, in a speech given before the US Congress, that:

> Cyber terrorism is the convergence of terrorism and cyberspace. It is generally understood to mean unlawful attacks and threats of attack against computers, networks, and the information stored therein when done to intimidate or coerce a government or its people in furtherance of political or social objectives. (Denning 2000:1)

Denning's argument is that cyber terrorism directly causes loss of life or other serious damage. This means the 'threat of attack on computers, networks' and attacks that could lead to 'explosions, plane crashes, water contamination or severe economic loss and even death' (Denning 2000:1). This conjures up a visual picture of graphic violence, of computer technology used as a lethal weapon. She argues that attacks against critical infrastructures, such as electric power or emergency services, are possible acts of cyber terrorism (Denning 2010:194).

Is Denning's description valid? Can the Internet be used to bring down an aeroplane? What is the evidence for her view? Weimann for example, takes a different view. He uses the term cyber terrorism in a different sense, arguing that: 'terrorists use of computers as a facilitator of their activities, whether for propaganda, recruitment, defaming communication or other purposes' could be forms of cyber terrorism (Weimann 2005:132).

To substantiate his argument, Weimann would need to show how terrorist's use of online videos and websites constitute the act of cyber terrorism. For example, are online videos of terrorist attacks a form of cyber terrorism? Or should we fear terrorists using steganography which may contain hidden messages in Arabic or Urdu?

Both of these views raise questions about how we define the term cyber terrorism, whether cyberspace is confined to the use of the Internet or also covers modes such as television, radio, fax, email and phone calls, and so on. This chapter examines the case for both these schools of thought but concludes that the current nature of terrorism provides more support for Weimann's argument, but that this conclusion could change if terrorists acquire more sophisticated skills in new technology.

Doomsday Scenario

According to Denning, cyber terrorism must be capable of wreaking actual damage on critical infrastructures of society, such as telecommunications, water supplies and economic and financial institutions. Denning argues that if terrorists have the capacity, training and technological skills then they could cause a cyber terror attack (Denning 2000).

She argues that a cyber terrorist attack could lead to death or bodily injury, through 'explosions, plane crashes, water contamination, or severe economic loss' (Denning 2000). As regards her first claim, that cyber terrorism causes explosions, it is clear that any explosive device (whether homemade or more sophisticated) is likely to cause major damage. How could computers be used to create such explosions? It is not clear, from Denning's writings, how this would actually work. One possibility is that she is referring to a hacker breaking into computer systems, successfully unlocking passwords and letting off a nuclear weapon or bomb (Awan 2010). Indeed, terrorist use of the Internet as a facilitator to get instructions on building a nail bomb, mounting to an explosion could be part of a cyber terrorist attack that Denning describes above. David Copeland, for example, unsuccessfully used online material to make a nail bomb with the intention of blowing up various locations in London (Hopkins and Hall 2000).

He used the Internet to facilitate his aims though he used cyber technology to aid his bomb making, it is questionable whether he would fall within the definition of a terrorist in the usual meaning of the word today. Furthermore, a Muslim convert by the name of Andrew Ibrahim attempted a similar mission by making explosives which he intended to detonate and cause mass murder (Gardham 2008). He also, like Copeland, had found material on the Internet which had helped him get the instructions on how to create these explosives which had the potential to kill and maim hundreds of people.

One question is, therefore, if somebody obtains instructions on the Internet on how to make a bomb, are they cyber terrorists? For Denning's argument to hold, computers should be *directly* used for the cyber terrorist attack. Copeland therefore is not a cyber terrorist because the computer in his case acts as a knowledgeable database on how to make a bomb. Denning argues that the computer *must be* the weapon (Denning 2001).

Hacking

Hacking has been defined as 'operations that exploit computers in ways that are unusual and often illegal, typically with the help of special software ('hacking tools'). Hacktivism includes electronic civil disobedience, which brings methods of civil disobedience to cyberspace' (Denning 2000:263).

Hackers are motivated by a variety of different reasons, one of the most common of which is fun and the challenge of hacking (Yar 2006). For example, Gary McKinnon, a UK resident, caused major damage to US security computers in the Pentagon, despite the fact that the US has one of the best ICT security systems in the world. McKinnon lost his appeal against extradition in 2009 demonstrating further that even if someone is not a terrorist but has used cyberspace for hacking then they may be treated as a cyber terrorist (Vegh 2002). Moreover, McKinnon's case has raised further doubts about how the US and UK deal with the threat of cyber terrorism.

There is some evidence to suggest that Denning's doomsday scenario has already happened. In Australia, in the Maroochy Shire, an individual successfully hacked into the electronic systems that controlled water supplies and caused severe water contamination. The attack was conducted by Vitek Boden who had been unsuccessful in a job application with the Queensland Council. Using a laptop, he was able successfully to disrupt the central pumping system and cause major damage to the sewage systems in rivers and parks all across Queensland. The concern regarding Boden's attack is that if this act was conducted by a terrorist than the consequences could have been much more severe (Hughes 2003). This example that supports this claim that the hackers with access to powerful computers could cause huge harm, but as most of the literature shows that the hackers with skills to do this do not have the same motivations as terrorists (Desmond 2002).

Motives

Hackers' motivations are testing systems and not bringing down an aircraft. Hackers have a high level of technological knowledge, spending endless hours honing their skills. But they do not intend to destroy the world. They simply enjoy the challenge of trying to disrupt computer systems. Their aims are not the same as terrorists.

Denning states that cyber terrorism '... covers politically motivated hacking operations intended to cause grave harm such as loss of life or severe economic damage. An example would be penetrating an air traffic control system and causing two planes to collide' (Denning 2000:241).

But there is no evidence to suggest aeroplanes have collided in mid-air as a result of terrorists hacking into air traffic control systems and been able to bring them down. Aircraft control systems are a potential target and aviation bodies rely heavily on computer networks to navigate aeroplanes in the sky. This critical infrastructure is vulnerable. NATS statistics showed air traffic controllers managed over 2,433,946 flights, in 2008 and NATS air traffic control handled more than 2.4 million flights (National Air Traffic Control Systems 2008). Electronic attacks on air traffic control therefore are possible, as they are clearly vulnerable and groups of hackers would be able to conduct cyber attacks against them using a broad range of cyber techniques such as malware, hacking, botnets, keystroke logging, phishing and denial of service which in turn has the potential to bring down aircraft.

More worryingly, insiders who have access to sensitive information about air traffic systems may well be pose a threat as they can use that information for terrorist related purposes. This is certainly true in the case of Rajib Karim who worked at British Airways as a computer analyst and used his considerable knowledge and expertise to send encrypted messages and codes to Al-Qaeda on how to cause a major terrorist attack at Heathrow airport (BBC News 2011). Although critical infrastructure is vulnerable to a cyber terror attack, to date no incident of magnitude has occurred. Therefore, groups like Al-Qaeda have to use the physical rather than cyber methods, namely suicide bombers, to create terror (Stohl 2007).

Another potential target for terrorists is the financial sector. Following the September 11 attacks, the US financial sector was hit very hard. A number of businesses, jobs, physical assets, bank accounts and the cost of repair meant the US felt both the physical, psychological, economic and financial damage within Wall Street. As the dust settled in New York, there was a chilly reminder that terrorists would use any means to cause havoc whether by a plane or simply by a click of a mouse. Furthermore, Al-Qaeda were quick to state that the destruction of the twin towers was intended to have as much a psychological impact as an economic one, as the world's currencies took a downturn leading to mass confusion in the financial sector (Kohlmann 2006).

Moreover, similar cyber attacks have intended to cause psychological damage as the Code Red worm did after it infected millions of servers in 2001 and the 'I Love You' virus in 2000 which simultaneously attacked 20 million Internet users and cost approximately $2.6 billion dollars to the US economy. The economic and social consequences of this kind of cyber attack should not be underestimated. Indeed, the Code Red worm and 'I Love You' virus were both perpetrated by hackers and not terrorists. They had different aims but similar consequences financially and open the scope for terrorists to use similar tactics (Gruner and Gautam 2001).

Simulation Exercises: The Evidence for Cyber Terrorism?

Support for Denning's argument that computers must be used as weapons in cyber terrorism is found in the Report for US Congress, 'Computer Attacks and Cyber Terrorism: Vulnerabilities and Policy Issues' where there were various experiments undertaken as a way of highlighting the potential threat of cyber terrorism. Part of the exercises involved the US Department of Defense (DOD) undertaking a simulation exercise that examined whether or not US ICT systems were able to protect and prevent a cyber attack. This exercise was called 'Eligible Receiver 1997' and was crucial in helping the US identify potential weaknesses they may have in the event of a cyber terrorist act.

Furthermore, another exercise called 'Eligible Receiver 2003' was used to try and play out whether the US military computer systems could cope with a cyber attack. Moreover, the Centre for the Study of Terrorism and Irregular Warfare at the Naval Postgraduate School in California issued a report entitled 'Cyber terror; prospects and implication' (Wilson 2003). This report issued a practical simulation exercise where actors were used to examine whether or not terrorists had the skills to mount a cyber attack. Their findings seem to suggest terrorists did not have the practical skills of doing such attacks.

Part of the process included using hacker's and practitioners with experience of warfare to be part of the study. The report showed that terrorists did not at the time (2002) have the sophisticated skills in information technology nor are they willing to use these tactics. However this example does also suggest that the terrorists lacked the skills to use cyber technology in the manner in which Denning predicts. Furthermore, to date, no terrorists have used cyberspace in this way. Terrorists aim to use tried and tested methods. Bringing down an aeroplane might kill innocent civilians and result in a loss of support from the community. A bomb against a legitimate target is preferable.

Cyber Terrorism Including a Wide Spectrum of Supporting Activities

The alternative approach to Denning is Weimann's argument which is that the Internet is simply a recruitment aid, and acts as a fundraising chat room. This form of cyber terrorism, Weimann states, '… can mobilise supporters to play a more active role in support of terrorist activities or causes' (Weimann 2005:132). Recruiters therefore may use more interactive Internet technology that they can use with online chat rooms, message boards and cybercafes, looking for enlisting support from the most naive and vulnerable and those that hold an identity crises (see chapters 4 and 5) namely young people (Sageman 2008).

The Internet is a safe haven for terrorists as they can remain anonymous, do not need to travel, and do not need to reveal their true identity. For example, the online terrorist Younis Tsouli who used the name *Irhaby* (terrorist) *007* to hide his real appearance had been trained and equipped to use computers as an agent for a cyber terrorist attack (Whine 1999). He was instrumental in preparing Al-Qaeda's online strategy and framework which consisted of propaganda campaigns, recruitment and translating Al-Qaeda material from Arabic into English (this included an Al-Qaeda e-book). In 2007, he was convicted in the UK for inciting terror through the use of the Internet. Academics, however, have made the point that no matter how influential cyberspace is for terrorist groups the use of actual physical domains for terror purposes is at the forefront of extremist group's ideological agendas. Geltzer, argues, that online terrorist material does not have the same impact as physical training camps have. He uses the example of the July 7/7 bombers in Britain who had less contact with online terrorist websites but instead evidence shows that they had taken part in a number of rigorous physical training sessions that required little use of computers (Geltzer 2008).

Forms of Communication

Cyberspace can also be used for propaganda, recruitment, training and indoctrination purposes. The Internet also offers advantages to terrorists in that they can hide their messages. Thus, terrorists have used sophisticated encryption tools so as to deceive as highlighted in the case of one of the September 11 bombers, Mohammed Atta, who was using encryption and secret coded messages via his MSN email account to communicate with the other 9/11 bombers (Walker 2006). One such tool that he used was steganography. This aims to hide information and create complex codes and in cases of cyber terrorism, this may be images, audio and text. Where the language is not one that is easily identifiable, it is easier to hide codes and more difficult for the security services to trace.

In order to tackle this problem and find out what these hidden codes mean there would need to be individuals with the appropriate language skills and insight into cryptic messages. MI6 continuously uses high-risk marketing strategies to hire people from ethnic minority communities to act as informants. This approach has been used before; for example, Special Branch recruited people from Northern Ireland in the early 1990s using the local population as informants who provided key intelligence on the Irish Republican Army (IRA). It is, however, more problematic and difficult to recruit from the Pakistani, Afghani, Yemeni and Somali communities because there is a history of mistrust between the Intelligence services and Muslim communities (Fenwick and Choudhury 2011).

For example, Project Champion, an initiative which was run by the police and various other agencies in the West Midlands (in the UK), consisted of installing a number of secret covert and overt cameras in predominately Muslim areas in order to gather intelligence about issues of counter-terrorism (Awan 2011b; Thornton 2010). Indeed, Innes et al. (2011) research on Muslim communities and their level of satisfaction for British policing of Prevent (Part of the UK Governments counter-terrorism policy) found that many young British Muslim men had a low satisfaction rating of law enforcement agencies such as the police. Thus, MI6 strategy to use the Muslim community as intelligence sources for key information on possible steganographic codes in Urdu and Arabic remains untried and untested.

Another form of propaganda is the use of online video games to train potential terrorists. This form of online video games offer real life simulation of war like scenarios where online gamers are able to fight in simulation exercises that are based on unpopular wars and foreign policies (such as Iraq or Afghanistan). Such games have the potential to ignite and nurture further extremism and also resentment. There is also a real possibility that online gamers will develop a violent culture and perspective through their experiences of warfare, and use it as a real life tool for committing a terrorist attack in the future (Freiburger and Crane 2008).

There have been a number of examples of where individuals have re-enacted those experiences online and wanted to relive the experience. Furthermore, there is an intense debate in the UK (at the time of writing) with respect to the impact of computer games such as 'Modern Warfare'. The game offers players the virtual sensation of fighting against either the Taliban or Al-Qaeda. Critics argue that the game risks losing its moral code as it encourages the killing of individuals (based on similar scenes that resemble what happened in Mumbai) which will only feed further extremism and antagonism. This is certainly not a passive experience and is meant to be as realistic as possible and it is this realism which has caused so much controversy.

Keith Vaz, MP argued that:

> I am absolutely shocked by the level of violence in this game and am particularly concerned about how realistic the game itself looks … I firmly believe that certain levels of violence should not be made into interactive entertainment. This would include acting as a terrorist (Cited by Kendall in *The Times* online 2009:1).

Recruitment

Websites are a powerful tool for extremist organisations. They can secure membership without directly approaching potential recruits and the messages on websites can reach thousands of people across the world. Atwan (2006) acknowledges that Al-Qaeda has become a web-based organisation that utilises cyberspace for terrorist purposes. Indeed, websites contain information about historical accounts, statistics and graphic imagery of terrorist material that can be downloaded and sent to millions of people. This helps create support and act as a recruitment tool. The key to such extremist ideology over the web is to create sites that cause further resentment for the West and allows international Muslim support by allowing its audience to reach to millions (Tsfati and Weimann 2002). Therefore websites are now being used by a wide range of terrorist groups who understand that a website is key to having a global reach. Furthermore, one of the core issues with terrorist websites is the potential to recruit innocent people who may have felt compromised and been allured by what they have seen online and thus become radicalised. Some examples of terrorist websites are included below:

Table 2.1   Terror websites

Organisation	Website
The Kurdistan Workers Party (PKK)	http://www.pkk.org/index.html
The Liberation Tigers of Tawul Eelum	http://www.eelamweb.com/
Hizbollah (Party of God)	www.hizbollah.org, www.moqawama. org www.almanar.com.lb
Hamas (the Islamic Resistance Movement)	http://www.palestine-info.com/hamas
Lebanese Hizbollah (Party of God)	http://www.hizbollah.org
Palestine Islamic Jihad (PIJ)	http://www.entifada.net/
The Popular Front for the Liberation of Palestine (PFLP)	http://www.pflp-pal.org/main.html
Kahane Lives Movement	http://www.kahane.org
Basque ETA Movement	http://www.batasuna.org/
Shining Path (Sendero Luminoso)	http://www.csrp.org/
Colombian National Liberation Army	http://www.eln-voces.com/
Armed Revolutionary Forces of Colombia (FARC)	http://www.farc-ep.org/
Al-Qaeda	http://www.alneda.com
Japanese Supreme Truth (Aum Shinrikyo)	http://www.aleph.to/index_e.html
Mujahedin-e-Khalq	http://www.iran-e azad.org/english/ index.html
Lashker-e-Toyba Pakistan	http://www.markazdawa.org.pk/

Furthermore, one of Al-Qaeda's media arms (known as '*As-Sahab*', which is Arabic for 'the clouds') has had a leading role in recruitment of a wide audience. According to Intel Centre, who monitor Al-Qaeda's media operations they argue that *As-Sahab* releases around 58 videos every day (Intel Centre 2007). Indeed, cyberspace is being increasingly used for hundreds of people who are posting questions to the Al-Qaeda leadership online. This view is reinforced by SITE in Washington, which described a question and answer session with Al-Qaeda's Ayman al-Zawarhi, as deeply 'disturbing' (Glasser and Coll 2005). Moreover, *As-Sahab* produced a further 90 videos in the year 2007. These videos of Osama Bin Laden and Ayman al-Zawarhi act as propaganda tools and aim to use information technology as a way for Al-Qaeda to reach a global audience.

Communication and Propaganda

Al-Qaeda are now using the Internet to promote and indoctrinate their audience by propaganda means through videotapes of its leaders condemning the West, selling T-shirts, flags and pictures of senior Al-Qaeda figures, CD Roms, DVDs and photographs all of the merchandise above act as recruitment message and advertise the Al-Qaeda brand globally. For example videotapes of the Baghdad sniper Juba are readily available on the Internet and are used by Al-Qaeda to show how foreign policy in Iraq has failed.

These videos show Juba killing American soldiers in Iraq without actually showing his face but show Juba as an immortalised figure and depicted as a freedom fighter. Some of the videos are available on the Internet with the aim of this propaganda to disseminate information through various online terrorist means. These videos, however, are seen in some communities as a justification for suicide attacks the key aim of this propaganda is to disseminate information through various online terrorist means (Juba 2007).

Furthermore, Omar Bakri, – (who was barred from entering the UK) – continued to use emails, chat rooms and online seminars to promote and broadcast his message of terror online using emails and chat rooms to keep in contact with those sympathetic to his cause. This use of the Internet allowed Omar Bakri to continue to preach his extremist views for recruitment purposes. It is also possible to use these chat rooms for terrorist funding online. For example, Paltalk has been heavily criticised for its unwavering regulation of its members and the messages its members are able to post (Shahda 2007). However, the issue of online forums does raise important civil liberties arguments that are based on freedom of speech and the right to express those opinions no matter how derogatory they are.

Below are some examples of discussions on the website and chat rooms:

Table 2.2   Paltalk links to forums

Paltalk	Overview of content
http://people.paltalk.com/people/users/ MUJAHIDEEN/index.wmt	Profiles include Mujahedin-Jihad. The profile evokes images of war as does the message within the profile.
http://www.paltalk.com/people/users/ JIHAD%20_J/index.wmt	Various Profiles, similar to the above; profiles includes description of war and destruction.
http://www.paltalk.com/people/users/ jihad_moh/index.wmt	Various profiles: Groups and discussions which relate to war.

These discussions clearly show a sense of anger, hatred and deep animosity for Western values and highlight a virtual community that is willing to post its views available online for all to see as a way of voicing their concerns in the debate surrounding cyber terrorism. Some of the examples of the images and profiles are discussed above and include debates and forums and images of Al-Qaeda.

A Tool of Terror

Whether the Internet is a tool of terror continues to be unclear. Some extremist organisations have used websites to show live online killing of Western hostages. This began with Nick Berg's and then Ken Bigley's and Daniel Pearl's killings. Since then there have been further cases of such executions with many British hostages being held as ransom in an attempt to persuade the UK to change its foreign policy. Using the Internet and videos to make such demands has changed the way information technology can be used (BBC News 2009).

Geltzer (2008) argues that both websites and chat rooms may provide grounds for Al-Qaeda to disseminate literature globally but that the central issue is not being tackled – that is how are websites or chat rooms linked to actual Al-Qaeda terrorist acts? Furthermore, he argues, that all that the Internet has done is too bring Al-Qaeda together to communicate more quickly but that these communications do not produce actual terrorist atrocities. Live executions, for example transmitted to a global audience, have become part of the cyber terrorist act, as it appears to be the direct link between the use of the Internet and a direct terrorist act. The aim is not only to cause fear but to humiliate and demonstrate power. As a result terrorist groups continue to broadcast these videos online.

Moreover the aim is not to create support or recruitment but to strike fear into the hearts and minds of people. These are the same hearts and minds that the former British Prime Minister Gordon Brown had stated needed to be won. The case of Edwin Dyer, a British hostage killed by Al-Qaeda in July 2009, highlights how Al-Qaeda now are using online videos to make demands against countries. In this case, the demand was for the release of Abu Qatada, a senior Al-Qaeda figure. The message which was posted by the group Al-Qaeda in the Islamic Maghreb (AQIM) stated that 'We demand that Britain release Sheikh Abu Qatada, who is unjustly [held], for the release of its British citizen. We give it 20 days as of the issuance of this statement ... When this period expires, the Mujahideen will kill the British hostage' (Rice 2009).

Furthermore, critics argue it does not matter whether Al-Qaeda use a fax or a telephone call any form of communication can still form part of the cyber terrorist act (Atwan 2006). Therefore no matter whether it is the Internet, websites, chat rooms, email, telephone or fax, it remains a form of communication used by Al-Qaeda which is part of the cyber terrorist attack as demonstrated in the Mumbai bombings where the suspects used mobile phones in order to directly communicate with terrorist leaders in Pakistan who gave the orders on the killing of innocent people.

Conclusion

The world's online population is currently estimated to be 1.5 billion, with 3 billion emails being sent every day, and every month 6 billion searches across the top 5 Internet search engines are made, half a million people signing up to Myspace, Facebook and Twitter daily and over 15,000 videos are updated on You Tube every day (Social Media Today 2010). This intense digital minefield creates ample opportunity for terrorists to use and exploit (Awan 2010). Cyber terrorism is any form of electronic media, that is, recruitment, propaganda and communication used in order to cause death and injure innocent people. It does not need to be water contamination or a plane falling from the sky it could actually be simply using an email address to contact someone who is planning a terrorist attack. Or it could be using a chat room to watch online terrorist videos which aim to nurture a hatred for Western democracy which could lead to a person taking part in a terrorist act. Although using an email to get in touch with an Al-Qaeda member or watching a video on YouTube of Bin Laden's speeches is not illegal, it could be argued that it is part of the final cyber terrorist attack.

Denning (2000) and Weimann (2005) have both argued that cyber terrorism is a real threat. The Denning argument has always placed the threat on the use of computers to destroy critical infrastructure, such as financial, military and governmental sectors. Conversely, the Weimann argument is that terrorists use the Internet as a means of propaganda and recruitment. A line has to be drawn between hackers and terrorists whose aims and goals are incomparable and different (Denning 2009). There have been a number of interpretations and definitions of the term cyber terrorism with the main arguments the myth versus reality debate and others describing what might be found in a *Die Hard* movie where cyber terrorism is depicted through the image a major blackout and poisonous gas descending upon the public with explosions, and aircraft falling out of the sky and thousands of people killed.

There is also an argument to be made that the Internet is a beneficial tool in helping governments combat and fight terrorists by being able to monitor their activities online and although cyberspace is a threat if in the wrong hands it also provides much-needed assistance to governments. Furthermore, terrorists, could argue that the Internet is as beneficial to them as it is governments as it can help them for example keep monitoring members of Al-Qaeda and other radical groups internationally who are using email or chat rooms to disseminate extremist literature or help fundraise terrorist activities from the luxury of their own home and therefore disrupting such cyber systems is in their interests.

Recruitment, propaganda and raising funds can now all be done online through websites. The UK, like the US, has implemented new policies in this matter and further changes can be expected in the near future as the threat of cyber terrorism becomes more noticeable. Therefore, the current nature of terrorism provides more support for Weimann's argument but this view could change if terrorists become more sophisticated in their skills. The editors suggest this wider definition is more useful in policing terrorism. In order to tackle this threat, there needs to be better international legal frameworks, the monitoring of terrorist activities, greater international cooperation, and exchange of information and analysis of communications all based upon the definition of a wide spectrum of cyber terrorism (Sarah and Richard 2003).

Further Reading

Awan, I. 2010. *The Threat of Cyber-Terrorism: Combating Cyber-terrorism and Online Crime and Law Series.* Derby: University of Derby. [Online]. Available at: http://www.derby.ac.uk/news/combating-cyber-terrorism-and-online-crime. [accessed: 10th March 2010]; also listen to the Podcast of the Lecture. [Online]. Available at: http://www2.derby.ac.uk/podcasts/bcl2011/disc_talk.wav [accessed:10 March 2012].

Embar-Seddon, A. 2002. Cyber-terrorism: are we under siege? *American Behavioural Scientist*, 45(6), 1033–44.

Foltz, B. 2008. Cyber-terrorism, Computer Crime, and Reality. *Information Management and Computer Security*, 12(2), 154–66.

Flemming, P., and Stohl, M. 2001. 'Myths and Realities of Cyber Terrorism', in *Countering Terrorism through International Cooperation*', edited by A.P. Schmid. Austria: ISPAC, 70–105.

Furnell, S. and Warren. M. 1999. Computer Hacking and Cyber Terrorism: The Real Threats in the New Millennium. *Computers and Security*, 18(1), 28–34.

Green, J. 2002. The Myth of Cyberterrorism. *Washington Monthly*. November. [Online]. Available at: http://www.washingtonmonthly.com/features/2001/0211.green.html) [accessed: 15 November 2010].

References

Atwan, A. 2006. *The Secret History of Al Qaeda*. Berkeley: University of California Press.

Awan, I. 2010. A Web of Deceit. *Public Service Review*, Home Affairs 22, 76.

Awan, I. 2011a. Slaying the Monster: Counter-terrorism Measures under Reform. *Criminal Law and Justice Weekly*, 175 (11), 151-152.

Awan, I. 2011b. Terror in the Eye of the Beholder: The 'Spy Cam' Saga in Birmingham: Counter-Terrorism or Counter-productive? *The Howard Journal of Criminal Justice*, 50 (2), 199–202.

BBC News. 2009. Fear Iraq bodies are UK hostages. [Online]. Available at: http://news.bbc.co.uk/1/hi/uk/8111003.stm [accessed: 12 June 2011].

BBC News. 2011. Rajib Karim: The terrorist inside British Airways .[Online]. Available at: http://www.bbc.co.uk/news/uk-12573824 [accessed: 9 June 2011].

Browne, L. 2010. Cyberattacks: EU Committee Report. Report of the European Union Committee on Protecting Europe against large-scale cyber-attacks. *5th Report, Session 2009–10, HLPaper68*. [Online]. Available at: http://www.publications.parliament.uk/pa/ld201011/ldhansrd/text/101014–0002.htm#10101424000811 [accessed: 27 July 2011].

Cabinet Office. 2010. *A Strong Britain in an Age of Uncertainty: The National Security Strategy*. (Cm 7953): [Online]. Available at: http://www.direct.gov.uk/prod_consum_dg/groups/dg_digitalassets/@dg/@en/documents/digitalasset/dg_191639.pdf?CID=PDF&PLA=furl&CRE=nationalsecuritystrategy [accessed: 29 June 2010].

Denning, D. 2000. *Cyber Terrorism Special: Oversight Panel on Terrorism Committee on Armed Services. U.S. House of Representatives*, 23 May 2000. [Online]. Available at: http://www.cs.georgetown.edu/~denning/inforce/cyberterror.html [accessed: 20 May 2009].

Denning, D. 2001. *Is Cyber Terror Next?. US Social Science Research Council*. [Online]. Available at: http://www.ssrc.org/sept11/essays/denning.htm [accessed: 10 March 2009].

Denning, D. 2009. *Activism, Hacktivism, And Cyberterrorism: The Internet as a tool for influencing foreign policy*. [Online]. Available at: www.rand.org/pubs/monograph_reports/MR1382/MR1382.ch8.pdf [accessed: 15 February 2010].

Denning, D. 2010. 'Terror's Web: How the Internet is Transforming Terrorism', in the *Handbook of Internet Crime*, edited by Majid Yar and Yvonne Jewekes. Willan Publishers, 194–212.

Desmond, P. 2002. Thwarting cyberterrorism. *Network World*, 19 (7):72–4.

Fenwick, H. and Choudhury, T. (2011) The impact of counter-terrorism measures on Muslim communities. *Equality and Human Rights Commission Research Report 72*. [Online]. Available at: http://www.equalityhumanrights.com/uploaded_files/research/counter-terrorism_research_report_72.pdf [accessed: 20 June 2011].

Freiburger, T. and Crane, J. 2008. A Systematic Examination of Terrorist Use of the Internet. *International Journal of Cyber Criminology*, 2(1), 309-319.

Gardham, D. 2008. Al-Qaeda Terrorists who brainwashed Exeter Suicide Bomber Still on the Run. *The Daily Telegraph*. [Online]. Available at: http://www.telegraph.co.uk/news/uknews/law-and-order/3204139/Al-Qaeda-terrorists-who-brainwashed-Exeter-suicide-bomber-still-on-the-run.html [accessed: 1 July 2011].

Geltzer, A. 2008. Six rather unexplored assumptions about Al Qaeda. *Critical Studies on Terrorism*, 1(3), 393–403.

Githens-Mazer, J. and Lambert, R. 2010. Islamophobia and Anti Muslim Hate Crimes: a London case study. *European Muslim Research Centre*. [Online]. Available at: http://centres.exeter.ac.uk/emrc/publications/IAMHC revised_11Feb11.pdf [accessed: 19 June 2011].

Glasser, S.B. and Coll, S. 2005. The Web as Weapon: Zarqawi Intertwines Acts on ground with propaganda campaign on the Internet. *Washington Post*. [Online]. Available at: http://msl1.mit.edu/furdlog/docs/washpost/2005-08-09_washpost_www_weapon_03.pdf [accessed: 1 July 2011].

Gruner, S. and Gautam, N. 2001. Extremist Sites Under Heightened Scrutiny. *The Wall Street Journal*. [Online]. 8 October. Available at: http://zdnet.com.com/2100-1106-530855.html?legacy=zdnn. [accessed: 3 May 2009].

Hopkins, N. and Hall, S. 2000. David Copeland: a quiet introvert, obsessed with Hitler and bombs. *Guardian*. [Online]. Available at: http://www.guardian.co.uk/uk/2000/jun/30/uksecurity.sarahhall [accessed: 18 June 2011].

Hughes, G. 2003. The cyberspace invaders. *The Age*. [Online]. 22 June. Available at: http://www.theage.com.au/articles/2003/06/21/1056119529509.html [accessed: 16 June 2011].

Innes, M., Roberts, C., Innes, H., Lowe, T., & Lakhani, S. 2011. Assessing the effects of Prevent policing. A report to the Association of Chief Police Officers. [Online]. Available at: http://www.acpo.police.uk/documents/TAM/2011/PREVENT%20Innes%200311%20Final%20send%202.pdf [accessed: 14 March 2012].

IntelCentre. 2007. *Al-Qaeda Messaging Statistics*. [Online]. Available at: http://www.intelcenter.com/QMS-PUB-v3-3.pdf [accessed: 19 June 2011].

Juba the Baghdad Sniper. 2007. *The Black Flag*. [Online]. Available at: http://www.blackflag.wordpress.com/2007/07/19/juba-the-baghdad-sniper-video/ [accessed: 10 February 2010].

Kendall, N. 2009. Modern Warfare 2-The Shocking Video game poised to smash records. *Times online*. [Online]. Available at: http://technology.timesonline.co.uk/tol/news/tech_and_web/gadgets_and_gaming/article6906968.ece [accessed: 10 November 2009].

Kohlmann, E. 2006. The Real Online Terrorist Threat. *Foreign Affairs*, 85(5), 115–24.

Lobban, I. 2010. *GCHQ Director Iain Lobban warns of 'real' cyber threat facing UK*. [Online]. Available at: http://www.thisisgloucestershire.co.uk/GCHQ-

Director-Iain-Lobban-warns-real-cyber-threat-facing-UK/story-11855429-detail/story.html [accessed: 1 July 2011].

May, T. 2011. 'CONTEST Speech. *Home Office.* [Online]. Available at: http://www.homeoffice.gov.uk/media-centre/speeches/contest-speech   [accessed: 20 July 2011]; Also see Travis, A. 2011. Counter-terrorism strategy driven by 'cyberjihad' threat. *Guardian* (July). [Online]. Available at: http://www.guardian.co.uk/politics/2011/jul/12/counter-terrorism-strategy-cyberjihad-threat [accessed: 13 July 2011].

National Air Traffic Control Systems. 2008. *Critical Infrastructure.* [Online]. Available at: http://www.nats.co.uk/article/253/270/nats_handles_more_than_24m_flights_in_2008.html [accessed: 30 September 2009].

Reid, L. 2010. Cyberattacks: EU Committee Report. Report of the European Union Committee on Protecting Europe against large-scale cyber-attacks. *5th Report, Session 2009–10, HL Paper 68.* [Online]. Available at: http://www.publications.parliament.uk/pa/ld201011/ldhansrd/text/101014-0002.htm#10101424000811 [accessed: 1 July 2011].

Rice, X. 2009. Al Aqida group demands release of Abu Qatada or British hostage will be killed. *Guardian.* [Online]. Available at: http://www.guardian.co.uk/world/2009/apr/27/alqaida-north-africa-hostages [accessed: 30 April 2009].

Sageman, M. 2008. *Leaderless Jihad.* Philadelphia: University of Pennsylvania Press.

Sarah, G. and Richard, F. 2003. Cyber terrorism? *Symantec White Paper.* [Online]. Available at: http://www.symantec.com/avcenter/reference/cyberterrorism.pdf [accessed: 12 February 2010].

Shahda, J. 2007. Paltalk hosts Al-Qaeda, Hizbollah, and Hamas chat rooms. *Mosquewatch.blogspot.com.* [Online]. Available at: http://mosquewatch.blogspot.com/2007/12/exclusive-paltalk-hosts-al-qaeda.html [accessed: 15 June 2011].

Social Media Today. 2010. *Statistics on Social Media.* [Online]. Available at: http://socialmediatoday.com/tompick/176932/best-social-media-stats-and-market-research-2010-so-far [accessed: 10 June 2011].

Stohl, M. 2007. Cyber terrorism: A clear and present danger, the sum of all fears. Breaking point or patriot games? *Crime, Law and Social Change.* 46 (4–5), 223–38.

Stuart, K. 2011. Why are Lulzsec and Anonymous hacking games companies? *Guardian.* [Online]. Available at: http://www.guardian.co.uk/technology/2011/jun/16/lulzsec-anonymous-hacking-games-companies [accessed: 1 July 2011].

The Terrorism Act 2000. (c.11), London: HMSO.

Thornton, S. 2010. *Project Champion Review.* [Online]. Available at: www.west-midlands.police.uk/ latest-news/docs/Champion_Review_FINAL_30_09_10.pdf [accessed: 10 March 2010].

Tsfati, Y. and Weimann, G. 2002. www.terrorism.com: Terror on the Internet. *Studies in Conflict & Terrorism,* 25(5): 317–32.

Vegh, S. 2002. Hactivists or cyber-terrorists? The changing Media Discourse on Hacking. *First Monday*. 7(10). [Online]. Available at: http://firstmonday.org/htbin/cgiwrap/bin/ojs/index.php/fm/rt/printerFriendly/998/919 [accessed: 2 July 2011].

Walker, C. 2006. Cyber-Terrorism: Legal Principle and the Law in the United Kingdom. *Penn State Law Review*,110, 625–65.

Wilson, C. 2003. *Computer Attack and Cyberterrorism: Vulnerabilities and Policy Issues for Congress. CRS Report for Congress.* [Online]. Available at: http://www.fas.org/irp/crs/RL32114.pdf [accessed: 22 March 2009].

Weimann, G. 2005. The sum of all fears? *Studies in Conflict and Terrorism*, 28, 129–49.

Whine, M. 1999. Cyberspace: A New Medium for Communication, Command, and Control by Extremists. *Studies in Conflict & Terrorism*, *22*(3), 231–46.

Yar, M. 2006. *Cybercrime and Society*. London: Sage Publications.

Chapter 3
Psychological Aspects of Cyber Hate and Cyber Terrorism

Jane Prince

In March 2011 the author was in a small regional northern European airport waiting for a flight home. Ahead in the queue to go through security was a blonde woman, in her early forties, dressed in T-shirt, cut-offs and sandals and clearly on her way to a holiday somewhere warm. She put her hand luggage on the scanner belt, it rolled halfway through, was stopped by the scrutiniser and reversed back to her. The security officer then pulled from the bag a 400 ml container of sunscreen lotion, looked at it, looked at the woman and said 'OK' and returned it to her (restrictions on carrying liquids on European flights mean all liquids had to be in containers of not more than 100 ml).

Clearly the security officer had a robust mental model of what constituted a terrorist and it appears that middle-aged women in holiday clothes flying out of a small airport did not match that model. The reliance on visual and contextual cues to establish categories for people is common in face-to-face interactions and, as a heuristic, is often very effective; however, in computer-mediated communication (CMC) with no visual cues and the need to rely on self-descriptions, language structures and syntax it is much harder to identify and categorise people. In particular the dominance of self-description (rather than tangible reality) in online communication allows for manipulation of others as well as making it difficult to identify the characteristics of the communication source. In using CMC in recruiting others for acts of terror or in establishing hate sites the use of a medium which is blind and deaf to reality can have its advantages.

What is understood regarding cyber hate and cyber terrorism from a psychological perspective? One of the problems faced by those theorising the psychological aspects of perpetrators of cyber terror is that few practitioners have been identified. Hence psychologists have had to draw on what they know of cyber communications, the psychology of those who engage in terrorism and broader theories of group membership, terrorist motivation, identity and social identity theories to explain the phenomena.

Cyber hate is understood as being the use of information and communication technologies (ICTs) to promote hate and to target the largely youthful and impressionable audiences that increasingly rely on these technologies. Hate-groups achieve their goals in four main ways: promoting ideology, promoting hatred of other racial or religious groups, exerting control over others and targeting opponents. Cyber terrorism is considered in this chapter broadly as being the use of information technologies to promote terrorism and to achieve terrorist goals. This may be through attacking the infrastructure of the web through viruses, hacking and so on, or through use of technology to organise terror attacks. Of interest then is the psychological aspects of the ways in which communication through ICTs differs from other modes of communication.

This chapter will return to the central issue facing those who try to theorise and challenge hate and terrorism on the Internet; this is the problem of defining the psychology of people who are essentially 'invisible'. The lack of information about the psychology of the terrorist is a consequence of the dearth of candidates for participation in research. For cyber terrorism the situation is even more problematic and its proponents even more inaccessible. Psychology has dealt well with theorising and explaining the consequences of terrorism and hate crimes for victims and the broader population (for example, Joshi and O'Donnell 2008, Laufer, Solomon and Levine 2010, Miller 2004) ; on a practical level, terrorism is a very slippery and dangerous subject for the collection of systematic and reliable data, and psychology has on the whole not dealt well with researching the terrorist himself (Silke 2003) apart from some research about the personality and motivation of the terrorist.

Weimann (2008) recognised the extent to which terrorists use CMC to plan, coordinate and execute their plans, freed from the constraints of physical space or the politics of a particular state with a medium which is uncontrolled, accessible to all and mobile. The geographical terrain of the cyber terrorist is even more unbounded than that of the face-to-face terrorist. I say this because while terrorist actions take place in a specific geographical locale, be that the Madrid metro system, the Kabul market place or a New York office block, the terrorist motivation can be driven by an imagined place, a land the terrorist has never seen or an idealised place of the future such as a re-established caliphate. However, locations for encounter are in the physical present; the terrorist planting bombs or the suicide bomber planning his own destruction can prepare for the physical context of his actions. He may calculate the best location for his explosion, anticipate the practicalities of achieving that place, plan out in advance strategies for screening out the humanity in the faces and bodies of intended victims or of any who may challenge him. For the cyber terrorist the conceptual space is different; whether planning a physical attack or coordinating a denial-of-service assault or a hacking venture, his geographical space is inchoate, nowhere and the results of his actions only have a tangible existence in the reaction of victims rather than in the blood of their bodies or the wreckage of their places of travel or of work. Tololyan (1989) called the geography of all terrorism 'a creature of time and place' (Tololyan 1989:101), an entity which occupies a narrative rather than a geographical space and this applies to the domain of the cyber terrorist enabling researchers a start to understand the motivation underpinning the action.

The constraints on the acquisition of empirical data have set limitations on the way in which the psychology of cyber terrorism has been theorised. Some researchers have focused on empirical data derived from studies of online aggressive behaviour such as flaming to develop theoretical models while others have drawn on existing psychological theory, in particular theory relating to psychopathology and to group membership, identification and moral disengagement. However, explanations consistently focus on the ability to manipulate and control others and this is explored next.

Social Identity Theory (Tajfel and Turner 1979)

Tajfel and Turner argued that identity derives to a large extent from group membership (whether family, ethnic, occupational or any other group) and that an individual's identity develops through a process of social categorisation, that is allocating self and others into social groups, us and them, in-groups and out-groups; social identity theory has as its core the assertion that members of in-groups will seek to elevate the status of their own group through valorisation of that group and through denigration of the out-group.

The process of establishing group membership is a three-stage one; firstly is the process of categorisation, secondly the process of social identification and finally that of social comparison. If we an individual can categorise people into a particular group then we can make assumptions about their characteristics, qualities and general merits; it is a cognitively advantageous process (and essential to everyday functioning) to be able to use categories or stereotypes to classify people and situations as this enables us to deal more rapidly with actions relating to them. Categorisation tells us about ourselves (for example, what we must support because we are Catholic, or Welsh or nurses) and what we should do; group norms are used as reference points to guide behaviour but to allow this we must be able to categorise both ourselves and others. It is during the second stage, that of social identification, that we adopt the identity of the group into which we have categorised ourselves; there is an affective significance to the group membership and self-esteem becomes entwined with continuing membership of that group.

The third stage is social comparison; once we have categorised ourselves as group members then to maintain self-esteem we need to compare ourselves with out-groups. This comparison includes consideration of group qualities (those positive things the group members have in common), group resources and group rewards. The process of social comparison makes it inevitable that resource allocation will be seen as unfair; by definition the in-group has the highest qualities and hence deserves more than the out-group.

This is a critical part of SIT as once groups see themselves as different, members inevitably develop out-group hostility either because there is competition for resources or as a result of competing identities. While a person may belong to many different groups these cannot be mutually conflicting. If they are conflicting the individual experiences dissonance and moves away from one group. Empirical support for Social Identity Theory is strong (for example, Hopkins and Reicher

1996, Liu and Hilton 2005, Lalonde 2002) and derives from both observation of real-life behaviour and empirical laboratory investigation (Tajfel 1982) and quasi-experiments such as Sherif's (1966) Robbers Cave study. It is important to note that in-group membership is a real and active part of the person's identity; manipulation therefore of in-and out-group characteristics can be used to promote actions hostile to the out-group and it is this manipulation, the emphasising of in- and out-group differences and entitlements which can facilitate the development of online terrorism where nothing is tangible and false representations of reality can be presented as fact. The process of out-group derogation legitimises the victimisation of others.

At this point the reader may ask 'so people belong to groups and don't like people who belong to other groups – so what?' Here the point is being missed. In Sherif's Robbers Cave study, in which children who were previously unknown to each other were taken to summer camp and arbitrarily assigned to groups for activities as is normal in such camps, it was found that the children developed an in-group pride coupled with an aggressive stance towards the other group which manifested itself in hate words, abuse, dislike and eventually physical violence. This was without any other communality between the boys in each group – no shared interests, religion, values or background. Sherif's initial and disturbing discovery that simply creating two groups and placing them in competition with each other led to animosity far beyond low-level rivalry with the potential for genuine hatred was further developed by Tajfel (1970) in his concept of minimal groups.

Tajfel argued that all that was need to create in-group pride and out-group hostility was for people to be told they were members of a group; the group did not have to be based around any specific interest or value system. In a series of studies involving the creation of artificial groups based on very unimportant distinctions (in one study he assigned boys to groups based on their alleged expressed preferences for contemporary art in a forced choice task) he found that not only did being assigned to a group lead to individuals identifying with that group but that one of the manifestations of that identification was a hostility to out-groups which led the focus of decision-making to be what would most disadvantage that out-group rather than what would most privilege the in-group. By merely being a group member, our cognitive, emotional and evaluative processes develop a tendency to orientate round that group, to seek to maintain it and to privilege it over any out-groups. It can be seen then that incorporating potential activists into a group (those characteristics which might make a person vulnerable to being drawn into such groups will be discussed later) requires only to identify an out-group and to identify a common organising characteristic for the in-group. For hate groups this is done through the identification of a perceived privilege the out-group has over in-group members. This might be civic (for example, perceived preferential treatment given to a particular religious or social group), economic (financial benefits accruing) or even status-oriented (members of that group have all the power). The British hate-group, the English Defence League, focuses on recruiting working class, white English males usually) living in areas of economic and social deprivation; it focuses its communications on mythical accounts of the material wealth (for example, housing cars, jobs) offered by the British state to undeserving immigrants. The Swedish National Democrats, an extreme right-wing group, focuses on similar issues and also on the 'privileges' given to homosexuals in Sweden (Lagerlof 2004). Such groups are using the net not just to present their view but to actively recruit new members.

Studies of ICT mediated communications form minority group members suggest that group-membership salience can be enhanced by active engagement. McKenna and Bargh (1998) studied the impact of membership of online groups for people with marginalised identities where the marginalisation was non-obvious (for example sexual preference); they found that those with marginalised but concealable identities engaged more in active posting than did people with marginalised visible identities (such as having a weight problem) and suggested that the opportunity to be with people of similar values was particularly attractive to those who did not easily voice their true identities. Moreover they found that active engagement with the group (posting rather than lurking) increased the group's importance to the individual. If one considers the position of a new recruit to a hate or terror group, certainly an identity which would have to remain hidden to the outside world, then encouraging that person to engage with the group discussions online would valorise that group membership for him and make him more susceptible to propaganda emanating from that source.

Berry et al. (2004) noted that the formation of cliques is the main recruitment mode for terrorist organisations. They developed software which is has been used for modelling the formation and dynamics of social groups and concepts. Their work was based on Sageman's (2004) account of terrorist organisations, based on his work in Afghanistan with the Mujahedin. Sageman's ideas challenged a view of the terrorist that s/he is psychologically flawed in some generalisable way; typically he said that the Mujahedin are psychologically healthy members of their society. What united them was communality of experience including a degree of social isolation as well as historical experiences which led to them forming social clusters (based on these common experiences). It is these clusters which are the basis of terrorist networks.

The model includes various conceptual agents which are used to locate societal and social concepts within the model allowing it to be manipulated (to explore different dynamics and outcomes) and allowing it to develop a predictive power. Within the model social networks – a world network connecting all members, an acquaintance network, a strong bond network, a mosque network (connecting all who attend the same mosque) and a clique network. Dependent on the individual's interaction with different networks different dynamics (and different social scenarios) can be explored. The role of the clique is paramount in the development of powerful networks; cliques are a product of acquaintance and strong bonds; cliques emerge through friendship and trust and this naturally extends to friends of friends becoming friends too. In simulations, changing opportunities for social contact impacted on the nature of the clique formed. In the real world this would suggest that rather than focusing on the charisma of an individual recruiter, it is important to impede communications between group members to prevent the formation of cyber-cliques. As with the material on social identity theory above this suggests that in combating cyber hate and cyber terrorism a critical point lies round recruitment of members and impeding the maintenance of information flow and the impact of social influence.

Social Influence and Social Identity Model of De-individuation Effects (SIDE)

Social Identity theory takes as given that it applies to small and large groups equally; it is the presence of a psychological group, a consequence of social categorisation, which produces social influence. How does this operate in situations where the out-group is either not present or where its nature is not immediately obvious. The SIDE model (Reicher, Spears and Postmes 1995) proposes that the social influence of factors at the social level in a group (norms, values, goals, assumptions and so on at the group level) are particularly powerful in their effects on group members when people are de-individuated. Individuation is the making of distinctions between members of a group, effectively undermining common causes within a group or even its reason for existence. De-individuation is best seen as a psychological state of lowered self-evaluation; being unknown causes a loss of a sense of self and individual identity and hence an increase in disinhibited behaviour. Reflections about the consequences of actions will be that these consequences will be for the group rather than for the individual. If a group is a 'whole' rather than viewed in terms of the characteristics of individual members then actions of that group are perceived as being a consequence of group rather than any personal qualities; the group becomes an agent in its own right.

Arguably group identities should be more powerful in situations where individual members are not in face to face interaction (for example in cyber-groups) as the qualities of the individual are to an extent invisible according to Postmes, Spears and Lea (1999). They argue that situations where groups do not meet face-to-face provide exactly the conditions 'predicted to maximise social influence exerted by social norms and social identities, according to the SIDE model' (Postmes, Spears and Lea 1999:167) and challenged the view that the inevitable anonymity associated with CMC would mean no opportunity for the development of a group identity or the influence of social norms. Rather this anonymity would, they argue, become more responsive to the group and to its values and norms. In a series of laboratory based studies (for example, Postmes et al. 2001) specific group norms were activated in a group and then that group were required to address a problem via CMC. Participants were allocated to one of two conditions – either they were completely anonymous (identified by a number) or they were identifiable by their picture (and those of the entire group) being presented on the screen. The induced social norm had a great impact on both the decision outcome and the interactional process dynamic when group members were anonymous but not when they were identifiable by pictures. The impact was in relation to the maintenance of the induced group norm. Later studies showed that anonymous groups assumed task-orientation more than did identifiable groups. If anonymity increases the significance of that group for its members then it would be expected that people would report higher group identification in the anonymous situation.

CMC appears to enhance the influence of social (group-related norm) factors within a group. It is likely that it also enhances the perceived differences between groups as self-categorisation theory (Turner 1987) would predict in that the meaningfulness of group identity is a consequence of a comparison of some sort, however unconscious, with a relevant out-group. Hence the anonymity between group members – or recruiters and potential recruits for cyber terrorism – has the potential to polarise attitudes towards a group's values and goals and those of out-groups. De-individuating environments may increase the influence of social stereotypes and prejudice. The hate-speech in online forums and discussion groups can serve to both reinforce the salience of the group identity and justify aggression and hostility to others. The de-individuating qualities of CMC with focus the attention of members away from individual variation and towards meaningful social identities shared in common. As the relevance of the social identity is enhanced then identification with the group increases; this is particularly the case when individual identities are hidden. Thus online group members affiliation with the group, its goals, its values and its methods are enhanced in the conditions of anonymity characteristic of online hate-groups and terror groups.

Computer-Mediated versus Face-to-Face Communication

While early studies of CMC focused on the importance of lack of visual and other social cues (for example, Social Presence Theory: Short, Williams and Christie 1976) more recent studies have focused on the role of de-individuation effects (for example, Sproull and Kiesler 1986) and research using the SIDE model to predict hostile behaviour. The research provides considerable insight into the nature of cyber hate and cyber terrorism. De-individuation theory proposes that during CMC individuals become less likely to monitor their own behaviour and less inhibited and hence more prone to impulsive behaviour such as flaming and cyber hate (Douglas and McGarty 2001). In a series of studies Douglas and McGarty attempted to extend existing theorising about hate-communications via CMC by applying the strategic aspect of SIDE. In particular they found that when in-group members were identifiable to an in-group audience they were more likely to produce generalisations in line with in-group norms when describing an out-group audience than if they were not being monitored by their in-group. In other words when what they were saying could be known to members of their 'group' they would use more stereotypical attitudes to the out-group. This has particular salience for understanding cyber hate and cyber terrorism when one considers the communication structures of a cyber cell; if it is believed that communication is being monitored by an in-group member (a cell leader for example) then hate speech and negative stereotypes and hostile expressions (to the out group) will be more likely. Identifiability brings about a stronger awareness of accountability to and motivation towards the group's norms; self-presentation motivation does affect the norm-related behaviour.

In part this serves the function of allowing group members to enact their identity; Douglas and McGarty use the term 'obligation' to describe this effect. Feeling accountable increases the tendency to voice ideas in a way which reflects (and uses language consistent with) group norms.

The psychology of online aggressive behaviour has been the focus of several research studies. Although cyber hate refers to a specific aspect of online aggression, the general concept of antagonistic or aggressive behaviour in CMC is a broad one and refers not only to the incitement of hatred but also to hostile or aggressive communications, including flaming and the use of keyboard symbols to substitute for the tonal emphasis in verbal communication. Such behaviour is at its highest level in real-time CMC interactions (Joinson 2003) though these are not necessarily characteristics of cyber hate or cyber terrorist groups. Online communication is characterised by its lack of any regulating feedback (for example, visual and tonal cues as to disapproval) and social anonymity. The lack of such feedback and the unreality of online environments may act as stimuli for aggressive and hostile online communication.

Whitney (2010) reports a study into online hate and terror websites. He noted the use of video-material both of terrorist actions and the consequences of retaliatory acts and the development of 'how-to' guides to encourage the construction of devices such as shoe-bombs. He also reported the developments of hate sites which allow those accessing them to play games in which they torture and murder particular groups; one example he cited was a site which allows users to 'bomb' the survivors of the Haiti 2010 earthquake. It is proposed that the use of games to encourage virtual hate crimes is a technique specifically targeted at the young. One outcome of this is to normalise hate-activities among this population. Pyszczynski et al. (2006) noted that support for violent military interventions by American forces was increased by reference to 'mortality salience' (reminders of death) amongst young politically conservative American college students, though not among the politically liberal. Hate websites such as the Haiti bombing site could be used to elevate levels of mortality salience and valorise young people to accept violence against other groups across political, geographic and ethnic divides. Terror Management theory (Greenberg, Pyszczynski and Solomon 1986) suggests that people can be motivated to support terror attacks on others through alerting them to a (perceived not actual) need for protection against some existential threat; reminders of death increases the willingness of group members to support aggressive and hostile acts against an out-group. Reminders of death lead people to adhere more closely to group norms, punish others for violation of those norms and react with hostility to any group whose views differ from those of their in-group. In a series of studies Pyszczynski et al. (2006) reported findings supporting this view; they argued that frequent reminders of death fan the emotions which sustain conflicts. Websites which display material such as videos of bombings, hostage executions, the aftermath of an attack and so on will enhance mortality salience and hence terrorist activity; it is then in the interest of those recruiting to hate or terror sites to maintain such images at the forefront of their websites. Once again it seems likely that the way to manage cyber hate and cyber terror psychologically is to focus on the prevention of recruiting new members.

One of the issues raised in developing understanding of the role of CMC in hate and terror crimes is the extent to which the anonymity of the medium and the lack of identity cues allows for deception and manipulation. CMC is gender, ethnicity ad age neutral; the cues to identity available are largely related to language use and these can be assumed. The online identity is taken as its self-description. Numerous incidents have been reported of deception relating to gender assumption (Ellison, Heino and Gibbs 2006) as well as deception in relation to health (for example, Feldman's 2000 account of Munchausen by Internet) and financial status (Campbell, Fletcher and Greenhill 2009).

Bowker and Tuffin (2003) investigated the deception strategies in online communication in a group of people who had strong motives for using deception in managing the presentation of self in online forums as a consequence of real-life experience, namely the disabled. Their perceptions of risk may be shared by individuals tentatively exploring cyber crime – a fear of being 'found out' and a fear of 'stranger danger'. Using a methodology involving discursive analysis the researchers identified two main repertoires involved in interaction – a 'keeping safe' repertoire, including knowledge of the dangers of disclosure to new untested communicators and a 'qualified deception' repertoire which included withholding personal information, reconstructing information (the deliberate construction of a false version of themselves, complete with life events prior to engaging with others with the specific goal of minimising risk associated with operating in a stigmatised identity). This qualified deception repertoire enable people to extend the nature of their online interactions as well as to explore identities not available in face-to-face interaction. What is of interest is the quality of the deception but also the psychological implications of it; the managed versions of themselves were plausible not only to others in the discussion groups but also to the participants themselves. The people they described themselves as being became desired possible selves; this has implications for the drawing in of novices to a terror or hate community using online recruitment. Deception online is much harder to identify than in face to face encounters.

Theory of Selective Moral Disengagement (Bandura 1990)

Selective moral disengagement refers to the ability to dissociate oneself morally from any negative outcomes of a specific behaviour by referring to a higher or alternative moral reference point. Moral rules are internalised throughout the period of maturation as the child moves from applying moral rules strictly without regard to context to a final stage of individual morality when judgements of fairness, best good for all and social justice are integrated into the person's moral repertoire (Kohlberg 1983); at this stage morality is about a broad conceptualisation of 'right' behaviour rather than simple rule following. Moral standards are used as a guide for good conduct and a deterrent for bad; the person sanctions himself for bad or immoral behaviour through affective and cognitive responses. Behaviour which breaks their moral codes brings self-condemnation. However, selective disengagement of internalised moral codes allows for a moral code to operate but with different behavioural outcomes dependent on context. Self-sanctioning can be disengaged by reframing the situation, by identifying some higher moral imperative (for example, patriotism or religious duty), by devolving personal agency to some other (for example, arguing an action was a group rather than an individual decision), downplaying the outcome of an action or by dehumanising or denigrating victims. History echoes with narratives of 'justified' acts of terrorism. For example when in thirteenth century England Jews were murdered by being thrown down wells, this was justified by the moral imperative to save Christian children from being kidnapped and murdered in order for the Jews to drink their blood. The Beslan (Russian Federation) school siege in 2004 which ended in the murder of over 300 people including 196 children was justified by the imperative to challenge the Russian oppression of the people of Chechnya.

Weimann (2008) identifies seven practices associated with moral disengagement. These are: the distortion of the relationship between the agents actions and its consequences through displacing responsibility for the action on compelling circumstances, the diffusion of responsibility through referral to group decisions, the dehumanising of victims by focusing on their symbolic qualities rather than their human ones, the use of euphemisms which sanitise actions and consequences (for example the use of the term 'collateral damage'), comparisons which draw attention to offences committed by the other rather than the consequences of one's own action, blaming the victim for provoking the aggression and the distortion of event sequences such as arguing an action was a response to a hostile act of the other party.

Personality, Individual Difference Disorders and Cyber Terrorism: Is There a Psychological Profile for a Terrorist?

One of the difficulties associated with describing the terrorist personality is that there is a shortage of participants whose characters to explore; few terrorists and even fewer cyber terrorists have been available to study and describe. Individuals engaging in criminal computer activities are believed to be more exploitive and manipulative than individuals who do not engage in criminal computer activity (Rogers 2003). Bachmann (2010) studied 124 individuals who had engaged in a specific area of computer crime, namely hacking. He found his participants had a significantly higher need for cognition (eager to learn and engaging with novel experiences, welcoming being confronted with challenges and solving them) than the general public and also higher propensity for taking risks. Their cognitive style was logical rather than intuitive and they displayed a very high level of confidence in their ability to overcome operational difficulties. They also preferred complex problems over simple ones. Parallels can be drawn between the goals of cyber criminals and those of cyber terrorists in that both need, in order to be successful, to engage complex problems and rise to the challenges they present.

It has been hypothesised that the violence and casual aggression displayed by instigators of hate crimes and of terrorism must indicate a pathological personality although, as mentioned above, studies of the specific groups of terrorists have not found any indication of psychopathology. Gottschalk and Gottschalk (2004) have reported research using the Minnesota Multiphasic Personality Inventory (MMPI), a measure designed and validated or assessing severe psychological and psychopathological disorders which has identified characteristics in contemporary terrorists which mark them out from both their predecessors and their fellow citizens of similar ethnicity. They argue, however, that focusing primarily on personality characteristics is not particularly useful in understanding the development of a terrorist; rather researchers should explore the integration between personality characteristics including psychopathologies and psychosocial orientation of terrorist. Contemporary terrorists they argue seem uninterested in presenting specific grievances with outlines of specific solutions – they seem more concerned with the publicity obtained for them through scenes of random violence. There is no demand for negotiation or for some form of recognition, nor for the release of jailed comrades – rather there appears to be terror for terror's sake coupled with an expansion of activities to a global context which is not selective in choice of targets or victims. Gottschalk and Gottschalk argue that terrorism is primarily motivated by the desire to create terror and that 'the political goals on behalf of which terrorists claim to struggle' (Gottschalk and Gottschalk 2004: 41) are nothing more than a medium through which their psychosocial orientation can be expressed. The MMPI tests found considerable similarity between terrorist groups (regardless of political or religious orientation) on schizophrenic tendencies, psychopathic deviation, depression and hypomania. When compared with control groups terrorists were more similar to each other than to their controls and the clinical profile of each terrorist group was closer to a 'general terrorist' profile than that of an ethnically-similar control. On the measure of pathological hatred too the terrorist were more similar to each other, regardless of political, social or religious affiliation than they were to controls from their own ethnic and religious background.

Gottschalk and Gottschalk then interviewed 57 terrorists using a semi-structured approach with interview being transcribed and then translated form Arabic or Hebrew into English and French then analysed using thematic analysis identifying themes. These oriented round group identity, ethnocentrism, racism and dehumanisation of other groups. The terrorists had a world view in which the out-group members are vicious, cunning, dangerous and effectively sub-human and deserving of any violence inflicted on them.

The connection is found then between the theory and the practice; there are few studies of actual terrorists and Gottschalk and Gottschalk's work seems to provide support for a model of terrorist psychology in which the theoretical accounts of social identity theory, de-individuation, social categorisation and out-group hostility outlined earlier in this chapter interacting with pathological psychological states to define a terrorist.

While the Gottschalk and Gottschalk study focused on those who were committing acts of terrorism in the Middle East (from both Islamic and Jewish terrorist groups), nonetheless their findings show an insight which is helpful in understanding the psychology of the cyber hate and terrorist activities. Other researchers have focused on hackers to explore the psychology of cyber terrorists. Rogers (2003) noted that although hackers were typically loners they had a desire for association with peers, something they fulfil via online chat rooms and groups of hackers.

Lachkar (2006) argued for terrorism and hate-crime behaviour to be linked to personality disorders. These are defined by DSM-IV-TR (American Psychiatric Association 2000) as being enduring patterns of behaviour which are located in the individuals orientation towards the external world and which are associated with disturbed, unrealistic and inappropriate patterns of behaviour of an individual which are associated in most cases with extensive disruption to the individual's personal and social life; these patterns of behaviour are inflexible and universal.

Lachkar's work focused on the link between characteristics of terrorists and those of individuals suffering from borderline personality disorder (BPD). This disorder (collection of symptoms and antecedents) was named 'borderline' because the behaviour it manifested placed the sufferer on the border between psychosis and neurosis. The key characteristic of the borderline personality is a failure to form a securely attached relationship (Bowlby 1982) leading in the case of people with BPD to a pattern of deficient affiliations and dependency needs, a consequence of the development of the belief that the person's needs (not attended to during maturation) are consequently something dangerous, to be engaged with impulsively and irrationally. Typically people with borderline personality disorder lack impulse control and fail to learn from experience; they also suffer from fears of abandonment and persecution and have a tendency to misperceive and manipulate reality. Lachkar (2006) describes the borderline personality as being 'dominated by shame/blame defences, persecutory abandonment identification, denial' (2006:316). Their problems are ones of illusion and perceived privation with a propensity for blaming others for all ills in their own lives; Lachkar argues that groups of individuals can manifest similar pathological tendencies, particularly when following a group leader, albeit an invisible one, whose delusions also involve perceptions of inequity and the responsibility of the 'other'. A leader can manipulate the fears and presumptions of members with themes of blaming 'the other' and the need for attack and retaliation. As with all groups individual members respond to information which reinforces the identity of the group (see Social Identity Theory material above). She proposes that children raised in traumatic environments such as war zones are vulnerable to identification with and attachment to leaders who embrace destruction; it is the vulnerability of those recruited by terrorists which needs to be explored and challenged.

Indeed Faria and Arce (2005) argue that the focus on prevention of recruitment to terrorist networks should orientate around openness. Of the four parameters they identify as being determinants of terror activity – deterrence policy, militancy, political opinion and the effectiveness of terrorism in achieving outcomes – it is political opinion which has the most impact on the recruitment of new members to a network.

Conclusion

It is a truism that the language is defined by those who use it; one person's terrorist is another person's freedom fighter. This chapter avoided such discussion as it is not relevant to the issues discussed. However, the case of a well-known contemporary cyber terrorist illustrates the problems in exploring the psyche of those who promote hate and terror while remaining invisible themselves in cyberspace: This is the case of Bradley Manning, the US soldier who is charged with being the source behind the 2010 Wikileaks' release of thousands of confidential documents from the US military relating to its activities in, among other places, Iraq and Afghanistan. Manning has been described as weak, geeky, psychologically flawed (*Guardian* 2011) and also as an intelligent, thoughtful young man, damaged by the breakdown of his parent's marriage and his volatile relationship with his father, but still planning and acting according to his moral and ethical code (Nicks 2010). Unfortunately his value to academics researching the 'personality' of cyber crime is likely to be limited as a year of solitary confinement and frequent interrogation is unlikely to have left him psychologically unchanged but he exemplifies the problem of giving a clear and clean definition of a cyber terrorist.

The material discussed in this chapter raises the question whether in challenging cyber hate and cyber terror it is helpful to focus on the psychology of the terrorist or whether it might be more effective to seek to understand what makes people vulnerable to recruitment to hate groups. The evidence is complex and seems to suggest that the online group might, through the very fact of its anonymity, be stronger than face-to-face groups in drawing in people to its norms and activities. However, denial of access is impractical as the web is truly global and mobile; the solution may be to focus on anticipating and preventing sites being set up as far as possible but also to focus on providing a social, political and economic climate which will make the attractions of discourses of terror and hate appear weak and tenuous, rather than powerful and real.

Further Reading

Silke, A. (ed). 2003. *Terrorists, Victims and Society: Psychological. Perspectives on Terrorism and Its Consequences*. London: Wiley and Sons.

References

American Psychiatric Association. 2000. *Diagnostic and Statistical Manual of Mental Disorders*. Fourth Edition, Text Revision, Washington, DC: American Psychiatric Association.

Bachmann, M. 2010. The risk propensity and rationality of computer hackers. *International Journal of Cyber Criminology*, 4, (1 and 2), 643–56.

Bandura, A. 1990. Mechanisms of moral disengagement, in Reich, W. (ed.), *Origins of Terrorism: Psychologies, Ideologies, Theologies, States of Mind*. Cambridge: Cambridge University Press, 161–91.

Berry, N., Ko, T., Moy, T., Smrcka, J., Turnley, J. and Wu, B. 2004. *Emergent Clique Formation in Terrorist Recruitment*. [Online]. Available at: http://vision.ucla.edu/tko/pub/aaai_aotp2004.pdf [accessed: 24 April 2011].

Bowker, N. and Tuffin, K. 2003. Dicing with deception: People with disabilities strategies for managing safety and identity. *Online Journal of Computer Mediated Communication*, 8 (2). [Online]. Available at: http://onlinelibrary.wiley.com.libezproxy.open.ac.uk/doi/10.1111/j.1083–6101.2003.tb00209.x/full [accessed: 20 January 2011].

Bowlby, J. 1982. Attachment and loss: retrospect and prospect. *American Journal of Orthopsychiatry*, 52 (4), 664–78.

Campbell, J., Fletcher, G. and Greenhill, A. 2009. Conflict and identity shape shifting in an online financial community. *Information Systems Journal*, 19 (5), 461–78.

Douglas, K. and McGarty, C. 2001. Indentifiability and self-presentation: computer-mediated communication and intergroup reaction. *British Journal of Social Psychology*, 40, 399–416.

Ellison, N., Heino, R. and Gibbs, J. 2006. Managing impressions online: self-presentation processes in the online dating environment. *Journal of Computer-Mediated Communication*, 11 (2), 415–41.

Faria, J. and Arce, D. 2005. Terror support and recruitment. *Defence and Peace Economics*, 16 (4), 263–73.

Feldman, M. 2000. Munchausen by Internet: detection of factitious illness and crisis on the Internet. *Southern Medical Journal*, 93, 669–72.

Gottschalk, M. and Gottschalk, S. 2004. Authoritarian and pathological hatred: a social psychological profile of the Middle Eastern terrorist. *The American Sociologist*, Summer, 38–57.

Greenberg ,J., Pyszczynski, T. and Solomon, S. 1986. The causes and consequences of the need for self-esteem: a terror management theory, in Baumeister, R. (ed.), *Public Self and Private Self*. New York: Springer-Verlag, 189–92.

Guardian. 2011. Bradley Manning: fellow soldier recalls a 'scared bullied kid'. [Online]. Available at: http://www.guardian.co.uk/world/2011/may/28/bradley-manning-video-transcript-wikileaks [accessed: 2 June 2011].

Hopkins, N. and Reicher, S. 1996. The construction of social categories and the processes of social change: arguing about national identities, in Breakwell, G. and Lyons, E. *Changing European Identities*. Oxford: Butterworth Heinemann.

Joinson, A. 2003. *Understanding the Psychology of Internet Behaviour*. Basingstoke: Palgrave Macmillan.

Joshi, P. and O'Donnell, D. 2008. Consequences of child exposure to war and terrorism clinical. *Child and Family Psychology Review*, 6 (4), 275–92.

Kohlberg, L. 1983. *The Psychology of Moral Development*. New York: Harper and Row.

Lachkar, J. 2006. Terrorism and the borderline personality. *Journal of Psychohistory*, 33 (4), 311–23.

Lagerlof, D. 2004. Hate on the net: Sweden. International Network against Cyberhate. [Online]. Available at: http://www.inach.net/content/inach-hateonthenet.pdf [accessed: 12 May 2011].

Lalonde, R. 2002. Testing the social identity inter-group differentiation hypothesis: 'we're not American eh!'. *British Journal of Social Psychology*, 41 (December), 611–30.

Laufer, A., Solomon, Z. and Levine, S. 2010. Elaboration on posttraumatic growth in youth exposed to terror: the role of religiosity and political ideology. *Social Psychiatry and Psychiatric Epidemiology*, 45 (6), 647–53.

Liu, J. and Hilton, D. 2005. How the past weighs on the present: social representations of history and their role in identity politics. *British Journal of Social Psychology*. 44 (December) 537–56.

McKenna, K. and Bargh, J. 1998. Coming out in the age of the Internet: identity demarginalization through virtual group participation. *Journal of Personality and Social Psychology*, 75, 681–94.

Miller, L. 2004. Psychotherapeutic interventions for victims of terrorism. *American Journal of Psychotherapy*. 58 (1), 1–16.

Nicks, D. 2010. Private Manning and the Making of Wikileaks. [Online]. Available at: http://ontd-political.livejournal.com/7403256.html [accessed: 6 June 2011].

Postmes, T., Spears, R., Sakhel, K. and De Groot, D. 2001. Social influence in computer-mediated communication: the effects of anonymity on group behaviour. *Personality and Social Psychology Bulletin*, 27, 1243–54.

Postmes T, Spears, R. and Lea, M. 1999. Social identity, normative content and 'de-individuation' in computer-mediated groups, in Ellemers, N., Spears, R. and Doosje, B. *Social Identity*. Oxford: Blackwell, 164–83.

Pyszczynski, T., Abdollahi, A., Solomon, S., Greenburgh, J., Cohen, F. and Weise, D. 2006. Mortality salience, martyrdom and military might. *Personality and Social Psychology Bulletin*, 32, 525–37.

Reicher, S., Spears, R. and Postmes, T. 1995. A social identity model of deindividuation phenomena. *European Review of Social Psychology*, 6, 161–98.

Rogers, M. 2003. The nature of computer crime: a social-psychology examination, in Turrini, E. (ed.) *Understanding Computer Crime*. New York: Auerbach.

Sageman, M. 2004. *Understanding Terrorist Networks*. Pennsylvania: University of Pennsylvania Press.

Sherif, M. 1966. *Group Conflict and Cooperation*. London; Routledge and Kegan Paul.

Short, J., Williams, E. and Christie, B. 1976. *The Social Psychology of Telecommunications*. London: John Wiley.

Silke, A. 2003. Becoming a terrorist, in Silke, A. (ed.) *Terrorists, Victims and Society: Psychological. Perspectives on Terrorism and Its Consequences*. London: Wiley and Sons.

Sproull, L & Kiesler, S (1986) Reducing social context cues: electronic mail in organizational communication *Management Science*, 32(11): 1492-1512

Tajfel, H. 1970. Experiments in intergroup discrimination. *Scientific American*, 223, 96–102.

Tajfel, H. 1982. Social psychology of intergroup relations. *Annual Review of Psychology*, 33, 1–39.

Tajfel, H. and Turner, J. 1979. The social identity theory of inter-group behaviour, in Austin, W.G. and Worchels, S. (eds). *The Social Psychology of Intergroup Relations*. Monterey, CA: Brooks/Cole, 33–48.

Tololyan, K. 1989. Narrative culture and the motivation of the terrorist, in Shotter, J. and Gergen, K. *Texts of Identity*. London: Sage, 99–118.

Turner, J. 1987. A self-categorisation theory, in Turner, J., Hogg, M., Oakes, P., Reicher, A. and Wetherall, M. *Rediscovering the Social Group: A self-Categorization Theory*. Oxford: Blackwell.

Weimann, G. 2008. The psychology of mass-mediated terrorism. *American Behavioral Scientist*, 52, 69–86.

Whitney, L. 2010. Wiesenthal study details online hate groups. [Online]. Available at: http://news.cnet.com/8301–1023_3–10469814–93.html [accessed: 23 March 2011].

Chapter 4

Cults

Brian Blakemore

There is no agreed and definitive definition of a cult; however, the main features in many definitions are similar, such as:

> a system of religious or spiritual beliefs, especially an informal and transient belief system regarded by others as misguided, unorthodox, extremist, or false, and directed by a charismatic, authoritarian leader

and

> a group of people who share religious or spiritual beliefs, especially beliefs regarded by others as misguided, unorthodox, extremist, or false

also

> an extreme or excessive admiration for a person, philosophy of life, or activity

(Encarta Dictionary nd)

All three elements of the above definition are likely to be present in a terrorist cult: a strong belief system that is anathema to others but excessively important to the cult, charismatic and authoritarian leaders who are revered by cult members and the total subservience of members to the aims and regime of the cult. A terrorist cult is one which: uses deceit to recruit new members, uses mind-control techniques on the new cult member to ensure they become dependent and obedient on the cult, and processes the cult members to such an extent that they are ready to attempt acts such as terrorism. However there is little if any recognition of mind-control in criminal justice systems:

> There are no legitimate treatments that are scientifically validated that appear in peer review journals, although they are effective clinically, Scheflin said. Therefore, they are vulnerable to challenge in the courts. That has to stop. There is no reason why people who are true victims of mind control or people who think they are victims and are wrong should not receive treatment when they need it or want it. (Dittmann 2002:30)

The Aum Shinri Kyo cult who conditioned its members to murder 19 people and injure thousands more by releasing gases that attack the nervous system, in Matsumoto and Tokyo, in the mid 1990s is according to Dubrow-Eichel comparable to Al-Qaeda: 'Their apocalyptic vision is similar in many ways … and their methods are very similar' (Long 2001:np). He especially points out their common 'adulation of a single charismatic leader' referring to Osama bin Laden and Shoko Asahara respectively, and their total 'conviction that God sent them to purify the world'. To the members of Al-Qaeda their enemies are likened to a disease to be eradicated demonstrating selective moral disengagement (see Chapter 2).

The word cult embodies the concept of undue influence in group behaviour (Dubrow-Marshall 2008). The cult may be on the edge of a society and or religion and will be ideologically driven. For terrorists this ideology is the justification for the physical attacks on both infrastructure and humanity. Thus the cult could be seen as a process that reorients members to such a state that they are able to commit cruel and violent acts. This links to the definition of terrorism contained within the UK Prevention of Terrorism (temporary provisions) Act 1989 of 'the use of violence for political ends' where the terms 'political ends' and 'ideologically driven' are interchangeable as formalised in section 1 of the UK Terrorism Act 2000. The perceptions of what is terrorism as opposed to fighting for freedom will inevitably vary between and within countries and individuals; Hudson (1999) uses the Sandinista National Liberation Front as such an example; they are labelled as a terrorist group by the ruling elite, while others in the general populace of Nicaragua thought of them as freedom fighters. Not all cults are terrorist cults and some only seek the right and space to be different from the mainstream of society in such as their thoughts, actions or dress.

Cult Typologies

There are various categories of terrorist cults: political, religious, ideological, nationalist, state sponsored and single issue (Staniforth 2009). Alternatively Hudson (1999) uses nationalist-separatist, religious fundamentalist, new religious and social revolutionary and right wing. These two classifications can be mapped as shown in Table 4.1 below.

Table 4.1   A comparison of cult typologies

Staniforth (2009)	Hudson (1999)
Political	right wing
Religious	religious-fundamentalist and new religious
Ideological	social revolutionary
Nationalist	nationalist-separatist
state-sponsored	-
single issue	-

The social revolutionary category above, maps to an ideological stance denoting cult beliefs around a radical cause, a religious belief or a political ideology, including anarchism. Hudson (1999) points out that despite some group's not fitting precisely just one type, the classifications are useful to better understand terrorist cults and their operations. Each campaign is potentially different, but there will be similarities within a specific typology that may enable better policing and subsequently reduction of terrorism. Hudson classifies the Irish Republic Army, Basque Fatherland and Freedom, the Palestinian terrorist groups and the Liberation Tigers of Tamil Eelam as nationalist and compares these groups with examples of the religious typology; the Islamic fundamentalist and the Aum Shinri Kyo groups. Staniforth (2009) argues that political and religious terrorists are often the most violent as they believe that their actions are justified and mandated by the cults belief system itself. Ideological terrorists can be extremely left wing or extremely right wing in their beliefs and seek a major social revolution. Nationalist groups often claim to represent the common people of an area and their culture, language and freedom of common identity. They may seek to have a government that represents this community by creating their own land by breaking away from an existing country or by uniting areas that are transnational. State-sponsored terrorism employs independent and possibly mercenary terrorist groups to do state's bidding: using a non-state-organisation enables the state to achieve its objectives without being formally linked to the attack and so reduces the likelihood of other states subsequent counter actions. Single issue groups do not seek to change the political or religious order in a state; they merely wish to change one particular policy or set of policies. Animal rights extremists, for example, have used unlawful attacks to terrorise those carrying out animal testing in laboratories as part of a campaign to improve the treatment of animals throughout society.

The religious and political aspects of the Al-Qaeda cult is also demonstrated in the manual found within three of the four cells that carried out the 9/11 attacks in 2001. This manual gave justification for violence by referring to early Islamic history when Muhammad totally reformed acceptable practices of working with non-Muslims and physically attacked them in order to establish Islam as a political force (Kippenberg 2005).

Recruiting to Cults

Some criminologists argue that poorer and marginalised people are more likely to become criminals (Murray 1990, 1999); however, criminals are not cult members and terrorists are not necessarily driven by financial gain. This begs the question: are some sections of society more likely to become terrorists and cyber terrorists than others? The psychology and location in society of the individual is important and is considered in more detail in Chapter 3. Krueger (2007) considered the demographics of terrorists by researching the backgrounds of 129 martyrs cited in a Hezbollah newsletter the Al-Ahd. He found (Table 4.2 below) that the martyrs were less likely to come from a low-earning background and were more likely have received a better secondary or tertiary education than the wider population. A previous study by Berrebi (2003) looked at Palestinian suicide bombers (Table 4.2) which produced broadly similar trends. In general terrorists tend to come from a range of backgrounds but disproportionately from well-educated and from middle-class or higher-earning families. For example, consider modern well-known revolutionaries: Fidel Castro, Ho Chi Minh, Leon Trotsky, Vladimir Lenin, Simon Bolivar (Levitt and Dubner 2009), Nelson Mandela and Bin laden are from relatively affluent and influential families. Members of the Bhagwan Shree Rajneesh religious cult were generally of above-average education from the middle class and previously had professional careers (Long 2001). Mohamed Atta, the alleged leader of the 9–11 suicide bombers, was 'a shy, considerate son of a lawyer and very bright' (Long 2001) and one of the Glasgow airport bombers was a practising medical doctor.

Table 4.2   The demographics of terrorists and the general public

	Krueger (2007)		Berrebi (2003)	
	Terrorists	General population	Terrorists	General population
Low earning	28 per cent	33 per cent	16 per cent	30 per cent
Middle class and good education	47 per cent	38 per cent	60 per cent	15 per cent

Hudson (1999) suggests that terrorists actively and deliberately target and recruit the expertise they need to carry out sophisticated acts of terrorism:

> Increasingly, terrorist groups are recruiting members with expertise in fields such as communications, computer programming, engineering, finance, and the sciences. Ramzi Yousef graduated from Britain's Swansea University with a degree in engineering. Aum Shinrikyo's Shoko Asahara recruited a scientific team with all the expertise needed to develop WMD. Osama bin Laden also recruits highly skilled professionals in the fields of engineering, medicine, chemistry, physics, computer programming, communications. (Hudson 1999:4)

Hudson (1999) also states that recruits may be unemployed and or poorly educated as in, the Gaza Strip, and suggests underlying motivations of boredom and seeking both action and a 'just' cause. Others recruits might be motivated to use specialist skills that they possess, such as bomb-making; thirdly he proposes that educated recruits may be following political or religious convictions and that this is a prevalent type found especially in western democracies. A more general list of causes is given by Wilkinson (1986): ethnic conflict, religious and ideological conflict, other traditions of violence, poverty, dealing with change, political inequities, weak governments and fundamental conflicts within a governing cadre, underdeveloped or threatening communications channels, formation and action by anti-establishment organisations. This is echoed and extended by Thiel (2009) who also includes discrimination, gender and western foreign policy with reference to Islamist terrorism.

There is much literature on religious cults generally targeting well-educated American teenagers and undergraduates in the 1970s which will be considered. According to Robbins (in Glock and Bellah 1976) from the late 1960s to the middle of the 1970s the emergence of a counterculture amongst American youth took place and this resulted in personal tumult and an identity crisis for many. This was a time also noted for the widespread use of psychedelic and or hallucinogenic drugs in this age group. This counterculture included activism on college campuses, supporting left-wing and anti-Vietnam War ideologies.

According to Enroth (1977) religious cults recruited in the USA in the 1970s mainly from 18–22 year olds who came from middle-class and relatively normal homes. Hussain (2011) names four British terrorists who were recruited on university campuses. Shelley Liebert, an ex 'Moonie' instructor (in Enroth 1977) describes two types of recruit: those experiencing failure by middle-class standards of the time, who may have left home, live in a dysfunctional family or have emotional problems and ongoing personal issues and or have dropped out of school or university, and they may have become part of a drugs subculture; alternatively, they might be from a group described as successful, idealistic and have a very secure personality. There were several different religious organisations that were actively recruiting such vulnerable youths to their cults and the similarity of their modus operandi was commented upon by Enroth (1977:12): 'Commonality of certain aims to certain means is so striking … Hallmarks of cultic conversion usually include the abandonment of a familiar life style; severing ties with friends and families; a radical and sometimes sudden change in personality …'. Such changes in personality may extend to changes in grooming habits, tone of voice, body posture, individual mannerisms and range and use of vocabulary. This was demonstrated by Mohammed Atta, suspected Al Qaeda leader of the 9–11 suicide bombers who ceased smiling and was seen to refuse to shake hands with a woman and grew a beard during his conversion process. His father found it hard to recognise the 9/11 attacker as his own son (Long 2001). More recent descriptions of Islamist terrorists suggest that they may be trained to hide their changed world view: Rajib Karim, a software engineer and member of Jamaat-Ul-Mujahedin, who obtained employment in British Airways to facilitate a plot to bomb a passenger laden aircraft, 'deliberately set about establishing a lifestyle which would not attract attention and those who worked with him were completely taken in by him'. (Twomey 2011:17).

Enroth (1977) found each cult had developed a strong message or mission that had very definite answers to the meaning of life and cites a case history of Lisa Bryant; Lisa was just over 14-years-old when she was attracted by the Hare Krishna movement. According to Lisa the cult had answers to the questions: why am I here and why do some people die young? Previously in her life she had only received replies from adults admitting that they did not know the answer to such questions. The cult manipulated such open and unknowing replies to argue and insist that outsiders know nothing, cannot understand and are inherently inferior. Cults in the 1970s and today appear to have definite, relevant and complete answers to today's problems and larger philosophical questions on the meaning of life that meets the needs for such clarity of purpose to the potential recruit. They are offering certainty in an uncertain world and a just cause to act and die for. For Chaudhury (2007) the progression from radicalisation to extremism is most likely to be associated with an individual searching for a definite self-identity during a period of crisis in their lives.

Conversion

The conversion (thought reform) modus operandi includes well-defined stages of progression and or status in the cult analogous to the colourful belts worn in some martial arts to show skill levels within the art. The cultic conversion process requires specified duties to prove ones devotion and rituals to mark progression to the next stage. Neophytes on the lower stages receive fewer privileges. There might be local interpretations and idiosyncrasies, Lisa Bryant (a case study in Enroth 1977) states each temple had a different way of doing things, depending upon the leader and the history of the original founders but all had rigid rules and busy daily routines.

The idea of keeping the neophytes busy is another similarity found in all these religious cults: Janice Evans signed over all possessions to the group and even let them open her mail; she obeyed all the rules and the officers in the cult. Her daily schedule was rigidly controlled; she was not even allowed to floss her teeth without first getting permission. New comers were called babes, then brothers and sisters, leaders had biblical names such as Caleb (Enroth 1977). Similar use of schedules, tasks and activities are described by Hussain (2007) and Nawaz (nd) in their conversion process to becoming radicalised Islamists. The manual used by the cells that carried out the 9/11 attacks used recitations, prayers and rituals to prepare the member, again very similar to keeping the member busy and the strict routines they must follow described earlier, the use of us (good) versus them (evil) rhetoric is also emphasised, the rituals are to purify the members' intentions and help them prepare for any planned terrorist act (Kippenberg 2005).

The linguistic use of terminology is part of the process to create a psychic boundary to distinguish the group and outsiders (Kanter 1972). According to some, Al-Qaeda use the Porsche 911 as a symbol of the materialistic and evil western way of life and that this may account for the significance of the date chosen for the 9–11 attack. This use of jargon and imagery is normal behaviour within cults. Jargon is value-laden and is used to dehumanise future victims, the general public and government. For example Islamist groups use the term 'the infidel' while revolutionary and anti-establishment terrorists have often used derogatory terms such as 'tools of the system', or 'pigs'.

Various models have been presented to describe the conversion process for new recruits. The Lofland-Stark process model (Lofland 1977) describes the total conversion process based upon that observed for the Unification Church (following Sun Myung Moon) and lists seven necessary conditions: three predisposing factors; firstly the potential convert must feel acute and persistent tensions in their world; secondly this tension is within a philosophical and or religious dimension; and thirdly the individual views themselves as a religious seeker. There are then 4 situational contingencies that must take place; the potential convert encounters a movement during this tumult in their life; they form an affective bond with one or more cult member; attachments outside the cult become severely reduced or severed thus neutralising any outside influences and finally intensive interaction within the group deepens resulting in conversion to the condition of a deployable agent.

As the potential converts complete more steps on their journey the probability of total conversion to the cult's world view increases. The various stages are not easy to measure and compare, so despite several complementary research programmes it a contested model. Snow et al. (1980:798) assert that social networks are the dominant factor in joining a cult and states that ' the probability of being recruited into particular cult is largely function of two conditions; links to one or more cult members through a pre-existing or emerging interpersonal tie; and the absence of counter veiling networks'. Arguably converting new members is mainly about the control of information to prevent critical thinking and little to do with the cult's true aims.

Singer (1995) lists five characteristics: deceit, dependency, debilitation, dread and desensitisation to model how cult members are recruited, moulded and converted. This again emphasises the step by step approach to reforming and restructuring the neophyte's way of thinking, so the process takes place subconsciously without the individual's perception.

Singer (1995) gives an example of deceit: students on campuses can easily be targeted by offering to talk about politics, philosophical or religious aspects of life. Potential converts will not be asked if they want to be a terrorist, such recruits would be both too few and too unreliable. Again Singer (1995) identifies isolation from friends and family as a key part of this process and this produces a dependency on the cult. One Al-Qaeda member, Al Owhali, claimed that he was first trained within a camp in Afghanistan for a month before being allowed to progress to the jihad camp. Once his training was finished and he was fully indoctrinated only then was the possibility of an act of terrorism discussed.

The second and third stages, dependence and debilitation, follow as the only messages the new member receives are now those of the cult and at this point, a new name, different dress and new ways of living are imposed in a rigid regime to mould both obedience and a new identity.

The fourth stage, dread, recognises the fear of punishment in the form of both formal and informal social control that members believe that they will endure if they were to challenge the cult's thinking, processes or actions. To avoid the anticipated repercussions from appearing to be less than totally committed to the cult's thinking new members try not to have any questioning thoughts lest they should inadvertently be vocalised.

The final stage, desensitisation, develops over time due to prolonged exposure to cultic influence. The new convert accepts that the cult is always right and that all others (outsiders) are always wrong, unclean and evil, and having reached this point of conversion cult members will not feel guilt for any of their subsequent terrorist thoughts or actions.

Lifton (1961) outlined the main characteristics in destructive cults based upon experiences of communist prisoner-of-war camps during the Korean War. His description included two aspects common to previous descriptions of the cultic process: an alluring and captivating principal who is likely to be an object of adulation as the original creator of the ideology behind the formation of the group, and the emphasis placed on thought reform. If Lifton (1961) is correct and Osama bin Laden was the focus of Al-Qaeda, and the religious and political views behind the aims of Al-Qaeda, are of a lower importance and the demise of bin Laden may severely weaken Al-Qaeda, unless an equally charismatic figure can fill this current void in the cultic identity.

The sixth and seventh stages in the Lofland–Stark model underpin a common observation that cults require impossibly high levels and constant proof of commitment and use argument, regime, fear and guilt to prevent recruits from leaving. They demand unquestioning faith and total commitment: 'if you leave you will endanger the salvation of your soul ... I was made to feel guilty if I ever wanted to be alone to think' (Enroth 1977:160) and 'young converts see themselves fighting selflessly for universal ideals of love and harmony and world unity in a world permeated by relativism, cynicism and selfish egoism' (Robbins and Anthony 1981:224). Osama bin Laden broadcast on a video tape:

> The brothers who conducted the operation, all they knew was that they have a martyrdom operation and we asked each of them to go to America, but they didn't know anything about the operation, not even one letter. But they were trained and we did not reveal the operation to them until they are there and just before they boarded the plane. (Jones 2002:83)

Converts are now so strongly indoctrinated into the cult's belief systems that they will carry out atrocities and acts of martyrdom. Steve Hassan, a former member of the Unification Church, says he would have been 'ready to die for the cause if necessary'. (Long 2001:np). Examples of such actions are as follows.

In Jonestown, Guyana where nearly one thousand members of the Peoples' Temple under their leader Reverend Jim Jones were either murdered by the upper echelon or committed mass suicide in 1978 (Hall in Robbins and Anthony 1981).

The Bhagwan Shree Rajneesh cult cell based in the USA carried out the first large-scale biological attack in US history in 1985. They poisoned 751 people who ate restaurant food that had been sprinkled with salmonella germs cultivated in the cult's laboratory (Long 2001).

Singer (1995) interviewed nearly 6,000 former cult members and found similarities between Bhagwan Shree Rajneesh and the People's Temple: both recruited and controlled members in much the same way. Al-Qaeda's indoctrination methods include thought-reform in both fundamentalist religious schools and around religious gatherings. Once in the cult, training camps were used to insulate the new member from contradictory viewpoints until 'totalistic identity' was affected (Long 2001). They would therefore appear to use the same thought-reform processes as described earlier. According to Lifton (1999), Al-Qaeda is not just a cult but also a social movement that is all the more threatening because of its wider appeal and because it does not depend singularly on cultic control:

> What we see is people who are not kids anymore engaging in a kind of institutionalisation and socialisation of terrorism,' he says. 'You depend for this kind of suicidal terrorism not only on fiercely extreme young people but on not-so-young people who become part of the group within which this is normal or desired behavior. (Lifton in Long 2001:np).

Lifton's work has been used as a framework to develop an objective measure of the level of influence exerted by any group (Chambers et al. 1994).

Social Identity Theory

Social Identity theory emphasises that the social world does not just impact upon the individual's thinking in an analogous way to the collision of one billiard ball with another (Dubrow-Marshall 2008); rather the world is inside the individual and so social identity is part of the individual's self-identity. Tajfel and Billig (1974) demonstrated this, splitting people into groups on random and minimal differences: preferences for paintings can easily and rapidly lead to group identification and prejudice (see Chapter 3). In Zimbardo's prison simulation (Haney et al. 1973) university students were randomly assigned roles as either prisoners or prison guards in a prison simulation. The students adopted attitudes and behaviours that were strongly based upon their assigned roles. Some of the guard's aggression levels were much higher and dehumanising than was initially expected in a short simulation study. This again shows the strong forces that groups, let alone cults, can play in changing the attitudes and behaviour of members when an individual is given a simple and strong role to play in a clear and an apparent cause.

Ferracuti (1982) suggested that terrorists exist in a subculture of their own and that this subculture has its own value systems. Wilkinson (1974) also supported this approach and stressed the need to incorporate the terrorists' prejudice and hatred and how this develops into a fanatical support for and participation in extreme violence. For Wilkinson (1974) then the terrorists can only be understood within their own ideologies, beliefs and lifestyles.

Shaw (1986) promotes the idea of a 'Personal Pathway Model' to becoming a terrorist. The model proposes that the prospective recruits will have low self-esteem. They may well grow up in families that are liberal but the individual experiences contradictions in the family values and is frustrated by the slow pace of reform. The family may well induce this alienation by having introduced and discussed some of the problems in their society. They may see themselves as unsuccessful as judged by the norms of their society. The motivation to belong to a terrorist group and the psychosocial situation is discussed more fully in Chapter 3 but equally importantly according to Shaw, confrontational policing or security measures (by the out-group) may provoke more active political activity by such individuals and hasten their progression from radicalisation through extremism to the role of a deployable agent within a terrorist cult (the in-group).

Post (1990) argues that the most enduring and ardent terrorist groups arise when the terrorists are from within the same families across generations and cites Northern Ireland and the Basque country as examples of this intergenerational, intrafamily and long-lasting terrorism. Post (1990) argues that anarchists such as the Italian Red Army, who seek to destroy their own society, experience more alienation and psychopathology than those continuing the fights initiated by their families.

A report by the MI5 security service (Travis 2008) found no typical profile of British citizens who had become terrorists; neither did the study find a standard conveyor belt producing such terrorists. Having strong religious association protected individuals from being radicalised. These findings are in accord with the case studies and models presented in this chapter. Furthermore the report claims that the role of radical clerics in recruiting such was less than in the past; arguably the Internet has supplanted this factor.

Cult Processes

Milieu Control is the total control of communications within a group to accomplish absolute control of the group. This control uses all possibilities of social control and is carried out by the leaders via a top down approach. This hierarchical model of control requires complete obedience from the lower orders and each order enforces this requirement downwards. The daily rituals and jargon are all part of structuring and reinforcing this social control. The leader is often remote to add to their mythical or religious status making them appear close to perfection or their god. Hudson (1999) states that terrorist groups are often totally dominated by a charismatic leader, such as Osama bin Laden or Shoko Asahara. He argues that such leaders make independent decisions then give strategies to their subordinate, for example to attack a country, but they do not become involved in the intricacy of operational details. These dominant leaders may listen to their immediate advisors, but they make the important decisions and expected these to be implemented without question.

Terrorists that have become part of the cult in order to gain a sense of purpose in their lives, as previously described, cannot easily be persuaded to change their position as this has become the only reason to exist (Post 1990). Furthermore the cult process will subdue any such tendency; for example, when some of the Red Army terrorist group objected to the group's strategy in 1972, these dissenters were tortured and then killed (Hudson 1999).

Many of the aspects of cult- and terrorist-cell-thinking can be termed 'Groupthink' (Janis 1972). This group of attitudes, behaviours and processes includes a false impression of invulnerability, unwarranted optimism resulting in extreme risk taking, belief in the group's morality being the correct and only value system of any meaning, a blinkered view of the outside world giving a one dimensional perception of the rest of society as an evil enemy, and finally total intolerance to the questioning of any shared key beliefs by a group member.

Thought reform can be defined in terms of several factors (Singer 1995:58–9): the body of knowledge centres on changing people without their realisation of the change process taking place, communication is directional and no debate is allowed, the organisation is rigid and focused upon its goals, the organisation is hierarchical and the neophyte has little knowledge of what goes on at higher levels, the group aims to retain the members forever, the organisation is deceptive, learning is a step-by-step approach to produce a deployable agent. The seven cultic practices identified by Weimann (2008, discussed in Chapter 3) are very similar to those given by Singer above particularly that there is no respect for individual differences (individuation see Chapter 3) and improper and unethical techniques are used. Dubrow-Marshall (2008) described the cultic process as one that develops a 'totalistic identity' in the convert and that this point of absolute conversion is an extreme point along a continuum of influence and persuasion.

Organisation Structures

Terrorist structures often grow organically and without a particular shape unless a conscious decision is taken and enforced to impose a structure on the organisation. The Irish Republican Army (IRA) used centralised and hierarchical structures (Staniforth 2009). This facilitated tight control of operations with policy determined at the top and strict enforcement of policy and actions throughout the organisation. This may contribute to splinter terrorist organisations that have broadly similar aims but seek to use different actions to achieve these. To limit the risk of leaks of information and hence avoid detection terrorist organisations often operate in cells and lateral communication is minimised. A terrorist manager in the structure may control only one or two cells. The enforcement of the operating system requires both a strong culture and rigorous control by those higher in the chain, exhibiting similarities to religious cults described earlier but making use of the stronger need to conform online if communication is being monitored by an in group member (see Chapter 3). Thiel (2009) suggests that Islamist terror cells range in size from 2 to 13 members.

Al-Qaeda changed from a centralised to a decentralised organisation after the Afghan–Russian conflicts to better equip Al-Qaeda to expand its remit to waging a global war on the west and has been described as a 'network of networks' (Staniforth 2009:28) and as 'a free floating organisational structure ...' by Thiel (2009:15). In such a structure the cells may form anywhere in the world and have relative independence of action. This suggests that the death of bin Laden will not reduce operational capability in the mid to short term but the loss of a charismatic leader may have more impact in the long term unless Al-Qaeda is a social movement (Lifton1999) rather than a cult. A decentralised cell structure not only supports 'group think' but magnifies the displacement of responsibility of its members and enables them to carry out even more inhuman activities and atrocities according to Della Porta (1992) based upon interviews conducted with left-wing militants in Italy and Germany. Furthermore the anonymity offered by cyber networks tends to enhance becoming part of a group and polarisation to the groups norms and values (see Chapter 3).

Arquilla (2001) speculates that the headquarters of a terrorist group may have a limited number of connections with the cells that make up the total organisation and that this limited chain of connections makes identifying other parts of the organisation or the leadership is very difficult task for investigators:

> networking, using the Internet, by the way, and the World Wide Web quite extensively has encouraged a much greater deal of connection, both within terror groups and between loosely knitted or Internetted terror groups. When we say 'all-channel connection' that simply means whoever in a network cell connects with others. If they can connect with everybody else in a cell, they have all-channel connection. (Arquilla 2001:np)

Virtual Cults, Swarming and Netwars

Arquilla (2001) coined the term 'netwars' to describe the contrast between the state with its political and national structures that are fixed, formalised and hierarchical against loosely linked, dispersed and fluid terrorist cells using the Internet, especially to aid their interrelationships and common purpose. He describes this informal group as:

> a distributed dispersed network of non-state actors, terrorists and to some extent criminals. I think we need to point out that Al Qaeda actually gets some of its financing from the drug business. What we are seeing is a kind of dark league of networked non-state actors who have a great deal of capability to do harm. (Arquilla 2001:np)

Such networks may be local or dispersed across the globe; they may use many and diverse forms of action at a time and place of their choice; they may not claim responsibility for their actions and so may remain in the shadows hidden from the intelligence searchlight. Netwar is used by Al-Qaeda which has demonstrated the power of this approach. This view is reinforced by the UK Government's position that 'Attacks on computer networks are among the biggest emerging threats to the UK, the government has said in its new national security strategy' (BBC News 2010:np). Arquilla (2001) calls for a holistic and collaborative response and emphasises the need to break down existing barriers in the formal institutions and structures so as to reconfigure present infrastructure to combat this mode of terrorism.

The Internet Social Network

The Internet network age may help link different societies across the globe and change the very nature of these societies to ones that are less parochial and nationalistic, ones that have a more common set of values, especially regarding human rights as demonstrated by the 'Twitter Revolution' and the 'Arab Spring' discussed previously in Chapter 1. In the same way as in the past commerce led to a spread of ideas around the world the Internet may now spread a new set of values and outlooks. The 'Big Society' suggested by David Cameron the newly elected Prime Minister of Great Britain may become the 'Global Society' within the near future. This may be an area that governments, institutions and individuals can support, develop and invest in to attack the root causes and mechanisms of terrorism and transnational crime. One such example of this is:

> Social Watch is an international network of citizens' organisations in the struggle to eradicate poverty and the causes of poverty, to end all forms of discrimination and racism, to ensure an equitable distribution of wealth and the realisation of human rights. We are committed to peace, social, economic, environment and gender justice, and we emphasise the right of all people not to be poor. (Social Watch nd:np)

Arquilla (2001) uses the analogy of the two-faced god Janus to emphasise the positive and negative characteristics of the Internet revolution: the integration of the civil society, versus the empowerment of terrorists, criminal actors and other anti-social elements.

For a negative example according to Musawi (nd:18–19):

> Jihadists use the Internet to create a virtual bubble in which they can behave according to what they perceive as the 'Salafist ideal', which they are determined to implement in real life ... Many of the threads and posts on these forums deal with general topics of religion and life, rather than only with 'Jihadist issues' ...

this reflects that Jihadists see their use of violence within the context of a larger religious framework for living a correct 'Islamic life'.

These Jihadist sites reflect the two faces of Janus analogy so the websites have safeguards to protect it from any incursion by factions wishing to propound any opposing propaganda messages: 'Non-members can view most discussions, but membership is required in order to take part and post a comment. To join, a prospective member must contact the administrators, whose permission is required for the applicant to login using a username and password' (Musawi nd:20).

Musawi also stresses that the website masters (part of the hierarchy) and members tend to be highly suspicious of new individuals who attempt to post news or discuss matters relating to Jihadist activities or any religious justifications for Jihadist strategies and actions.

Conclusion

All cults share certain broad characteristics which follow from their common definition above, the modus operandi of achieving their aims and also the types of people they target to recruit to their cause. However, there will be local variations within different parts of any terrorist organisation.

Singer (1995) summarises these thought-reform processes in three categories: first, to destabilise the individuals' existing sense of themselves; secondly, to make the individuals completely reinterpret their view of life, the world and everything; and thirdly to develop the individuals into new people who is subsequently totally dependent upon the cult and this dependency makes them a reliable deployable agent of that cult.

Comparisons with cults from the 1970s are useful in understanding terrorist cults of today. The religious converts of the 1970s defied rational arguments and attempts to demonstrate alternative viewpoints and modern terrorist groups are equally irrational and are unlikely to act as predicted by rational analysis. Many of the terrorist groups cannot be dealt with on the precept that they are willing to negotiate on their principles and work towards a compromise solution regarding their aims and objectives.

Further reading

The website of the International Cultic Studies Association (ICSA) at: http://www. icsahome.com/default.asp/
The Quilliam foundation website at: http://www.quilliamfoundation.org/

References

Arquilla, J. 2001. *Global Q & A: Netwar – Fighting a Global Terrorist Network.* [Online]. Available at: http://www.fpa.org/topics_info2414/topics_info_show. htm?doc_id=85640. [accessed: 3 March 2011].

BBC News. 2010. Cyber attacks and terrorism head threats facing UK. [Online]. Available at: http://www.bbc.co.uk/news/uk-11562969 [accessed on 30 March 2011].

Berrebi, C. 2003. *Evidence about the Link between Education, Poverty and Terrorism among Palestinians.* Princetown: Princetown University Industrial relations working paper.

Chambers, W., Langone, M., Dole, A. and Grice, J. 1994. The group psychological abuse scale: a measure of the varieties of cultic abuse. *Cultic Studies Journal*, 11(1), 88–117.

Chaudhury, T. 2007. *The Role of Muslim Identity Politics in Radicalisation* (A Study in Progress). London: DCLG.

Della Porta, D. 1992. (ed) Social Movements and Violence. Greenwich (Conn.): JAI Press.

Daner, F. 1976. *The American Children of Krishna.* New York: Holt, Rinehart and Winston.

Dittmann, M. 2002. Cults of hatred. *The Monitor*, American Psychological Association. [Online]. 33 (10), 30. Available at: http://research.apa.org/ monitor/nov02/cults.aspx. [accessed: 1 March 2011].

Dubrow-Marshall, R. 2008. The influence continuum- the good the dubious and the harmful – evidence and implications for policy and practice in the 21st century. Inaugural professorial lecture, 9 December. Pontypridd :University of Glamorgan.

Encarta Dictionary. [Online]. Available at: http://uk.encarta.msn.com/encnet/ features/dictionary/ dictionaryhome.aspx. [accessed: 1 March 2011].

Enroth, E. 1977. *Youth, Brainwashing and the Extremist Cults.* Exeter: Paternoster Press.

Ferracuti, F. 1982. A sociopsychiatric interpretation of terrorism. *The Annals of the American Academy of Political and Social Science*, 463,129–41.

Glock, C. and Bellah, R. (eds).1976. *The New Religious Consciousness.* Berkeley: University of California Press.

Haney, C., Banks, C. and Zimbardo, P. 1973. Interpersonal dynamics in a simulated prison. *International Journal of Criminology and Penology*, 1, 69–97.

Hudson, R.A. 1999. The sociology and psychology of terrorism: who becomes a terrorist and why? *Federal Research Division, Library of Congress.* [Online]. Available at: http://www.loc.gov/rr/frd/pdffiles/Soc_Psych_of_Terrorism.pdf. [accessed: 28 February 2011].

Hussain, E. 2007. *The Islamist: Why I* Joined Radical Islam in Britain, What I Saw Inside and Why I Left. London: Penguin.

Hussain, G. 2011. Threat of campus extremists must never be ignored. *Daily Express*, 12 June, 8.

Janis, L.1972. *Victims of Groupthink*. Boston: Houghton-Mifflin.

Jones, M. 2002. Restitution awards in Pennsylvania and on the federal level: how civil restitution has evolved into a criminal penalty and the effect on Usama bin Laden's wallet for the September 11th attacks on America. *Duquesne Business Law Journal*. [Online]. 4, 2001–2002, 83. Available at: http:// heinonline.org/HOL/Page?handle= hein.journals/duqbuslr2 &div=18 &g_ sent=1 &collection=journals [accessed: 24 March 2011].

Levitt, S.D. and Dubner, S.J. 2009. *Super Freak-onomics*. London: Penguin.

Lifton, R.J. 1961. *Thought Reform and the Psychology of Totalism*. New York: Norton.

Lifton, R.J. 1999. *Destroying the World to Save It: Aum Shinrikyo, Apocalyptic Violence and the New Global Terrorism*. New York: Metropolitan Books – Henry Holt and Company.

Lofland, J. 1977. *Doomsday Cult: A* Study of *Coversion, Proselytization, and Maintenance of Faith*. New York: Irvington.

Long, J. 2001. Cults, Terrorist Groups Share Chilling Similarities, Experts Say. [Online]. *The Oregonian*, 9 November. Available at: http:// www.rickross. com/reference/ alqaeda/ alqaeda25. html. [accessed: 15 March 2011].

Kanter, R.M. 1972. *Commitment and Community*. Cambridge, Mass.: Harvard University Press.

Kippenberg, H.G. 2005. Consider that it is a raid on the path of god: the spiritual manual of the attackers of 9/11. *Numen, International Review for the History of Religions*. [Online]. (1). Available at: http://www.jstor.org/pss/3270442. [accessed: 24 March 2011].

Krueger, A.B. 2007. *What Makes a Terrorist?* Princetown: Princetown University Press.

Murray, C. 1990. *The Underclass*. [Online]. Available at: http://justice4victims. org/theunderclass.aspx [accessed: 15 May 2011].

Murray, C. 1999. *The Underclass Revisited*. Washington, DC: The AEI. Press Publisher for the American Enterprise Institute.

Musawi, M.A. nd. Cheering for Osama: how jihadists use Internet discussion forums. [Online]. Available at: http://www.quilliamfoundation.org/. [accessed: 7 April 2011].

Nawaz, M. nd. In and out of Islamism. [Online]. Available at: http://www. quilliamfoundation. org/. [accessed: 7 April 2011].

Prevention of Terrorism (temporary provisions) Act 1989 (c.4). London: HMSO.

Post, J. 1990. Current understanding of terrorist motivation and psychology: implications for a differentiated antiterrorist policy. *Terrorism*, 13(1), 65–71.

Robbins, T. 1988. *Cults, Converts and Charisma*. London: Sage.

Robbins, T. and Anthony, D. (eds). 1981. *In Gods We Trust: New Patterns of Religious Pluralism in America*. New Brunswick, NJ: Transaction.

Shaw, E.D. 1986. Political terrorists: dangers of diagnosis and an alternative to the psychopathology model. *International Journal of Law and Psychiatry*, (8), 359–68.

Singer, M.T. 1995. *Cults in Our midst*. San Francisco: Jossey-Bass Publishers.

Snow, D.A., Zurcher, L.A. and Ekland -Olson, S. 1980. Social networks and social movements: a microstructural approach to differential recruitment. *Amercican Sociological Review*, 45(4), 787–801.

Social Watch (nd) http://www.socialwatch.org/. [Online]. Available at: http://www.socialwatch.org/ [accessed: 21 February 2012].

Staniforth, A. 2009. *Blackstone's Counter –Terrorism Handbook*. Oxford : PLND, OUP.

Tajfel, H. and Billig, M. 1974. Familiarity and categorization in intergroup behaviour. *Journal of Experimental Social Psychology*, (10), 159–70.

Terrorism Act. 2000. (c.11), London: HMSO.

Thiel, D. 2009. *Policing Terrorism: A* Review of Evidence. London: The Police Foundation.

Travis, A. 2008. MI5 report challenges views on terrorism in Britain. *Guardian*. [Online]. Available at: http://www.guardian.co.uk/uk/2008/aug/20/uksecurity. terrorism1 [accessed: 1 July 2011].

Twomey, J. 2011. BA computer expert 'in plot to bomb packed jet. *Daily Express*, 2 February, 17.

Wagenlehner, G. 1978. Motivation for Political Terrorism in West Germany, in *International Terrorism in the Contemporary World*, edited by Livingston, M.H. Westport, Connecticut: Greenwood Press, 195–203.

Weimann, G. 2008. The psychology of mass-mediated terrorism. *American Behavioral Scientist*, 52, 69, 69–86.

Wilkinson, P. 1974. *Political Terrorism*. London: Macmillan.

Wilkinson, P.1986. Terrorism: International Dimensions, in *The New Terrorism*, edited by Gutteridge, W. London: Mansell Publishing, 29–56.

Chapter 5

Hate in a Cyber Age

Geoff Coliandris

Introduction

'Jumping off the gw bridge sorry.' This brief yet chilling message was reportedly posted on Facebook by American student, Tyler Clementi, minutes before he is believed to have jumped into the Hudson River after video of him having sex with another man was streamed live onto the Internet (Pilkington 2010). Two fellow students (one, a roommate) now face 'invasion of privacy' charges though a political and legal storm has erupted over the question of whether 'hate crime' law prosecutions may be more appropriate (Hu 2010). The case is important for several reasons beyond its obvious tragedy. First, it provides an insight into the kinds of torment experienced by those who may be perceived as somehow different; second, it suggests how people can be victimised at the hands of people they know and possibly trust; third, it illustrates the difficulties involved in categorising and dealing with the type of offending behaviour alleged; and fourth, it shows the serious consequences which can flow from the convergence of what Pilkington (2010) terms 'age-old habits' (for 'teenage pranks') and the 'huge social power' of new information and communication technologies (ICTs).

This chapter will explore the complexities of hate crime and its associated concepts. There will be a particular emphasis on its cyber forms. An interdisciplinary approach is used to advance the argument that hate crime cannot be meaningfully reduced to simple or single explanations or solutions. The aim will be to develop understanding with a view to supporting improvements at the policy and practice levels among a broad range of services.

Definitional Challenges

Though 'hate crime' is now well established on the criminal justice agendas of societies such as the UK (Iganski 2010) as a concept, it remains elusive: no universal definition exists. Several reasons for this can be suggested: hate crime is inherently complex; it involves meaning; it evokes powerful emotive responses; and those meanings and responses are socially and historically contingent and variable.

The concept of 'hate' raises particular challenges. For some, alternative concepts such as 'prejudice' and 'bias' are preferred (see Hall 2005, Jacobs and Potter 1998). However, according to Iganski (2010) the concepts of 'prejudice' and 'bias' are only marginally less problematic than 'hate' given that one can be biased or prejudiced in favour of or against something or someone.

Perry (2001: 10) offers what is widely seen as a particularly comprehensive attempt at definition. For her:

> Hate crime ... involves acts of violence and intimidation, usually directed towards already stigmatised and marginalised groups. As such, it is a mechanism of power and oppression, intended to reaffirm the precarious hierarchies that characterise a given social order. It attempts to re-create simultaneously the threatened (real or imagined) hegemony of the perpetrator's group and the the 'appropriate' subordinate identity of the victim's group. It is a means of marking both the Self and the Other in such a way as to re-establish their 'proper' relative positions, as given and reproduced by broader ideologies and patterns of social and political inequality.

Interestingly, Perry's (2001) definition establishes the direction of the dynamics of hate crime where such behaviour is seen as being perpetrated by dominant (hegemonic) groups against (perceived) subordinate groups. Chakraborti and Garland (2009) argue that Perry's definition enables a clear distinction to be made between hate crime and 'borderline' expressions of hate such as terrorism. In their view, terrorist attacks such as the London bombings of 7 July 2005 should not be seen as hate crime for two main reasons: first, the victims of these bombings were from diverse ethnic, national, religious and cultural backgrounds and were not killed because of their membership of a historically marginalised or disadvantaged group; and second, the bombings were neither perpetrated by dominant groups nor aimed at keeping subordinate ones 'in their place' (Chakraborti and Garland 2009: 103). Waddington (2010), however, points out that there are cases where members of white majority sections of a community allege racial hatred offences committed by members of ethnic minority populations. As Chakraborti and Garland (2009) go on to acknowledge, we are left with the 'conundrum' of whether anyone, regardless of status or background, can be a victim of something termed a 'hate crime' or whether the term should be reserved for the experiences of disadvantaged minority groups.

Yet despite the identified limitations of the term 'hate crime' it also has merit. Chakraborti and Garland (2009) argue that its merit lies in its 'symbolic value' where the term is seen as offering a way of 'reaffirming society's condemnation' of these type of offences. The term also provides a 'rallying point' for a broad range of concerns and interests linked to oppression and bigotry (2009: 155).

Operational Definitions

Professionals engaged in tackling hate crime need operational or working definitions to guide and support their practice. However, operational definitions are also variable in the context of broader social, political and historical developments. Bowling (1999) explores the changing nature of official responses to violent racism in the UK. In particular, he notes the transformation in recent decades from its being seen as a 'personal trouble' of minority ethnic people themselves to a 'public issue' of central concern to local and central governments.

The UK (New Labour) government sought to progress the countering hate crime agenda through legislation (for example, the Crime and Disorder Act, 1998 with its provisions for 'racially' and 'religiously' aggravated offences) and policy. Their *Hate Crime: The Cross-Government Action Plan* document (Her Majesty's Government (HMG 2009)) provides, among other things, operational definitions of 'hate crime' (race hate crime is used here as an example; for other types of incidents substitute 'religion', 'sexual orientation', 'disability' or 'transgender' as appropriate). Here, hate crime is seen as:

> any criminal offence which is perceived, by the victim or any other person, to be motivated by a hostility or prejudice based on a person's race or perceived race (HMG 2009: 53)

The hate crime action plan also provides a definition of 'hate incident'. Thus, a 'hate incident' is defined in the same way only replacing criminal offence with the term 'non-criminal incident'. Several reasons can be suggested for framing the definitions in this way and for distinguishing between 'hate crime' and 'hate incident', including:

- To emphasise the importance of a victim-centred approach to hate crime reporting. Here, it the perceptions of the victim (or the person acting for them) that are prioritised over police officer discretion.
- To emphasis the seriousness of all types of hate-related incidents, regardless of whether they meet criminal prosecution standards.
- To support 'intelligence-led' and 'community intelligence'-based policing (See Chapter 7 *Knowledge Management* and Chapter 8 *Intelligence Gathering and Police Systems* for further reading on the concept of 'intelligence') approaches which rely on a range of open information flows related to crime, criminals as well as 'quality of life' issues.

The UK Association of Chief Police Officers' (ACPO) hate crime manual (ACPO, 2005) provides strategic, tactical and operational guidance based around working definitions of 'hate crime' and 'hate incident' – which are essentially identical to those in the *Hate Crime: The Cross-Government Action Plan.*

At the time of writing, the publication of a 'refreshed' ACPO hate crime manual is overdue. It is believed the refreshed manual will include updated guidance on national minimum standards of investigation, the recording hate incidents and crime as well as Internet hate crime (see Her Majesty's Government 2009).

Hate Crime, Social and Historical Change

It has been acknowledged that offences now recognised as hate crimes have a long history in societies such as the UK (Hall 2005). Harris et al. (2009) historical perspective on hate, for example, notes that British anti-Semitism can be traced back via the popular oral culture of the Middle Ages. Yet despite the idea that hate crime represents a constant feature of the social and historical landscape, its nature, extent and consequences continue to change within the context of wider social, cultural, economic, political and technological developments. As with 'crime' in general, 'hate crime' is 'relative' and 'historically and culturally contingent' (Perry 2003).

In recent decades, attention (particularly from social scientists) has increasingly turned to what many see as the major social and political transformations occurring in societies such as the UK. Various terms have emerged to describe these transformations, including 'late-modernity, 'post-modernity' and 'post-industrial' (Giddens 2009). While the precise nature and consequences of these changes remain contested, a number of features have been agreed upon of interest to hate crime studies. According to Robins (2002) these include:

- the role and impact of globalisation (a force which contributes to a growing mobility across frontiers of goods, commodities, services, information, communications, cultural products and people);
- the rise of global networks and information flows supported by powerful new technologies;
- challenges to the established 'certainties' of earlier social, political and economic arrangements through the rise of new forms of global enterprise [legitimate and otherwise];
- challenges to the concept of identity (at both the personal and the collective levels).

Hate Crime, Identity and Difference

As suggested by Robins (2002), globalisation is impacting concepts of 'identity' which, it can be suggested, are key to any exploration of hate crime. Woodward's (1999) concept of 'identity in crisis' suggests how individuals and groups may be struggling to engage with these change processes. The concept of 'identity in crisis' supposes that individuals and groups situated within these major social and political upheavals are engaged in a constant process of identity construction and negotiation (see Chapters 3 and 4 on psychology and cults for further reading on these issues). This process results from the human search for meaning and security in an otherwise uncertain and unpredictable world and is associated with a new kind of 'identity politics' (Muir and Wetherell 2010).

Perry's (2001) concept of 'doing difference' also addresses questions of identity. In her view, doing difference involves engaging in 'identity formation'. Such formations can relate to a range of intersecting identities and hierarchies constructed along lines of sexuality, 'race', gender, class and other markers of difference. In this perspective hate crime is understood as a response by dominant groups to threats posed by (perceived) subordinate groups who somehow transgress 'sacred boundaries', forget their 'place' or 'step out of line' within existing socio-cultural arrangements and hierarchies (Perry 2001: 55). This perspective links to psychological theories that seek to explain how inter-group conflict can arise. Cole and Cole (2009), for example, discuss 'Realistic Threat', 'Symbolic Threat' and 'Integrated Threat' theories. Together, these theories rely on the concept of 'in' and 'out-group' conflict that arises over negative expectations, competing values, competition over scarce resources and perceived threats (actual and symbolic).

A topical and volatile identity 'fault line' in contemporary societies arguably relates to questions of religious affiliation. Cole and Cole's (2009) work on radicalisation and terrorist violence among British Muslims highlights the centrality of concepts of identity in inter and intra-group relations. As they argue, the internal diversity of the British Muslim population (along lines of ethnicity, nationality as well as different traditions of Islam) leads to a lack of a 'uniform sense' of Muslim social identity. Yet within mainstream society, there are those who perceive British Muslims as a homogeneous group possessing (negative) stereotypical features. One expression of this situation is Islamophobia. Chakraborti and Garland (2009: 159) define 'Islamophobia' as 'prejudice towards, or hatred of, Islam or those of the Islamic faith'. Though not a new phenomenon (Chakraborti and Garland 2009) the nature and dynamics of Islamophobia continue to be shaped by wider social and political developments. Pantazis and Pemberton (2009) develop this theme, arguing that in the context of the present day 'War on Terror' as the 'principal conflict of our time', Muslim identity in the UK has been constructed in terms of the 'new suspect community' (replacing the Irish). They suggest that this situation is associated with the implementation of a specific official counter-terrorism agenda, the construction of official discourses which identify Muslims in certain ways and through the use of negative representations of such groups. Pantazis and Pemberton (2009) highlight the dangers involved, suggesting that once a community is treated as 'suspect' by police the public are encouraged to do the same. They explain this disturbing development in terms of the emergence of a 'permission to hate' which pervades society.

The Multiple Dimensions of Hate Crime

Iganski (2010: 355) warns of the limitations of attempting to look 'deep into offenders' souls' when seeking to understand and counter hate crime. Such an approach, he argues, does not bring us close to the 'lived reality' of victims' experiences of hate crime. Alternative approaches to understanding and dealing with hate crime focus on wider concerns. Thompson's (1998) 'PCS. Analysis' (P-personal; C-cultural; S-structural) draws attention to the different dimensions of oppression and discrimination and their interconnectedness. The PCS analysis usefully shows how factors at the personal level (such as individual thoughts, actions and attitudes) connect to cultural factors (including shared meanings, jokes, negative stereotypes and negative imagery) as well as to structural/ societal factors (such as the patterned inequalities and divisions in societies and institutions based around questions of class, gender, 'race', ethnicity, faith, ability/ disability and sexual orientation for example) Sir William Macpherson of Cluny's Inquiry (Macpherson 1999) into the police handling of the investigation into the 1993 racist murder of London teenager Stephen Lawrence explored the contested concept of 'institutional racism'. The Inquiry settled on the following definition:

> The collective failure of an organisation to provide an appropriate and professional service to people because of their colour, culture, or ethnic origin. It can be seen or detected in processes, attitudes and behaviour which amount to discrimination through unwitting prejudice, ignorance, thoughtlessness and racist stereotyping which disadvantage minority ethnic people. (Macpherson 1999: 28)

Sibbitt's (1997) ground-breaking study of the perpetrators of racial harassment also explores the connections between the personal and the social through the concept of the 'perpetrator community'. This concept suggests the reciprocal relationship between individual perpetrators of hate crime and their wider community. As she observes:

> The views held by all kinds of perpetrators towards ethnic minorities are shared by the wider communities to which they belong. Perpetrators see this as legitimising their actions. (Sibbitt 1997: vii)

In this view, perpetrators' actions are legitimised and shaped by their community which in turn is served by the perpetrators' actions. Together, these views highlight the importance of addressing the multiple dimensions and factors of hate crime.

The Spectrum of Hate Crime

The *Hate Crime: Cross-Government Action Plan* (HMG 2009: 2) refers to a 'spectrum' of hate crime running from 'abuse and harassment through to violent extremism'. This view suggests a wide range of possible incidents and/or crimes which may be included under the umbrella term 'hate crime'. In a recent review of anti-social behaviour, the UK coalition government clearly links both 'anti-social behaviour' and 'hate crime' as key priorities when they explain:

> Our ultimate aim is to ensure that where a community or victim is suffering anti-social behaviour or a concerted campaign of hate crime – particularly the sort of targeted, persistent harassment seen in a number of high-profile cases – the police and other local agencies take the problem seriously, take the necessary steps to stop it permanently, and protect vulnerable victims. (Home Office 2011: 27)

Chakraborti and Garland (2009) suggest that the concept of a 'continuum of violence' can be adapted and applied to hate crime. Their earlier research into rural racism, for example, found that victims reported both 'low-level' forms of racist harassment (such as 'verbal abuse', 'unnecessary or persistent staring', the throwing of stones or other objects, the 'blocking of driveways' and racist 'humour') as well as 'high-level' racism (such as physical assault and attempted petrol bombing). While both levels of incident clearly affected victims, the researchers found that it was the cumulative 'drip-drip' effect of the so-called 'low-level' incidents embedded as a constant feature of everyday life which caused the greatest degree of concern to rural minority ethnic households (Chakraborti and Garland 2009: 34). This view is echoed in the British government's *Cyber Crime Strategy* (Home Office 2010: 12) which observes that 'research has found that 'minor' hate crimes can produce as much emotional harm for victims as so called 'serious offences".

Another expression of hate is referred to as 'hate speech' defined by Jewkes and Yar (2010: 633) as:

> Any form of speech or representation that depicts individuals or groups in a derogatory manner with reference to their 'race', ethnicity, gender, religion, sexual orientation, or physical or mental disability in such a manner as to promote or provoke hatred.

Harris et al. (2009) highlight the elusive nature of the concept of 'hate speech' and the practical difficulties facing those charged with policing it. They suggest three main ways of approaching this difficulty: first, by arguing that certain statements or modes of expression are placed in a *sui generis* category of 'hate speech' because of their offensive nature; second, by defining hate speech by reference to the speaker's intent; and third, by acknowledging that the meaning of hate speech is elusive but recognising there is a 'core' of meaning upon which 'reasonable people' could agree.

Hate Crimes as Communicative Acts

Hate crimes can be seen as possessing communicative properties. A suggested distinguishing feature of such crimes is their capacity to create an impact beyond the immediate experiences of victims. The concept of 'message crimes' seeks to explain this phenomenon. Perry (2003: 19) argues that hate crimes, as message crimes:

emit a distinct warning to all members of the victim's community: step out
of line, cross invisible boundaries, and you too could be lying on the ground,
beaten and bloodied.

Thus hate crimes are capable of 'sending a message' to particular communities
that their presence/activities are being monitored and (negatively) evaluated.

The 'Signal Crimes Perspective' (SCP; Innes 2004) argues that signal crimes
and signal disorders (which can include hate crimes/incidents) act as warning
signals to individuals and groups about their exposure to risk. These signals
influence individual and group perceptions of security and can lead to adjustments
in behaviour to any perceived changes in the risk/threat/harm environment. The
SCP enables policing agencies to respond through 'control signals' (such as
high visibility patrols or other focused interventions) that target issues deemed
important to particular stakeholders. The concepts of message crimes and signal
crimes usefully explain how particular events can have seemingly disproportionate
impacts on specific people and groups in particular social and historical contexts
due to the meanings attached to them.

The Problems of Escalation

Hate crime consists of what Iganski (2010) terms 'everyday' and 'extreme'
offending. In recent years, the question of escalation in terms of a progression
from the relatively low-level to the high-level consequences of hate crime has
assumed a new importance in the light of high profile cases involving allegations
of agency failures in protecting victims. The ACPO Hate Crime Manual warns that
'progressive escalation of violence, left unchecked, leads to increasingly serious
injury and even death' (ACPO, 2005: 67). In a recent speech on disability hate
crime, the British Director of Public Prosecutions, Keir Starmer, QC (Starmer
2011) citing the Fiona Pilkington case.

> In October 2007 Fiona Pilkington drove to a lay-by near Earl Shilton,
> Leicestershire with her severely disabled daughter, Francecca Hardwick. There,
> she set light to the vehicle with the couple inside. Their deaths followed several
> years of abuse, torment and anti-social behaviour at their home in Barwell from
> a gang of local youths that was targeted on the family members. The family also
> included a son with learning difficulties. Official investigations into the case
> have identified a number of police failings in terms of the quality and level of
> protection afforded the family. In particular, police failed to see the family as a
> 'collective vulnerable family unit' and to link and prioritise individual incidents
> reported (IPCC 2011: 179) warned of the dangers of advising hate crime victims
> to ignore all but the most serious of incidents.

A dated yet still highly influential approach to the manifestations of prejudice and discrimination and the dangers of escalation is found in 'Allport's Scale' of prejudice and discrimination (Allport 1954). The Scale consists of five levels where 'antilocution' represents the least extreme level of expression and 'extermination' the highest. Examples of behaviour or expression at each level include the following.

Antilocution

Bad-mouthing; racist jokes; discussion of prejudices with like-minded people; use of negative stereotyping and imagery. The lowest level of expressions of prejudice.

Avoidance

Actively avoiding members of particular groups; social isolation strategies.

Discrimination

Prejudice into action; unfair or unequal treatment; limiting an individual's opportunities on the basis of one or more perceived markers of difference; denial of services.

Physical attack

Physical attacks on persons or property leading to harm or damage.

Extermination

The most extreme expression of prejudice/discrimination; 'The Final Solution'; genocide; 'ethnic cleansing'.

Allport's Scale has been adopted by UK police services to inform training, strategy and operations (for example, see National Police Training 1997). In particular, it can be used to emphasise the importance of early intervention and to highlight the dangers of allowing relatively low-level prejudice/discrimination to foster a climate of further and more extreme expressions of negativity. It should be noted that escalation is not seen as inevitable.

While Allport's Scale is largely derived from the experiences of the Jews in Nazi Germany, there is scope to apply it to other settings (see Rogers and Lewis 2007, Clements 2006). For example, 'extermination' may be interpreted as 'getting rid of' an individual from the organisation through a range of behaviours designed to demonstrate extreme hostility to their presence in the workplace. Alternatively, it could be taken to mean forcing a person or family to leave a house or area in present day society.

The Paradox of Increased Connectivity: Internet as Both Opportunity and Threat

Commentators have highlighted the 'Janus-faced' character of the Internet. It brings both opportunities and threats for questions of security and progress. In his study of 'old' and 'new' forms of terrorism, Neumann (2009: 11) suggests how the 'tools of globalisation' are being exploited and appropriated by extremists 'to spread violence and hatred'. Along similar lines, Bobbitt (2008) in his study of modern terrorism, draws on the concept of the 'connectivity paradox' to suggest the dual-nature of modern ICTs. On the one hand, and as noted, increased connectivity has enabled social progress through greater opportunities to combine diverse resources, skills and ideas, while on the other, these same societies (their systems and by extension, their citizens) have become more and more vulnerable through their increasing dependence on such technologies.

Computer-Mediated Communication, Cyber Violence and Cyber Hate

Computer-mediated communication (CMC) is concerned with the diverse ways new technologies are permeating and impacting everyday life and its diverse social interactions (Thurlow et al. 2009). CMC is particularly focused on the role played by ICTs in identity formation and the construction of what Rheingold (1993) terms 'virtual communities'. From a CMC perspective, hate crime can be understood as one of a myriad activities enabled by technology. Along these lines, Herring (cited in Thurlow et al. 2009) identifies four categories of 'cyber violence'. These may be seen as sharing convergences with the concept of 'cyber hate' in that they rely on ICTs and have the potential to produce harms. The types of cyber violence identified are:

- online contact leading to offline abuse (which may lead to unlawful behaviour);
- cyber stalking (tracking an individual's actions online with illegitimate intent);
- online harassment (unwanted, unreciprocated and unnecessary communications which can include personal threats and may contravene law);
- degrading representations (which can include disrespectful and/or harmful representations through image or text).

The concept of 'cyber hate' has become increasingly well established in the relevant literature fields though it too raises conceptual difficulties. In their study of online White supremacist groups, Douglas et al. (2005: 68) explain cyber hate in the following terms:

Increasingly, hate groups use the Internet to express their viewpoints, sell their products, and recruit new members ... [t]his phenomenon, called cyberhate, has taken the form of hatred against particular social groups such as gays and lesbians ... and advocacy of terrorism ... [h]owever, the most common example of cyberhate is racial hatred as seen in the case of White supremacists in the United States.

CMC draws on diverse disciplines in developing the field, including sociology and psychology. Relevant concepts used which offer insights into hate crime are as follows.

Disinhibition

Johnson (1998: 44, cited in Thurlow et al. 2009: 62) describes 'disinhibition' as an 'apparent reduction in concern for self-presentation and the judgment of others.' It links to the notion of 'anonymity' and suggests the actual or perceived freedom from constraints and freedom from responsibility associated with CMC.

De-individuation

A term appropriated from sociology and psychology, 'de-individuation' suggests the 'subjugation of the individual to the group and a concomitant reduction in self-focus' (Thurlow et al. 2009: 63).

Polarisation

CMC researchers have found a tendency in online groups towards extreme views and an absence of contradictory or moderating voices. Psychologist Patricia Wallace (1999, cited in Thurlow et al. 2009) explains how online communications can lead to the intensification of the individual leanings of the group members towards extremes. 'Strength in numbers' becomes a calculation for such individuals though this may also involve a false sense of security.

Flames or Flaming

Often understood to be 'hostile and aggressive interactions' in CMC such as: inflammatory remarks; vicious verbal attacks; derogatory, obscene or inappropriate language; and overheated prose (Thurlow et al. 2009: 70).

Organised Cyber Hate: The Case of the Far Right

Of growing academic and policing concern is the rise of the so-called 'Far Right' (see Whine 2003). This umbrella term encompasses a range of ideologies, groups and movements typified in the US, UK and Europe by white supremacist groups, militias, neo-Nazis, 'Holocaust Deniers' and so-called 'Christian fundamentalists' (Perry and Olsson 2009, Whine 2003). Common themes uniting these diverse groups suggested by Gerstenfeld (2004), Hall (2005) and Williams (2010) include ideological-based claims to superiority; calls for racial segregation (partial or total); an immigration focus; power differentials (usually involving 'dominant' groups who perceive themselves as 'threatened' by perceived subordinate groups); religion (while not all Far Right groups claim a religious basis, some do and seek to explain their activities in terms of 'God's work'); and populism (here, Far Right groups pursue strategies aimed at undermining mainstream political parties' achievements and which seek to exploit popular 'fears' and 'resentments' while broadening their appeal and moderating their rhetoric).

Britain has its own history of Far Right politics. Matassa and Newburn's (2007) study explores the activities of far-right wing historical groups such as Combat 18, the National Front and, more recently, the British National Party. A more recent study by Meleagrou-Hitchens and Standing (2010) focuses on the 'Blood and Honour' (B&H) international network's British origins and activities. In particular, they note the key role played by the Internet in the activities of the B&H network (for example, in enabling the publication of an 'official' online magazine').

Perry and Olsson (2009: 190) explore the case for an 'emerging globalisation of a virtual community of hate' enabled by new ICTs. In their view, the Internet amplifies messages and ideologies and creates space for a sense of belonging and identity to emerge that allows otherwise separate interests to unite and to be recruited. Elsewhere, academic and community voices have criticised contemporary UK government security strategies for their 'bias' and 'disproportionality' in targeting Muslims while neglecting other forms of extremism including that stemming from Far Right politics (House of Commons 2010).

Policing Hate Crime: Police and Partnership Problems

While the responsibility for tackling hate crime has largely fallen to professional police services as part of their wider reducing crime and disorder reduction and improving public safety remits, the contemporary landscape of crime control and security is more complex and 'pluralised' (Crawford 2007). These pluralised arrangements now encompass other bodies including those from the public, private and voluntary sectors as well as communities themselves. These arrangements have been institutionalised with mixed results across the UK on a statutory footing through landmark law reforms such as the Crime and Disorder Act of 1998. Over the past decade or so, a range of issues to do with UK statutory partnerships have been identified which suggest less than optimal working relations and conditions. Together with police-specific issues, this suggests a set of important barriers that have the potential to mediate the effectiveness of countering hate crime strategies. Police-specific problems centre on are as follows.

Historical Tensions between Police and Minority Groups

Bowling (1999) traces key historical developments in British police-community relations that have contributed to a legacy of mistrust. This includes large-scale events such as the 1981 Brixton disorders as well as the consequences of specific incidents such as the New Cross house fire of the same year that killed 13 young black people. These cases, in different ways, involve claims of police bias, disinterest and/or other failings in terms of the services they provide, particularly to minority ethnic victims and communities.

Lack of Trust between Police and Communities

Victims lack trust and confidence in the police for a variety of reasons including a fear of not being taken seriously and of secondary victimisation by police (see Bowling 1999. The Macpherson Inquiry (1999: 19) noted that Duwayne Brooks (Stephen Lawrence's friend and a witness to the murder) was 'the victim of racist stereotyping' at the hands of police as well as being a victim of the traumatic events of that night.

Police Culture

Features of 'cop' culture such as 'prejudice', 'conservatism', 'solidarity' and 'isolation' and the embedded tensions between 'response' (as 'real police work') and 'community' policing (as somehow less meaningful) inhibit the provision and development of fair, professional and needs-based services to victims and communities within a diverse society (see Reiner 2010, Foster 2007).

Over-Policing and Under-Protection

Williams and Robinson's (2004) study of hate crime victims among lesbian, gay and bisexual communities found that police services and reporting decisions were adversely affected by several factors including victims' simultaneous perceptions of police 'harassment' and being 'unprotected'.

Lack of Diversity within the British Police

Her Majesty's Inspectorate of Constabulary (1996) noted how weaknesses in the recruitment, retention and progression of female and minority ethnic officers were linked to low levels of public trust and confidence.

The Process-Incident Contradiction

Bowling (1999) argues that the traditional approach of the British police in favour of responding to 'calls' for assistance as individual and isolated incidents neglects the wider social dimensions of hate crime. The social process approach involves situating individual experiences in the wider social context. It more effectively detects the connections between incidents, suggests the value of a multi-pronged response and allows the cumulative effects of victimisation to be more effectively identified.

Disconnects between High-Level Policy and Frontline Police Practice

Bowling's (1999) concept of a 'hierarchy of police relevance' usefully suggests how police officers use informal working norms and rules to categorise incidents into 'good' or 'rubbish' categories. The frontline policing culture allows for a 'natural agenda' of police work to develop which may conflict with higher-level policy priorities. Within this hierarchy of relevance, hate crimes tend to be categorised at the lower end of the scale with particular consequences for victims and wider communities. Lipsky's (1980) concept of 'street-level bureaucracy' also highlights the mediating influences of individual frontline officers' discretion in the everyday implementation of law and policy.

Problems have also been identified at the level of statutory partnerships. Coliandris and Rogers (2008) summarise these as:

- inter-organisational conflicts over aims, priorities, practices and interests
- intelligence-sharing weaknesses
- resourcing issues and lack of skills
- 'blurred boundaries'
- differential power relations
- a lack of emphasis on crime prevention.

Policing Cyber Hate: Problems and Challenges

Cyber hate perpetrators exploit the well-documented appeal of the Internet in much the same way as other cyber criminals. Its attractions, according to Jewkes (2010), Sandywell (2010) and Whine (2003) centre on the following features:

- anonymity
- sophistication
- opportunities for empowerment
- virtually instantaneous information transmission
- manipulability of electronic information
- affordability, popularity and accessibility
- potential as a 'force-multiplier' capable of enhancing the power and reach of extremist messages or relatively powerless individuals/groups

However, as Whine (2003: 242) argues, governments and policing authorities seeking to take legal action against those who post hate material online face two major issues. They have to balance 'the right of free expression with the protection of human dignity' and they must 'determine under whose jurisdiction' any offence has been committed. The defining features of the Internet are, after all, its dynamic, borderless, networked and globalised character and for some, the defining property of the Internet is its commitment to, and opportunities for, open and unregulated speech.

Governments have adopted different strategies to regulate online hate. Wall (2001: 171, cited in Sandywell 2010: 60) distinguishes between five levels of Internet regulation: 'policing by Internet users themselves; the internet service providers [ISPs]; corporate security organisations; state-funded non-public police organisations; and state-funded public police organisations.' In the UK, there is evidence, in varying degrees, of each of the five levels being invoked. The UK government has a history and suggested future policy intention of working with a range of partners, including ACPO, ISPs and the European Office for Democratic Institutions and Human Rights (ODHIR; see HMG 2009).

In the US, the approach has been different largely due to the protection afforded to speech (even where deemed 'offensive' or 'hateful') by the First Amendment to the Constitution. Henry (2009) describes two novel approaches to combating hate speech online, both of which involve American non-governmental organisations. The first involves the Southern Poverty Law Center and its 'Intelligence Project' which aims to expose online hate speech through active monitoring of websites. Here, the Internet becomes a 'weapon' against hate. In the second approach, the Anti-Defamation League brings offensive content to the attention of ISPs and reminds them of their obligations under agreed terms of service or codes of conduct.

Inevitably though, given the nature and scale of the challenges involved, efforts to effectively regulate cyber hate will require multidimensional strategies. These will need to operate transnationally as well as accounting for localised conditions. They will need to resort to the principles of law enforcement, problem-solving (Problem-oriented policing (POP) is associated with the work of Herman Goldstein (1990) who pioneered the concept within US law enforcement. It has been introduced somewhat unevenly into British policing with mixed results (see Bullock et al. 2006). Essentially, POP requires a fundamental orientation towards deeper problems rather than individual incidents, and calls for a renewed emphasis on the mobilisation of police and community resources in an effort to reduce demands on policing and to deliver longer-lasting solutions, education, active risk assessment/ management), intelligence-led policing, partnership working, and situational and social-oriented preventive approaches (Rogers (2006) helpfully distinguishes between 'situational' and 'social' crime prevention approaches. The former are more focused on opportunity reduction, situational factors and target-hardening strategies while the latter emphasis the need for more socially or community based programmes and interventions that aim to change social environments and the motivations of offenders/those at risk of offending) if they are to be effective in trying to counter this multifaceted phenomenon. Cyber hate regulation will also require authorities to respond creatively and flexibly: as discussed, the form and dynamics of hate crime are constantly shifting and authorities will be required to adapt positively to emerging new threats and opportunities. Chan's (2007: 674) suggestion that the police have been more 'enthusiastic' about technologies that advance 'traditional' law enforcement objectives of 'arrest and conviction' raises important questions about the nature and extent of police adaptation to the emerging range of anti-social/criminal cyber activities and, cyber hate in particular. This, together with the relative unregulated and unregulatable dimensions of the Internet suggest significant policing challenges ahead.

Conclusion

Hate crime remains an elusive concept yet its harmful and corrosive consequences for individuals, groups and societies are clear. Emerging powerful technologies have presented new opportunities for the perpetrators of hate. Cyber hate represents the convergence of two major social forces: the 'old' (human propensities towards prejudice, discrimination and hostility) and the 'new' (powerful ICTs). However, these new technologies can also be effectively exploited by authorities: this will require them to respond through creative and flexible multidimensional strategies that draw on the potential of partnership synergies, diverse perspectives and shared knowledge, skills and resources operating in dynamic and globalised contexts.

Further Reading

Two particularly accessible texts addressing the complexities of hate crime are Hall's *Hate Crime* (2005) and Chakraborti and Garland's *Hate Crime: Impact, Causes and Responses* (2009). The latter includes a section on the more 'invisible' and 'borderline' forms of offending such as disablist hate crime as well as a useful glossary. There is a shortage of texts dealing specifically with cyber hate. However, Jewkes and Yar's (eds) *Handbook of Internet Crime* (2010) provides a comprehensive set of readings on many aspects of cybercrime, with some references to online hate.

References

Association of Chief Police Officers (ACPO) 2005. *Hate Crime: Delivering a Quality Service (Good Practice Guide and Tactical Guidance)*. Association of Chief Police Officers. London: ACPO.

Allport, G.W. 1954. *The Nature of Prejudice*. Reading, MA: Addison-Wesley.

Bobbitt, P. 2008. *Terror and Consent: The Wars for the Twenty-First Century*. London: Penguin Books Ltd.

Bowling, B. 1999. *Violent Racism: Victimisation, Policing and Social Context*. Revised Edition. Oxford: Oxford University Press.

Bullock, K., Erol, R. and Tilley, N. 2006. *Problem-Oriented Policing and Partnerships: Implementing an Evidence-Based Approach to Crime Reduction*. Cullompton: Willan Publishing.

Chakraborti, N. and Garland, J. 2009. *Hate Crime: Impact, Causes and Responses*. London: Sage Publications.

Chan, J.B.L. 2007. Police and new technologies, in *Handbook of Policing*, edited by T. Newburn. Cullompton: Willan Publishing, 655–79.

Clements, P. 2006. *Policing a Diverse Society*. Oxford: Oxford University Press.

Cole, J. and Cole, B. 2009. *Martyrdom: Radicalisation and Terrorist Violence among British Muslims*. London: Pennant Books.

Coliandris, G.A. and Rogers, C. 2008. Linking Police Culture, Leadership and Partnership Working. *Police Journal*, 81, 111–25.

Crawford, A. 2007. The pattern of policing in the UK: policing beyond the police, in *Handbook of Policing*, edited by T. Newburn. Cullompton: Willan., 136–68.

Douglas, K.M., McGarty, C., Bliuc, A.M., and Lala, G. 2005. Understanding Cyberhate: Social Competition and Social Creativity in Online White Supremacist Groups. *Social Science Computer Review*, 23(1), 68–76.

Foster, J. 2007. Police cultures, in *Handbook of Policing*, edited by T. Newburn. Cullompton: Willan, 196–227.

Gerstenfeld, P.B. 2004. *Hate Crimes: Causes, Controls and Controversies*. Thousand Oaks, CA: Sage.

Giddens, A. 2009. *The Consequences of Modernity*. Cambridge: Polity.

Goldstein, H. 1990. *Problem-Oriented Policing*. New York, NY: McGraw Hill Inc.

Hall, N. 2005. *Hate Crime*. Cullompton: Willan Publishing.

Harris, C., Rowbotham, J. and Stevenson, K. 2009. Truth, Law and Hate in the Virtual Marketplace of Ideas: Perspectives on the Regulation of Internet Content. *Information & Communications Technology Law*. [Online]. 18(2), 155–84. Available at: http://www.informaworld.com/smpp/content~content=a 912569992~db=all~jumptype=rss [accessed: 28 May 2011].

Henry, J.S. 2009. Beyond Free Speech: Novel Approaches to Hate on the Internet in the United States. *Information & Communications Technology Law*. [Online]. 18(2), 235–51. Available at: http://www.informaworld.com/smpp/content~con tent=a912572577~db=all~jumptype=rss [accessed: 28 May 2011].

Her Majesty's Government (HMG). 2009. Hate Crime – The Cross Government Action Plan. [Online]. Available at: http://library.npia.police.uk/docs/homeoffice/hate-crime-action-plan.pdf [accessed: 28 May 2011].

Her Majesty's Inspectorate of Constabulary (HMIC).1996. *Developing Diversity in the Police Service. Equal Opportunities Thematic Inspection Report.* London: Home Office.

Home Office. 2010. *Cyber Crime Strategy.* Cm. 7842. London: TSO.

Home Office. 2011. *More Effective Responses to Anti-Social Behaviour.* London: TSO.

House of Commons. 2010. *House of Commons Communities and Local Government Committee Preventing Violent Extremism, Sixth Report of Session 2009–10*, HC 65, Norwich: TSO.

Hu, W. 2010. Legal debate Swirl's in Charges in a Student's Suicide. *New York Times.* [Online]. Available at: http://www.nytimes.com/2010/10/02/nyregion/02suicide.html?_r=1 [accessed: 2 April 2011].

Iganski, P. 2010. Hate crime, in *Handbook on Crime,* edited by F. Brookman, M. Maguire, H. Pierpoint and T. Bennett. Cullompton: Willan Publishing, 351–65.

Independent Police Complaints Commission (IPCC). 2011. IPCC report into the contact between Fiona Pilkington and Leicestershire Constabulary 2004–2007. [Online].IPCC Reference 2009/016872. Available at: http://www.ipcc.gov.uk/news/Pages/pr_240511_pilkington.aspx? [accessed: 28 May 2011].

Innes, M. 2004. Signal Crimes and Signal Disorders: Notes on Deviance as Communicative Action. *British Journal of Sociology*, 55(3), 335–55.

Jacobs, J. and Potter, K. 1998. *Hate Crimes: Criminal Law and Identity Politics.* Oxford: Oxford University Press.

Jewkes, Y. 2010. Public policing and Internet crime, in *Handbook of Internet Crime*, edited by Y. Jewkes and M. Yar. Cullompton: Willan Publishing, 525–45.

Jewkes, Y. and Yar, M. 2010. *Handbook of Internet Crime.* Cullompton: Willan Publishing.

Lipsky, M. 1980. *Street-level Bureaucracy. Dilemmas of the Individual in Public-Services.* New York, NY: Russell Sage Foundation.

Macpherson, Sir W. 1999. *The Stephen Lawrence Inquiry: Report of an Inquiry by Sir William Macpherson of Cluny*. Cmnd. 4262–4. London: HMSO.

Matassa, M., and Newburn, T. 2007. Policing and terrorism, in *Handbook of Policing*, edited by T. Newburn. Cullompton: Willan Publishing, 467–500.

Meleagrou-Hitchens, A. and Standing, E. 2010. Blood & Honour: Britain's Far Right Militants [Online]. The Centre for Social Cohesion. Available at:http://www.socialcohesion.co.uk/files/1266928262_1.pdf [accessed: 28 May 2011].

Muir, R. and Wetherell, M. 2010. Identity, Politics and Public Policy. [Online]. The Institute for Public Policy research (ippr). Available at: http://www.ippr.org.uk/publicationsandreports/publication.asp?id=742 [accessed: 28 May 2011].

National Police Training (NPT). 1997. *Equal Opportunities and Community and Race Relations Minimum Effective Training Levels,* Harrogate: National Police Training.

Neumann, P.R. 2009. *Old and New Terrorism.* Cambridge: Polity Press.

Pantazis, C. and Pemberton, S. 2009. From the 'Old' to the 'New' Suspect Community. Examining the Impacts of Recent UK Counter-Terrorist Legislation. *British Journal of Criminology,* 49(5), 646–66.

Perry, B. 2001. *In the Name of Hate: Understanding Hate Crimes.* London: Routledge.

Perry, B. 2003. Where Do We Go from Here? Researching Hate Crime. *Internet Journal of Criminology.* [Online]. Available at: %20Do%20We%20Go%20 From%20Here.%20Researching%20Hate%20Crime.pdf [accessed: 28 May 2011].

Perry, B. and Olsson, P. 2009. Cyberhate: The Globalisation of Hate. *Information & Communications Technology Law.* [Online]. 18(2), 185–99. Available at: http://www.informaworld.com/smpp/content~content=a912569634~db=all~j umptype=rss [accessed: 28 May 2011].

Pilkington, E. 2010. Tyler Clementi, student outed as gay on Internet, jumps to his death. *Guardian.* [Online]. Available at: http://www.guardian.co.uk/ world/2010/sep/30/tyler-clementi-gay-student-suicide [accessed: 10 April 2011].

Reiner, R. 2010. *The Politics of the Police.* 4th Edition. Oxford: Oxford University Press.

Rheingold, H. 1993. *The Virtual Community.* New York, NY: Harper Collins.

Robins, K. 2002. What in the world's going on?, in *Production of Culture/Cultures of Production,* edited by P. Du Gay. London: Sage, 11–66.

Rogers, C. 2006. *Crime Reduction Partnerships.* Oxford: Oxford University Press.

Rogers, C., and Lewis, R. (2007). *Introduction to Police Work.* Cullompton: Willan.

Sandywell, B. 2010. On the globalisation of crime: the Internet and new criminality, in *Handbook of Internet Crime,* edited by Y.Jewkes and M.Yar. Cullompton: Willan Publishing, 38–66.

Sibbitt, R. 1997. *The Perpetrators of Racial Harassment and Racial Violence.* Research Study No. 176. London: Home Office.

Starmer, K. 2011. Prosecuting disability hate crime: the next frontier – DPPs speech to the University of Sussex. [Online]. Crown Prosecution Service website. Available at: http://cps.gov.uk/news/articles/prosecuting_disability_ hate_crime [accessed: 11 March 2011].

Thompson, N. 1998. *Promoting Equality: Challenging Discrimination and Oppression in the Human Services.* Basingstoke: Macmillan Press.

Thurlow, C., Lengel, L. and Tomic, A. 2009. *Computer Mediated Communication: Social Interaction and the Internet.* London: Sage.

Waddington, P.A.J. 2010. An examination of hate crime. *Police Review,* 118, 6077, 14–15.

Whine, M. 2003. Far right extremists on the Internet, in *CyberCrime: Law Enforcement, Security and Surveillance in the Information Age,* edited by D. Thomas and B.D. Loader. London: Routledge, 234–50.

Williams, M.H. 2010. Can leopards change their spots? between xenophobia and trans-ethnic populism among western European far right parties. *Nationalism and Ethnic Politics.* [Online]. 16(1), 111–34. Available at: http://www. informaworld.com/smpp/content~db=all~content=a919551764 [accessed: 2 April 2011].

Williams, M. and Robinson, A. 2004. Problems and prospects with policing the lesbian, gay and bisexual community in Wales. *Policing and Society,* 14(3), 213–32.

Woodward K. 1999. Concepts of identity and difference, in *Identity and Difference,* edited by K. Woodward. London: Sage Publications, 7–62.

Chapter 6

Policing the Global Phenomenon of Cyber Terrorism and Extremism

Imran Awan

Cyber warfare is a major threat to British national security. With a variety of technological advances, the potential to attack, for example, the national electric grid and cause economic and physical damage is a real one (Tier 1 Risk-Cabinet Office 2009b). What used to be described as possible cyber attacks have become a present threat (Stohl 2007). Indeed, air traffic control depends on ICT, as do the armed forces, the electricity grid, transport and the financial sectors; therefore an attack on these systems could be considered an act of cyber warfare. Moreover, governments across the world now fear that terrorist groups are developing the ability to hack into critical infrastructure, such as air traffic control and be able to unleash death and destruction, depicting the doomsday scenario, described in detail (see Chapter 2). The chapter will examine government policies in relation to the threat of cyber terrorism and uses empirical evidence to look at the implementation of such laws and evidence. The UK security service monitor's the use of the Internet and cyber activities in the context of its counter-terrorism policies (known as CONTEST) which aims to combat the threat of terrorism and now extremism in the realms of cyberspace (HM Government 2011).

Policing Cyber Terrorism

You should contact your local police

In an increasingly complex world of cyber crimes, cyber threats, cyber hate and terrorist related incidents on the web; the police have to play an important role in policing cyberspace. With this heightened sense of fear and anxiety surrounding the threat of cyber terrorism in the UK, a new unit was created known as the Counter Terrorism Internet Referral Unit (CTIRU) by the Association of Chief Police Officers (ACPO) in March 2011. Through the use of an anonymous referral system for members of the public (Direct Gov 2011) individuals are encouraged to notify the police of any suspicious material which is terrorist related and is subsequently removed. Thus, the unit's main aim is to get local communities to work in a partnership with the police by reporting suspect terrorist material on the Internet.

ACPO's broader strategy utilises both intelligence based policing models and community policing models in the fight against extremism in cyberspace. The unit is a blend of police officers and staff from various forces across the UK (which include the Counter Terrorism Units, Counter Terrorism Intelligence Units and the Metropolitan Police Service Counter Terrorism Command) who are all tasked with removing unlawful terrorist material (see Chapter 2 for discussion on terrorist material on the web) that is on the Internet and which has the potential to begin a process of radicalisation (Weber 2008).

The Internet has become a valuable database for those who wish to prey on vulnerable people; however it is not clear whether this initiative by ACPO to counter extremism will actually help counter a terrorist attack in the future, as many of these terrorist websites or material will simply move elsewhere under a different domain name. Furthermore, the premise of such a strategy implies a measure of trust and confidence from within communities; however, controversial counter-terrorist legislation, and heavy handed police raids, means many communities remain deeply suspicious of police tactics when it comes to tackling terrorism.

The referral site does provide members of the public with a list of content that may be regarded as unlawful terrorist material, that is, material which is violent in nature, for example videos that show beheadings of Western hostages (such as Daniel Pearl – see Chapter 2 for further discussion on online executions) on the Internet which they are encouraged to report. Once a user clicks onto the referral site a heading page appears with the title 'what makes offensive content illegal; seen something online that's worried you?' (Direct Gov 2011). The referral site uses counter-terrorism legislation, under the Terrorism Act 2000 and Terrorism Act 2006, to identify more specifically material that is potentially illegal in nature; this may for example be information which is shared that may be useful to terrorist organisations; or material that may encourage people to commit or help with acts of terrorism; and finally material that glorifies or praises terrorist attacks (Direct Gov 2011). Therefore, some examples of illegal terrorist content online could be sermons or writings, videos of terrorist attacks (see Chapter 2 for discussion on websites and extremist videos), chat rooms and forums that encourage acts of terrorism and in some way advocate religious acts of violence (Weimann 2008). The problem with policing cyber terrorism in this way is that it allows for state censorship, that is, people not being able to openly express their views on chat rooms or forums through fear of prosecution.

Global Cyber Attacks

Cyber terrorism has become an international legislative issue which requires countries to pursue cyber terrorist acts via their own traditional modes of legal practice as well as using cyber crimes to prosecute those involved. However, as countries begin to understand the nature and threat of cyber terrorism they have also begun using a broad range of multifaceted agreements and protocols that allows member states to take the necessary measures to ensure anyone who illegally accesses information and interferes with computer data has committed an offence (EU Council Framework Decision on Attacks against Information Systems, Article 2 and Article 4). This form of partnership work has led to the Budapest Convention on Cybercrime (2001) which is a broad and comprehensive treaty that deals with ICT related crime and cyber crimes in general by making member states have national legislation in place that will help tackle the cyber threat. One of the key objectives of the convention is prosecuting those involved in cyber hate crimes (see Chapter 5), generic cyber threats that include wider terrorist use of the Internet (see Chapter 9 on national security strategies for more detail) (Council of Europe 2001).

Moreover the EU Council Framework Decision on Combating Terrorism under Article 1 states that all member states must work together where a cyber attack has taken place. A cyber attack in this context has to be one that seriously intimidates a population or seriously destabilises a constitution – the paradox being that there is still no universal definition of the term cyber terrorism (Wykes and Harcus 2010; see Chapter 2 for further discussion on the meaning of cyber terrorism).

In May 2007, Estonia came under siege for almost 3 weeks from hackers using sophisticated modes of technology. They were able to deface and cripple a number of governmental, financial and political websites. This attack is not the first of its kind as similar incidents of cyber attacks have taken place against different countries. However, such cyber attacks do highlight the vulnerability of countries to computer-based crime and is one the reasons for national agreements (discussed below). The attacks in this case were political in nature and came to the surface when a war memorial to the Red Army was removed from the capital by the government (Traynor 2007).

The extent of the damage caused in Estonia and the reverberations of the consequences for the international community meant there was a need for further international agreements that protect countries against similar cyber attacks. The hackers in this case redirected users of the government sites to powerful graphic and visual images of Soviet soldiers in war battle lines and also left quotations and speeches from Martin Lurthur King. The images and speeches also acted as a motivational tool for the demonstrators giving them hope, trust and confidence. Before this incident, the Estonian government had invested heavily in protecting itself from such cyber attacks. It had mechanisms which, it argued, could combat this threat. For example an Information Computer Technology infrastructure in place to deal with the threat and had created the Estonian Computer Emergency Services (CERT), a body committed to thwarting hackers. However, such was the nature of these attacks that the Estonian government is looking to the EU community for more help and much more in the way of national and international protocols that can help member states against such attacks.

Furthermore, cyber attacks in July 2009 arose when North Korea mounted a sustained cyber attack on South Korea and the United States. Seoul's National Intelligence Service argued that the attack was both well coordinated and organised by hostile hackers (BBC News 2011). Moreover, this attack came amidst the Obama administration pledging to make cyber security a priority. The US has already established an inter-agency cyber security and a military cyber command, yet has still been the victim of a sustained attack (see section below on US cyber security policy).

Pakistan and India

Similar cyber attacks have arisen in Southern Asia in India and Pakistan as part of the conflict over Kashmir. Pakistan hackers successfully shut down the Indian Army website (www. Indianarmy.nic), resulting in the disruption of services in the military and economic sectors leaving serious implications for Pakistan and India's relationship (Denning 2008). The Indian government's response to these cyber attacks was to engage in a cyber attack that immediately shut down one of Pakistan's leading newspaper *Al-Fajr* (also known as 'Dawn').

Since those attacks a number of hackers have begun to work in partnerships in small well coordinated groups in an attempt to gain control in cyberspace. Some of those groups called the Patriotic Indians, H20, and Hindustan Hackers Organisation have been involved in a series of cyber attacks against the Pakistan government and been able to deface the Pakistan governmental official website on more than one occasion (www.pakgov.uk). Furthermore, Pakistan-based hacker groups calling themselves Milw0rm were able to hack into the Bhabha Atomic Research Centre websites defacing both the website and at the same time leaving anti-Indian sentiments. It appears that hackers from both Pakistan and India are well equipped to mount such attacks with the intention of causing severe disruption.

The fact is that countries are not immune from such attacks. It does not matter how much they create defence mechanisms or how heavily they may have invested in protecting themselves from these attacks, as the skills and abilities of hackers grow to match them. While media attention has focused on the possibility of a war between India and Pakistan, those groups that want to plot in the dark, have been able to conduct cyber attacks.

Moreover, there is evidence since 2008 to suggest that the Pakistan government would like to introduce the death penalty for those involved in future acts of cyber warfare including those they would class as cyber terrorists (Associated Press of Pakistan 2008). This is a step back for a country promoting its liberal and democratic outlook to a country seen as too weak on those converged in cyberspace. In an already fragile situation between these two countries, anything which exacerbates the conflict will further lead to a volatile situation. The use of computers could be more dangerous, deadly and potent than the use of a bomb.

International Agreements

There are a number of protocols and conventions in place to tackle the threat of cyber crime, which include the Convention of Cyber Crime of the Council of Europe, the EU Council Framework Decision on Attacks against Information Systems, the EU Council Framework Decision on Combating Terrorism (Council of Europe 2008). Moreover, the UN Convention has numerous multilateral conventions and protocols relating to how member states should combat violent acts of terrorism. There are, however, no universal conventions that directly cite cyber terrorism as a major issue, but instead they do discuss IT related crime and also include within that sphere the issue of terrorism, violence and cyber crime.

The European Councils Report on the threat of cyber terrorism concludes that: 'With respect to cyberterrorism and the use of the Internet for terrorist purposes it is important to note that all criminal provisions contained in the conventions and protocols are worded in general terms' (Council of Europe 2008:59).

The most prominent UN conventions and protocols that relate to terrorism is the Unlawful Seizure of Aircraft Convention, which creates rules and offences that are used for the civil aviation sector and secondly the Convention on the Unlawful Acts of Severe Violence at Airports which is where dangerous acts of violence at airports are deemed to be criminal offences (Council of Europe 2008). The aim of these conventions in terms of cyber terrorism is the impact of terrorists using such technology to manipulate and control air traffic systems. Furthermore, there are a number of conventions that make criminal offences where crimes are committed against governments or heads of state, for example, the Convention on the Prevention and Punishment of Crimes against Internationally Protected Persons makes it an offence for anyone who commits an act of kidnap or the murder of a government head of state by a (terrorist). Moreover, the Council of Europe Report states that 'Such an attack could be committed, for example by manipulating a hospital computer in order to kill a person protected by the Convention' (Council of Europe 2008:57).

Furthermore, the International Convention against the Taking of Hostages makes it an offence where a person threatens to kill or injure another person whom they have taken as a hostage. This in particular could be where a terrorist group might hold a hostage and then through the use of extremist websites and videos make certain demands (see Chapter 2 for discussion on extremist videos). Moreover, there are conventions that directly relate to the physical protection of nuclear material; the International Convention for the Suppression of Terrorist Bombings which addresses the unlawful use of explosives and other lethal devices and the Convention for the Suppression of Unlawful Acts against the Safety of Maritime Navigation. All of the above conventions establish international rules that make it an offence for someone to unlawfully possess material that might cause death or injury or cause damage to property.

The Council of Europe Convention on Cyber Crime (C of E 2008), however, remains the most potent convention as it addresses both cyber crime and cyber

terrorism in generic terminology. The convention provides four broad categories
to tackle cyber crime and includes offences against the integrity of computer data,
illegal interception, data and system interference, and finally the misuse of devices.

The Convention on Cybercrime also creates international agreements that
directly assess computer-based cyber crime offences. Under Article 4 and Article
5 the convention examines data interference and system interference that relate
to alterations of computer systems. As the Council of Europe Report on Cyber
crime states that 'the Cybercrime Convention covers all types of interference with
data and computer systems that-as shown-are a prerequisite for terrorist's attacks
on computer systems carried out by means of the Internet' (Council of Europe
2008:52).

The EU Council Framework Decision on Combating Terrorism takes into
account more than just the actions of the perpetrator it takes into account the mens
rea (intent) of the individual concerned. The convention does recognise traditional
criminal law codes of member states (United Nations 1999). The mens rea is
the part of the definition of the offence which describes the fault element that
is, the prosecution must prove in order for the defendant to be found guilty. The
most commonly used mens rea terms are where the perpetrator has been reckless,
grossly negligent, or in terrorist cases someone who may have used the Internet
to instil terror and fear. The burden of proof rests solely with the prosecution who
must prove all the elements of the offence beyond a reasonable doubt.

UK Policy on Cyber Security

In the UK the response to the threat of cyber terrorism developed from the cyber
security strategy (Cyber Security Strategy 2009a). This includes enlisting the
support of ex-hackers (based at GCHQ in Cheltenham) to monitor potential cyber
terrorist threats from across the world (see Chapter 9 for a further discussion on
national security agendas). The UK now acknowledges like its close ally the US,
that Al-Qaeda may be capable of causing real damage to UK critical infrastructure
through the use of computers. Therefore the UK strategy focuses not only on the
threat of cyber terrorism but also on cyber crime, fraud and identity theft in general.
It was anticipated that with the help of enlisted hackers the UK could counter any
cyber terrorist attack. In July 2009, Lord West, the cyber security minister at the
time, stated that; 'We know terrorists use the Internet for radicalisation … but there
is a fear they will move down the path (of cyber attacks)' (BBC News 2009a).

The UK strategy on cyber security is unique in that it is the first of its kind to
be implemented alongside the National Security Strategy. This is an important
step, since in the past Britain has relied on the e-crime unit run by the Metropolitan
police to tackle cyber security issues. However, since cyber terrorism has become
a global phenomenon and the UK may be a potential target, combating such a
threat has become a key priority both legally, politically and socially. As part of the
strategy an office for cyber security was initiated in order to help the government

make key decisions on cyber crime, fraud and the creation of the cyber security operations centre that will monitor potential threats to businesses and the public – this includes cyber terrorism. Both of the above centres aim to create safe and secure systems, awareness and cultural change, developing policy, regulatory issues and look at international engagement, governance roles and responsibilities. The then Prime Minister of Britain, Gordon Brown, stated that: 'Just as in the nineteenth century we had to secure the seas for our national safety and prosperity, in the 20 century we also have to secure our advantage in cyber space' (Norton 2009).

The UK cyber security strategy is thus focused on building partnerships with inter agency departments: 'Whilst we expect terrorist groups to continue to favour high-profile conventional operations over cyber attacks, we must be vigilant against any future increase in capability that might be directed against UK interests at home and overseas' (Cabinet Office 2009b: 13).

Critics, however have, argued that such media hype surrounding policy on cyber terrorism will only lead to terrorists developing and further there online tactics. Stohl (2007) states that:

> It is clear that despite the continuing reality that cyber terror remains a potential threat rather than an ongoing series of events, there has not developed a sense of security, comfort or complaisance in the popular press but rather a fear that this year or next is 'in fact' the year of maximum danger. (Stohl 2007: 223)

The UK government has stated that its cyber strategy for national security embraces human rights, the rule of law, justice, accountability, tolerance and freedom. Furthermore, this approach is meant to be a fairer and objective way of tackling such a threat. Previous cyber security policy was run by the National Information Assurance Strategy – which tackled information technology communications disputes. The UK government argues that, because critical infrastructure such as power supply, water and sewage, economic services, transport, health and defence are technologically important, then the potential to hack into these systems and cause destruction remained. The cyber strategy thus examined the issue of the Internet as a safe haven for terrorists as it offers anonymity yet has the possibilities of causing real destruction. The strategy will focus its attention on potential actors (terrorists) who wish to pursue criminal activities.

> Terrorists and violent extremists use cyber space for communication, coordination, propaganda, fundraising, radicalisation, and recruitment, providing them with an unprecedented opportunity to access a wider global community … the strategy also recognises terrorists as potential actors willing to take out cyber attacks or use it as a recruitment tool. (Cyber Security Strategy 2009b: 13)

Securing Britain in an Age of Uncertainty

The most recent National Security Strategy in 2010 sets out two clear objectives: (i) firstly, to make sure the UK is resilient and secure by protecting the public, economy, infrastructure, territory and ways of life from all major risks; and (ii) to build a stable world, by reducing the likelihood of risks affecting the UK or its interests overseas, and applying instruments of power and influence to shape the global environment and tackle potential risks (Cabinet Office 2010). The British government aims to make the cyber security strategy one that is multifaceted and tackles the complex myriad of sophisticated cyber attacks against the UK, yet also balances the issue of human rights with national security. The current review states that the UK must take the threat seriously, so much so that it refers to cyber terrorism, in the Tier 1 risks which include international terrorism, cyber attacks, major natural hazards and an international military crisis between states that draws in the UK. Organised crime is put into Tier 2 risk and energy security and an attack on a UK overseas territory in Tier 3 category.

Table 6.1   (Risks: UK threats to national security are categorised into three tiers)

Tier 1: Threats	Tier 2: Threats	Tier 3: Threats
Risks are international terrorism	Organised crime	An attack on UK land
Cyber attacks, major natural hazards and an international military crisis between states that draws in the UK.	Energy security	And an attack overseas

(Cabinet Office 2010)

Furthermore, the security review seeks to look to the future where an attack could come from anywhere; for example a new computer virus could take over a computer system and cause huge economic and financial damage. For example, the 'Stuxnet' virus infected an Iranian power station and gained control of the system leaving the Iranian government's nuclear programme seriously undermined (Fildes 2011) (see Chapter 1 for further discussion on the 'Stuxnet' virus). This was such a complex and sophisticated attack on the Iranian industrial control systems in the Middle East that the UK government feared that this scenario might be repeated against UK infrastructure increasing the cyber threat landscape for the UK.

US Policy on Cyber Security

The American government strategy on cyber security is contained in the Cyber Security 'Assuring a trusted and resilient information and Communications and Infrastructure' Report (2009). The Obama administration has made it one of its key priorities to tackle cyber security and has begun moulding a policy on cyber security that will tackle the threat of cyber terrorism:

> Threats to cyberspace pose one of the most serious economic and national security challenges of the 21st century for the United States and our allies. A growing array of state and non-state actors such as terrorists and international criminal groups are targeting U.S. citizens, commerce, critical infrastructure, and government. These actors have the ability to compromise, steal, change, or completely destroy information. (Cyber Policy Review 2009:1)

Policy frameworks on cyber security in the US can be traced back to 1998 with the Presidential Decision Directive 63 which was aimed at working with organisations to protect the US against a cyber attack. In 2003, the National Strategy to Secure Cyberspace was introduced alongside the Homeland Security Presidential Directive which uses homeland security as a means of tackling the *new* cyber threat. Moreover, the Comprehensive National Cyber Security Strategy (2007) was introduced that would oversee counter-terrorism policies and look at the vulnerabilities of a cyber attack against US infrastructure. The US policy has also strengthened federal leadership and accountability for cyber security as well as building the capacity for a digital nation. All these initiatives clearly demonstrate the US commitment to combat cyber terrorism.

US policy on cyber security is reliant upon a number of factors. For example, appointing a new cyber security policy based upon the National Security Council Directorate. Part of this campaign is to work in collaboration with experts in the field of cyber security.

The Director of National Intelligence (DNI) stated that: 'the growing connectivity between information systems, the Internet, and other infrastructures creates opportunities for attackers to disrupt telecommunications, electrical power, energy pipelines, refineries, financial networks, and other critical infrastructures' (cited in Cyber Policy Review 2009 at: 1-2). The US strategy therefore is focused on protection of its cyber security through various means such as deterrence, resilience, incident response and recovery policy.

UK Legislation

The Counter Terrorism Internet Referral Unit (CTIRU) has a responsibility under the Terrorism Act 2006 within the UK to serve notices to anyone who has committed an offence under the Terrorism Act. This section of the Act also contains provisions about the encouragement of terrorism and the dissemination of terrorist publications in cyberspace. This allows for an officer to arrest and charge a person who they believe are using terrorist-related material on a website that could be understood to be 'direct' or 'indirect encouragement' or 'glorification' of a terrorist act.

The Terrorism Act 2006 created a number of new offences related to cyberspace. These include: (i) the 'encouragement' 'and or glorification' of terrorism, making it a criminal offence now to 'directly' or 'indirectly encourage' others to commit acts of terrorism; (ii) the dissemination of terrorist publications – this includes the loan or sale of terrorist publications; (iii) preparation of terrorist acts – this includes people planning to carry out acts of terrorism; and finally (iv) training for terrorism – anyone who gives or receives training in terrorist techniques may be prosecuted; the Act also criminalises attendance at a place used for terrorist training. Furthermore, the Terrorism Act 2006 also created offences such as holding and collecting material on the computer (The Terrorism Act 2006).

What is Encouragement?

Section 1 of the Terrorism Act 2006 creates the offence of encouragement of terrorism. This covers direct and indirect encouragement, and the glorification of terrorism. The wording of the encouragement offence may lead to unlawful prosecutions as the requirement of indirect and direct encouragement will be open to many interpretations that could be made by a jury.

Under the offence of 'direct encouragement', it must involve a 'statement which must be likely to be understood by some or all of the members of the public to whom it is published' as a 'direct encouragement' to them to commit an act of terrorism. The offence may also allow the prosecution of innocent people, even though in theory they are entitled to their beliefs and should be able to speak their minds without fear of retribution.

Dissemination

Section 2 of the Terrorism Act 2006 creates the offence of dissemination of terrorist publications. The legislation stipulates that a person commits an offence of disseminating terrorist material if his or her conduct intends to be 'direct or indirect encouragement' or prepares, commissions and instigates an act of terrorism. Moreover, it is an offence if a person is reckless with his or her conduct in the commission or preparation of such acts, including disseminating material.

Furthermore, for the purposes of the legislation any person who distributes or circulates terrorist material including publication of such material may be committing an offence; further if they intend to 'sell or use that material; or lend such publication; or offer such a publication in sale or loan; or provide a service to others which enables them to obtain, read, and listen to such publications, or to acquire it by means of gifts, as well as sales or loans; and in the UK transmitting the contents electronically' may make one liable for prosecution in British Courts (The Terrorism Act 2006).

Possession

Section 57 of the Terrorism Act 2000 makes it an offence to possess articles connected with an act of terrorism. Under the Terrorism Act 2000 a person commits an offence if he or she possesses an article that may give rise to some form of reasonable suspicion that this possession is connected with committing, preparation or instigating an act of terrorism. Furthermore, section 57 states what a possible defence for a person charged with such an offence is, that is, if it is proved that the article in question was not on the premises at the same time as the accused was, or was on premises of which the accused was the occupier (The Terrorism Act 2000).

Collection

Section 58 of the Terrorism Act 2000 provides offences relating to the collection of information which may be useful to someone who commits or prepares acts of terrorism. A person commits an offence if he collects or makes a record of information of a kind likely to be useful to a person committing or preparing an act of terrorism, or he possesses a document or record containing information of that kind.

Furthermore, like s57 there is a possible defence for a person charged with an offence under this section if they can prove that he or she had a reasonable excuse for his act or possession of such material. For example, five men in May 2011 were held under the Terrorism Act 2000 for taking photographs of a British nuclear power site near Sellafield, although the arrests were made under s41 of the Terrorism Act 2000, that is, where an officer requires only 'reasonable suspicion' that they may be involved in a terrorist act. However, it does emphasise the broad nature of s58, that is, collecting images and photographs for an act of terrorism (Glendinning 2008). Furthermore, the Terrorism Act 2000 s12 deals with support of cyber activities relating to proscribed organisations (The Terrorism Act 2000).

Balance of Human Rights versus Security

The case of Samina Malik has raised more questions about the right to freedom of expression in cyberspace. Malik is known as the 'lyrical terrorist' because of the poetry she wrote and was convicted under s58 of the Terrorism Act for 'collecting terrorist material'. On appeal, her conviction was quashed, mainly because the jury found it difficult to infer whether or not she had any intent when writing this poetry (Dodd and Carter 2011).

The case of Samina Malik highlights how broadly s57 and s58 could be interpreted. In her trial the court heard how she had a stock of material that might be useful to terrorists which she had on her computer. Her case also raises important civil liberties issues in terms of what people can and cannot say on websites and what they download in an increasing age of social networking and tweeter, and so on.

Conclusion

Cyber terrorism is not a conventional form of warfare. This is a war being fought now in cyberspace, where guns, bombs and artillery do not have the same impact as a small bug, worms and viruses in a digital battlefield. Countries have taken the threat of cyber terrorism seriously and thus invested heavily in their ICT infrastructure. At the present moment there is a need for a more centralised approach to dealing with cyber terrorism related issues and a more universal convention that directly deals with cyber terrorism as opposed to the vague terminology of current European Conventions. There needs to be more emphasis of balancing freedom with security because there is a clear conflict when it comes to someone being able to passionately express their own opinion without fear of possible prosecution because it may incite terror related incidents.

At present UK legislation does not do enough to tackle the issue of cyber terrorism but instead we have a number of leading cases that highlight the problem of legislating against cyber crimes and terrorism. Indeed, in a landmark ruling in February 2008 (R v Zafar 2008) five young men from Bradford were acquitted of charges of possessing extremist propaganda as they had no intention of using the material. The men were alleged to have downloaded extremist material on computer hard drives and discs which were stored electronically but were not intended for use for terrorist purposes under s57 and s58 of the Terrorism Act 2000. The main reason for the acquittal was the problematic nature of proving intent and linking it with actual terrorist activity.

Furthermore, a similar case arose in 2008 where a research student had been held under the Terrorism Act for downloading terrorist material, that is, The Al-Qaeda Training Manual. The student who had downloaded a copy of Al-Qaeda's training manual was researching in the area of counter-terrorism. Although he was never charged this case does raise serious questions about cyber-related offences and UK counter-terrorism laws (BBC News 2009b). Moreover both the above cases highlight the problematic nature of sections 57 and 58 of the Terrorism Act 2000 that makes it an offence to possess or collect articles connected with an act of terrorism. Furthermore, there needs to be much more emphasis placed on working with local communities and supporting multifaceted approaches to dealing with the threat of cyber terrorism in the future.

Further Reading

Grabosky, P. 2007. Requirements of prosecution services to deal with cyber crime. *Crime, Law and Social Change*, 47, 201–23.

Hanlon, M. 2007. Attack of the cyber terrorists. *Daily Mail*. [Online]. Available at:http://www.dailymail.co.uk/sciencetech/article-457504/Attack-cyber-terrorists.html [accessed: 26 May 2011].

Lee, H., Plambach,T., and Miller, M. 2006. *Henry Lee's Crime Scene Handbook*. London: Academic Press.

Levi, M. 2008. White-collar, organized and cyber crimes in the media: some contrasts and similarities. *Crime, Law and Social Change*, 49, 365–77.

Pool, J. 2005. Technology and Security Discussions on the Jihadi Forums. *Jamestown Foundation*, October 11.

Powell, B., Carsen, J., Crumley, B., Walt, V., Gibson, H., and Gerlin, A. (2005). Generation Jihad. *Time*, 166, 56–9.

Thomas, T.L. 2003. Al Qaeda and the Internet: The danger of 'cyberplanning.' *Parameters*, 33(1), 112–23.

Weimann, G. 2004. Terror on the Internet: The new Arena, The New Challenges. Paper presented at the *International Studies Association* (ISA), Annual Conference, Montreal, Quebec, Canada, 17–20 March.

References

Associated Press of Pakistan. 2008. *President promulgates ordinance to prevent electronic crimes.* [Online]. Available at: http://www.app. com.pk/en_/index. php?option=com_content&task=view&id=58277&Itemid=1 [accessed: 9 June 2011].

BBC News. 2009a. UK has cyber attack capability. [Online]. Available at: http://news.bbc.co.uk/1/hi/uk_politics/8118729.stm [accessed: 27 June 2009].

BBC News. 2009b. Student was studying terrorism. [Online]. Available at: http://news.bbc.co.uk/1/hi/england/nottinghamshire/7415685.stm [accessed:12 May 2009].

BBC News. 2011. Governments hit by cyber attack. [Online]. Available at: http://news.bbc.co.uk/1/hi/technology/8139821.stm [accessed:15 June 2011].

Cabinet Office. 2009a. *Cyber Security of the United Kingdom: Safety, Security and Resilience in Cyber Space. Norwich: The Stationery Office.* [Online]. Available at:http://www.official-documents.gov.uk/document/cm76/7642/7642.pdf [accessed:10 March 2011].

Cabinet Office. 2009b.*The National Security Strategy of the United Kingdom: Update Security for the next generation.* (Cm 7590). [Online]. Available at: http://www.official-documents.gov.uk/document/cm75/7590/7590.pdf [accessed: 30 June 2009].

Cabinet Office. 2010. *A Strong Britain in an Age of Uncertainty: The National Security Strategy.* (Cm 7953). [Online]. Available at: http://www.direct. gov.uk/prod_consum_dg/groups/dg_digitalassets/@dg/@en/documents/digitalasset/dg_191639.pdf?CID=PDF&PLA=furl&CRE=nationalsecuritystrategy [accessed: 29 June 2010].

Council of Europe. 2008. *Cyberterrorism – The use of the Internet for terrorist purposes.* (January). France.

Cyber Policy Review. 2009. *Cyber Security Policy Assuring a Trusted and Resilient Information and Communications and Infrastructure.* [Online]. Available at: http://www.whitehouse.gov/assets/documents/Cyberspace_Policy_Review_final.pdf [accessed: 2 July 2010].

Direct Gov. 2011. *Reporting Extremism and Terrorism.* [Online]. Available at: http://www.direct.gov.uk/en/CrimeJusticeAndTheLaw/Counterterrorism/DG_183993 [accessed: 25 May 2011].

Dodd, V. and Carter, H. 2011. Sellafield terror arrests prompt London police raids. *Guardian.* [Online]. Available at: http://www.guardian.co.uk/uk/2011/may/03/five-arrested-sellafield-terrorism-act [accessed: 8 June 2011].

EU Council Framework Decision on Attacks against Information Systems. (Article 2 and Article 4). Council Framework Decision 2005/222/JHA of 24 February 2005 on attacks against information systems *Official Journal L069*, 16/03/2005 P. 0067-0071. [Online]. Available at: http://eur-lex.europa.eu/LexUriServ/LexUriServ.do?uri=CELEX:32005F0222:EN:HTML [accessed: 23 March 2012].

EU Council Framework Decision on Combating Terrorism. (Article 1). Council Framework Decision of 13 June 2002 on combating terrorism (2002/475/ JHA). [Online]. Available at: http://eur-lex.europa.eu/smartapi/cgi/sga_doc?s martapi!celexapi!prod!CELEXnumdoc&lg=EN&numdoc=32002F0475&mo del=guichett [accessed: 23 March 2012].

Fildes, J. 2011. Stuxnet Virus Targets and Spread Revealed. [Online]. Available at: http://www.bbc.co.uk/news/technology-12465688 [accessed:1 July 2011].

Glendinning, L. 2008. Lyrical terrorist has conviction quashed. *Guardian*. [Online]. Available at: http://www.guardian.co.uk/uk/2008/jun/17/uksecurity. ukcrime [accessed:10 June 2011].

HM Government. 2011. *Prevent Strategy*. Presented to Parliament by the Prime Minister and the Secretary of State for the Home Department by Command of Her Majesty. [Online]. Available at: http://www.homeoffice.gov.uk/ publications/counter-terrorism/prevent/prevent-strategy/prevent-strategy-review?view=Binary [accessed: 14 June 2011].

Norton, T. 2009. GCHQ steps up strategy to combat cyber-attacks, Brown announces. *Guardian*. [Online]. Available at: http://www.guardian.co.uk/ politics/2009/jun/25/cyberspace-war-computer-hacking-fraud [accessed: 29 June 2009].

Stohl, M. 2007. Cyber terrorism: a clear and present danger, the sum of all fears. breaking point or patriot games?. *Crime, Law and Social Change*, 46 (4–5), 223–38.

The Terrorism Act 2000. (c.11), London: HMSO.

The Terrorism Act 2006. (c.11), London: HMSO.

Traynor, I. 2007. Russia accused of unleashing cyberwar to disable Estonia. *Guardian*. [Online]. Available at: http://www.guardian.co.uk/world/2007/ may/17/topstories3.russia [accessed:19 June 2011].

R v Zafar. 2008. EWCA Crim 184.

United Nations Manual on the Prevention and Control of Computer Related Crime. 1999. *International Review of Criminal Policy no. 43 and 44*.

Weber, L. 2008. Virtual Jihad. *Forbes List*. [Online]. Available at: http://www. forbes.com/2008/05/16/virtual-jihad-terrorism-oped-cx_slw_0519jihad.html [accessed: 14 February 2011].

Weimann, G. 2008. Al Qaida's extensive use of the Internet. *CTC Centenial*, 1(2), 607.

Wykes, M. and Harcus. D. 2010. Cyber-Terror: Construction, Criminalisation and Control, in *The Handbook of Internet Crime*, edited by Majid Yar and Yvonne Jewekes. Cullompton: Willan Publishers, 214.

Chapter 7

Knowledge Management and Cyber Terrorism

James Gravelle

Introduction

Cyber terrorism has been for some time a threat to national security (Hyslop 2007, Colarik 2006). Although the concept of cyber terrorism is not new to the United Kingdom, the level of organisation and determination demonstrated by modern-day terrorist networks is dramatically different (Makarenko 2007). No longer driven by a single political objective or confined to one specific geographical area, Al-Qaeda for example operates on an international scale, fuelling its worldwide campaigns with religious rhetoric, propaganda, sophisticated weaponry and technology. The terrorist's objective is simple; to create a maximum level of fear or terror in a maximum number of civilians using any methods whatsoever, conceivably making the possibility of a chemical, biological, radiological, nuclear or cyber attack a realistic prospect. The availability of new and ever changing technology keeps terrorist networks supplied with new methods and devices to spread propaganda and enable the continuation of their radicalisation initiatives, new surveillance and reconnaissance techniques, without mention of the appropriation of specialist, more advanced weaponry (Coliandris and Rogers 2008). Perhaps as important, new technology is enabling global terror networks and implanted cells to develop operational plans, share data and information on potential targets and develop novel tactics. Consequently, security services gather increasing amounts of intelligence and evaluate the modus operandi of the modern day terrorist which reveals increasing levels of sophistication which is making terrorists a formidable threat.

Cyber Terrorism, Knowledge Management and Security

It is crucial to gain an accurate perspective of what knowledge-management offers for tackling cyber terrorism for any country's security services. The world of policing has always been complex, with the police having to deal with the impact of social change, latterly the forces of globalisation, changes in technology and the evolution of society and economy. Luen and Hawamdeh (2001) states that:

> Police work by its very nature is dynamic, complex and stressful ... fast
> challenging, complex and demanding problems involving crime, prevention,
> incident management, investigation and community policing. (Luen et al.
> 2001:312)

This is especially true when evaluating the changes that cyber terrorism has prompted. The security services in recent years have revolutionised their tactical approach to dealing with the rise of cyber terrorism and terrorism more broadly (Home Office 2006, Home Office 2009, James and Forest 2007 and Henderson 2009). The security services have increased levels of surveillance, security encryption and in recent years have manipulated cyber terrorist's computers, finances and in some instances focused on disrupted Internet resources (Meng 2006). It should be noted that all security services are required to remain as efficient and innovative as possible. A basic complexity when implementing knowledge-management is that this can have significantly different meanings within different organisations, demonstrating that knowledge-management is not easily defined or implemented. Business, science, technology, the public sector, governments and the security services will inevitably select a definition which best fits their current working practices and ethos (Dalkir 2005). Many such organisations which engage in both public and private cooperations have often attempted to single out one key fragment of knowledge-management and apply this in isolation to benefit their organisation. An over reliance on the introduction and development of technology, strategic leadership, business strategies and the failure to redefine working cultures are all reasons why organisations are not always successful when implementing knowledge-management (Frappaola 2006). Chan et al. (2002) notes that the police, for example, have always been reliant on knowledge, on the information they acquire and are information-driven. Luen (2001) suggests that as a direct consequence police officers are knowledge-workers and they seek to assimilate large quantities of knowledge within their working day and practices. Police officers and other support staff will undoubtedly come into contact with a vast quantity of intelligence in the form of criminal and community information. This intelligence may prove useful in detecting many offences including those linked to cyber terrorism providing it is assimilated and analysed within the relevant intelligence systems. Providing it is implemented appropriately, knowledge-management could act as the vehicle to successfully deliver this service. This should not only enable the police to deliver a timely, efficient and effective service, but will enable them to meet other goals set by their respective governments. In times where demands on policing are increasing and funding is clearly problematical, there is increased pressure from all quarters including the external customer, internal users and government to increase the efficiency, effectiveness, economic viability and quality of the service that is being provided. Now police forces, not just in the UK, but internationally, are turning to knowledge-management for a solution. Collier (2001) makes reference to the intellectual capacity of the police both as individuals and as an organisation.

Knowledge management aims to 'funnel' the flow of this knowledge through both the appropriate individuals and the organisation itself.

Knowledge Processes

The diagram below (Figure 7.1) illustrates the relationship between the different categories of knowledge.

Figure 7.1   Dean's knowledge continuum model

Data is viewed as being 'raw facts', a series of figures, numbers or digits (*Collins English Dictionary* 1996). To further contextualise the meaning of data and typify an everyday example, data would be collected in the form of large stores on numbers, for example, 192.0.2.1, or NN 163 254. These figures alone do not show where the crimes occur, the circumstances in which they occurred, at what time of day or night they happened or the nature of forensic evidence found. Data in itself has no intrinsic meaning and yet organisations and businesses are insistent on capturing and storing large quantities of data, in the belief and hope that the greater the quantity of raw data captured, the more accurate and precise outcomes may be (Tiwana 2008). For data to be actionable and have meaning for an organisation processes must be carried out to evaluate and appraise data. Unfortunately, many organisations simply store rather that process data. This mindset often over-focuses on the quantitative approach, concerned with capturing figures and numbers. The qualitative approach tends to be a secondary consideration. The second stage in the process is to transform data into information. In this stage, it is essential that some relevance or purpose be attached to the data (Drucker 1995). To future illustrate this stage, raw data collected would be given meaning, for example, IP Address -192.0.2.1 and grid reference location is NN 163 254. Davenport et al. (1998) makes reference to the different methods of attaching meaning to data, thus transforming it into information:

- **Condensing** – Data will often come in large quantities, frequently in binary digits or numbers, for example, within the police crime figures that will have little meaning to most users, except perhaps the professional analyst. The dataset must be summarised and condensed, to show an overall position, pattern or trend.
- **Contextualising** – Data may be collected for a number of reasons, be it to keep track of governmental targets, measure performance or calculate the frequency of crime occurrences. To contextualise the data, this reason must be attached for its collection, that is, to examine trends or patterns in cyber attacks.

- **Calculating** – similar to condensing, the data must be processed and analysed to attain a meaningful and concise picture, illustrated by graphs or figures. Within the police service, this task is often conducted by non-policing analysts or statisticians.
- **Categorising** – in a similar vein to contextualising, the unit of analysis must be known.
- **Correcting** – any erroneous data should be removed and any gaps within the dataset replaced, or at least accounted for. This will improve validity at the analytical stage.

Dean and Gottschalk (2007) add an additional layer to the hierarchy or continuum, stating that information needs to be translated into intelligence prior to becoming knowledge. Information must be analysed, examined and appraised by an officer, intelligence officer or crime analyst, before becoming knowledge. Using the same example, an intelligence officer would cross reference the IP address and grid location with other intelligence to identify hotspots, trend patterns or a list of possible suspects. Similarly, for intelligence to be transformed into knowledge there must be an attachment of belief, prior experience, knowledge, truth or judgement (Dean and Gottschalk 2007). Collier (2006) further suggests that there must be a cognitive process in which the information is made useful, thus enabling conclusions to be drawn. These components are essential and underpin knowledge to reach the highest point within the 'knowledge continuum'. Prior experiences assist workers who have extensive tacit knowledge, which may include experience, know-how, judgement, insight, heuristics, rules of thumb and skills (Rumizen 2002), enabling them to be more efficient and effective when assessing information. Individuals who have large stores of tacit knowledge gained from years of experience will be more effective at problem-solving, resulting in these people being paid relatively well and holding senior management positions. In this instance, this would enable an officer to identify the most probable and likely suspect based on previous experience and judgement. Intertwined with experience is judgement, which a knowledge-worker must attach to the information to determine how the information obtained will be analysed resulting in a decision or action. Similarly, police officers will use a heuristic approach, a way in which a process has historically or executed based on their assumptions, values and beliefs, which may result in good or bad working practices depending on the heuristic method of working adopted by the worker.

Types of Knowledge

There are predominantly two contrasting types of knowledge that need to be collected and managed within the police service and security services in order for its effective use. It will be essential to understand these two types of knowledge, prior to evaluating how knowledge-management has been operationally applied.

Tacit Knowledge

Tacit knowledge incorporates many forms of intelligence which are intangible. Tacit knowledge is difficult to convey, often the only way to express this would be through conferences, meetings, apprenticeships or mentoring (Frappaola 2006). Otherwise referred to as implicit knowledge, this is the knowledge that officers would carry around with them, growing with experience and when dealing from new situations. In more recent years, organisations have begun to realise the real value of tacit knowledge, recognising that it has great potential for business. 'Headhunting' and offering large cash incentives for individuals who possess experience, know-how and insight has become commonplace in private industry.

The diagram below (Figure 7.2) illustrates the different types of tacit knowledge that a police officer will need to effectively acquire to deal with situations which he or she may encounter throughout the course of their duties. The cognitive dimension will constitute the knowledge the knowledge already possessed by the officer; for example, this is used when the officer consciously decides to work harder. The technical dimension is affiliated with the knowledge of the different tasks which need to be performed. This may include knowledge on how to stop and search, application of law, legislation or fill in police forms. The final dimension in the context of policing is the social element. The police 'culture' element will differ depending on subculture, particularly that between managerial and operational roles. This tacit social dimension will be the knowledge of rules, heuristics, team working and the need to be protective of one another. This particular dimension has a major impact on police culture in general; for example this will ultimately determine how effective and efficient officers are at carrying out their role and will determine how they interact with members of the public.

Explicit Knowledge

In contrast to tacit knowledge, explicit knowledge can be expressed in documents, doctrines, crime figures, schematics, orders and models. This type of knowledge can be expressed and recorded, shared and entered into a database (Rumizen 2002), which can be transmitted among individuals in formal or organisational terms or language. The difficulty with this type of knowledge is the potential volume and quantity of data available and the challenge is to be able to effectively disseminate the knowledge among individuals (Frappaola 2006). Traditionally, it is in this area where organisations including the police service have focused their efforts, disseminating doctrines and orders through the use of information technology. Undeniably, police officers are now required to be more reliant on data, information, intelligence and knowledge resulting in the creation of a knowledge society and knowledge-workers.

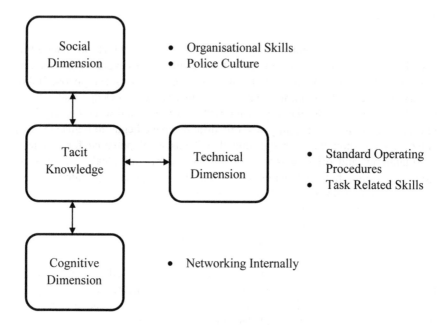

Figure 7.2   Multidimensional model of tacit police knowledge

The Police as Knowledge-Workers

The modern police service and its practitioners must have the understanding and ability to create and process knowledge, enabling them to problem-solve and conduct criminal investigations. Brodeur and Dupont (2008) comment on the increasing importance placed on concepts such as data, information, data mining and knowledge-work. This has invoked the development of new policing paradigms, most notably, 'intelligence-led policing' which relies heavily on such concepts as intelligence, knowledge and data (Ratcliffe 2008). A typical British police officers time spent dealing directly with crime appears marginal, as the amount of time spent in the police station was recorded by Ericson and Haggerty (1997) to be as high as 50 per cent. Although many politicians and strategic police managers have attempted to rationalise the role of the police officer, to reduce bureaucracy and administrative duties and introduce new technology enabling officers to update databases while on patrol, much of a police officer's time is still spent reviewing evidence, gathering intelligence and complying with the necessary rules and procedures at the station, instead of remaining on the front line, visible to the public (Home Office 2001). This study commissioned for the Home Office found that 43.1 per cent of an officer's time was spent in the police station. Of this time spent working from the station, a disproportionate high amount of time was spent conducting investigations and making enquiries (Home Office 2001). It is for this reason, Ericson and Haggerty (1997) note, that police officers have become 'knowledge-workers'. The wider implication of this is that the environment in which knowledge-workers operate has developed into a 'knowledge society', or network' (Böhme and Stehr 1986). For the police, this brings with it its own specific difficulties linked in part with the complexities surrounding the policing structure. The compartmentalisation, also referred to as 'silos' or 'multilateralisation' of the police, combined with the increasing levels of operation required of the police, has resulted in the need to communicate, share data, intelligence and knowledge internally within and between department, incorporating in the process its partner agencies throughout the national boundaries and overseas. Conventionally, there are two distinct types of knowledge-workers. Firstly, there are those traditional workers who 'produce knowledge'. Most notably these may include scientists or those employed within the research and development field. These knowledge 'producers' are among the minority, as most knowledge-workers fall under the second category, knowledge 'users' (Williamson 2008). These knowledge 'users' or 'practitioners' utilise the produced knowledge and apply it to solve problems. Although the police are considered as being knowledge-workers (Ericson and Haggerty 1997). Drucker (1995) states that the criteria for becoming a knowledge-worker includes the need for a 'formal education'. Historically, the police service in England and Wales has not required its officers to have a 'formal education', unlike some international law enforcement agencies, most notably the Federal Bureau of Investigation (FBI 2009). As a consequence of this, British police officers and police officers from other courtiers have little training or experience on how to formally produce or utilise knowledge to its maximum potential. De Lint (2003) also challenges the notion that police officers qualify as being knowledge-workers, noting that the police are in a privileged position of being the gatekeepers for the criminal justice system and although they process a vast amount of information, the distinction between information and knowledge must be maintained. Simple data processing and information gathering differs considerably from complex knowledge working.

The Role of Knowledge-Management

Knowledge-management offers an approach for all of the relevant security agencies involved at local, national and international levels to use intelligence efficiently and effectively, and plays a central role in the implementation strategies for dealing with cyber terrorism (Gravelle and Rogers 2009). One useful definition of knowledge-management, incorporating many of its key components is as follows:

> Knowledge management is the deliberate and systematic coordination of an organisations people, technology, process and organisational structure in order to add value through reuse and innovation. This coordination is achieved

through creating, sharing and applying knowledge as well as through feeding the valuable lessons learned and best practises into corporate memory in order to foster continued organisational learning. (Cited in Dalkir 2005:3)

As the successful development, implementation and conclusion of any anti cyber terrorist strategy is so clearly reliant on intelligence, the successful implementation of knowledge-management systems will enable the organisations and individuals involved to maximise coordination, as they create, share and use knowledge. For each organisation to maximise potential pay offs, it must integrate every aspect of the above definition into its working practices. To achieve this, detailed inspection must be taken at each stage of the knowledge-management cycle (Figure 7.3) which is explained in detail below.

Discovering Knowledge

The first stage of the cycle is concerned with the creation of data and intelligence, where an organisation consciously adopts the process or ideology of knowledge-management. A theoretical understanding of key concepts such as 'knowledge' 'data' and 'intelligence' and where these fit into both the cycle and how these affect the support organisations involved will be essential. In addition, any organisation and its individual components need to understand the philosophy of knowledge-management, understand its purpose and how it supports that organisation. Without this understanding of knowledge-management and its intentions, useful applications, evaluations and worthwhile outputs will be impaired.

Generating Knowledge

The cycle then progresses to organisational learning, where through examining information and intelligence acquired the organisation can develop in terms of contingencies and strategic preparation. In addition, at this stage of the process, knowledge-management systems and tools are refined and developed, which in the context of any anti-cyber terrorist strategy is essential. Being able to store information, in the long term, enables the efficient dissemination and processing of data in a much more effective, efficient and purposeful manner.

Evaluating Knowledge

Following this phase, the cycle advances to the evaluation of knowledge. It is at this stage where strategic management plays a crucial role. Having collected the data, stored it within the knowledge-management system, the processing and scanning of such intelligence can begin. Local intelligence officers, for example, could scan the data and produce intelligence reports, with information such as specific individuals of interest, suspicions of a particular activity or hotspots. From this evaluation strategic plans and contingencies can be reviewed and prepared.

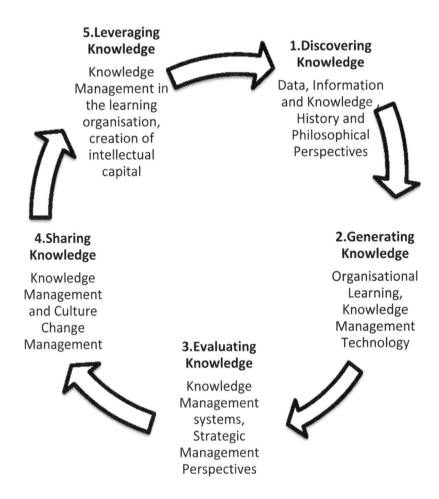

Figure 7.3   Knowledge-management cycle

Sharing Knowledge

The penultimate stage of the process involves the sharing of knowledge. Fundamental to the success of the overall anti-cyber terrorist strategy, the dissemination and sharing of intelligence is vital, sharing internally between departments as well as with partner agencies both at home and abroad. This stage of the process must not be underestimated given the characteristics and activities of modern cyber terrorists. This stage is problematic for the police services and security agencies across the world (see Chapters 6 and 9).

Leveraging Knowledge

Leveraging completes the cycle. This stage is where the overall intellectual capacity of the organisation is amplified and enhanced. Within the context of any government's cyber terrorism strategy, this means that many of the organisations involved such as the security services, police, governments and partner agencies use intelligence that is coherent, up to date and critically evaluated. Clearly, each stage interlocks and it is essential that every agency involved fully complies with each individual stage of the process. For the strategy to be entirely successful, these links must be made, maintained and nurtured between all relevant organisations. If an organisation fails at any one of these stages, for example intelligence sharing, the consequences could be profound.

Problems in Application

The problems for many organisations attempting to use knowledge-management have been their over reliance or focus on the development of knowledge-management systems, which would meet the criteria for storage and retrieval but would seldom support other activities such as creating, integrating, analysing and employing such knowledge. For the police or any security service to overcome such issues, it must not see knowledge-management as simply managing, moving and storing data. This mechanistic perspective will prove detrimental to the organisation if managers focus solely on managing knowledge. The real goal of both the organisation and strategic management should be on the dynamic aspect, or the context and culture in which the knowledge is being generated. Although knowledge itself cannot be managed, the context and the environment in which it is used must be objective focused and target driven. The organisation must be 'dual visioned' as it must see not only the technological aspects but must understand the human dimensions to successfully promoting knowledge-management (Dean and Gottschalk 2007). Security services such as the police have been effective in collecting and collating information and data which comprise stage one and two of the knowledge-management cycle. Problems appear to arise, however, when there is a need to analyse, process, share and use the intelligence to formulate comprehensive strategies when dealing with cyber terrorism. The response from the police service, for example, following assessment of intelligence has traditionally and predominantly been focused solely on enforcement, relating only to stages one, two and three of the knowledge-management cycle.

Organisations will attempt to single-out knowledge-management definitions to meet their specific needs dependent on their organisation's internal drivers. Some organisations will be driven by commercial pressures, some by internal pressures from the workforce and others by governmental pressures. The police service in the UK, for example, often considers that information technology equates to knowledge-management (Dean and Gottschalk 2007). An over reliance simply on the introduction and development of technology, and not analysing why organisations fail to successfully implement knowledge-management is an issue (Frappaola 2006). This adds strength to the argument that organisations can become disillusioned, and are less successful in their attempts to implement a full and comprehensive knowledge-management system that encapsulates every aspect which impacts directly on the overall delivery and coordination of their activities. This may have major implications on the performance, image and effectiveness of anti cyber terrorism strategies.

Successful implementation of knowledge-management will be achieved when organisational coordination is maximised, as it creates, shares, and applies knowledge appropriately. Particularly within large businesses and public sector organisations, coordination can be difficult to maintain and monitor. Coordination is concerned with:

> Integrating or linking together different parts of an organisation to accomplish a collective set of tasks. (Van de Ven et al. 1976:332)

With large numbers of employees, departments and strategic management spanning wide geographical areas, effective organisational coordination becomes problematic. Nevertheless it is particularly important to ensure that an organisation remains coherent, focused and constant in pursuing its overall policy objectives at all times. Another concern for national and international police and security agencies is that of their work culture. Within an organisation such as the police, for example, it is inevitable that a strong work culture exists. The somewhat nebulous subject, 'culture', develops as a result of a 'mix of informal prejudices, values, attitudes and working practices' which exists most prominently within the lower or more junior ranks of any police service (Newburn and Neyroud 2008:203). This issue has been well researched with findings published by such as Reiner (2010), Ianni and Ianni (1983) and Waddington (1999). Many organisations develop a work culture which becomes embedded within the organisation. This is defined as:

> The deeper level of assumptions and beliefs that are shared by members of an organisation that operates and projects unconsciously an organisation's view of itself and environment. (Grieve et al. 2007:116)

As noted previously, knowledge-management seeks to change the way people work. The success of implementing a knowledge-management package, and ultimately the fate of the strategies for dealing with cyber terrorism will depend on the ability to share information both internally, with other officers and externally with partner agencies. Traditionally, the police environment has been compartmentalised, with the police rarely sharing knowledge (Luen and Hawamdeh 2001). The dynamics of the various British dedicated police units has resulted in the creation of specialist departments or divisions being set up to perform a defined task, or meet a set of narrowly defined objectives. As a result knowledge sharing between departments can be sporadic and at times non-existent, resulting in silos of unconnected intelligence and knowledge. As has been argued policing is a complex activity often requiring different solutions, departments or different agencies to interact to tackle problems. This approach is replicated throughout most western European countries. Unfortunately, some departments fail to fully comprehend the link between their work and the work of others. This approach has resulted in a failure to engage with the wider and more complex concepts of 'policing'. In a recent study conducted by Rogers (2008), British police managers were of the opinion that police information or intelligence should be available only to police and is often simply too sensitive to share with other 'crime fighting organisations'. Such cultural manipulation demonstrates how staff will sometimes attempt to control both defining and attaining objectives. Clearly, to be successful, staff need to adopt an open-minded approach, with a willingness to share knowledge and build trust between organisations. Flanagan (2007) reported that to succeed, the working culture within the police must change and must adopt a new approach to policing in the UK. Not only will the workforce need to adapt, but the organisation as a whole must fully embrace change open-mindedly to ensure success. Staff need to change their core beliefs, adapting to change by changing the way they operate. This becomes ever more significant when evaluating the exchange of data, both within police and security organisations and between its partner agencies. Clearly, knowledge-management systems need to be coterminous with partnerships. Bichard (2004) concludes from research into the effectiveness of intelligence based recording and sharing between public agencies that such systems often simply could not communicate effectively with one another. Bichard further concluded that the development of locally themed IT systems did not have the capacity to communicate with each other. As a direct consequence, the public enquiry concluded that this resulted in 'poorly informed decision-making', undermining efficiency, effectiveness and economic viability (Bichard 2004:129). A failure of the system clearly would affect the success of any partnerships forming between other 'crime fighting agencies' and the police. Nationally within the United Kingdom, the picture is as complex, further demonstrating that little progress had been made in the development of a national IT system, where different agencies could readily engage in intelligence sharing. Knowledge management offers a unified process, or set of rules where if implemented within each organisation will standardise the way in which intelligence is used by providing an 'end to end' process. This model of knowledge (knowledge-management) will apply both within and between agencies acting as a benchmark, protocol and an overarching philosophy.

Overcoming the Limitations

Although not a simple panacea for the problems discussed knowledge-management offers a real and robust option for overcoming the problems of data sharing and the cultural differences between organisations. Security organisations need to encourage and create knowledge communities, thus stimulating communication, a cooperative and supportive working environment. Every knowledge-management system (KMS) essentially has three key components including the socio-cultural, organisational and technological elements to structure knowledge for individual knowledge-workers, groups, departments and the various organisations participating (Dean and Gottschalk 2007). Dean further defines four typologies that relate to knowledge-management systems (KMS) that can offer a solution to overcome some, but not all of the current limitations of tackling cyber terrorism.

Information Management Systems (IMS)

As previously noted, the policing landscape throughout the western world is becoming ever more stressed and complex with acts of cyber terrorism committed over wide geographic areas. Information Management Systems aim to use relational databases to communicate relevant knowledge rapidly. An example of such a database would be 'COPLINK' in the UK. In essence, the system has two elements, the first being 'connect'. This aims to disseminate the information to all police officers. The second element 'detect' is aimed primarily at the detectives and the crime analysts, where the databases deploy the same information from the 'connect' element to make links, associations and build lines of potential enquiry.

Geographic Information Systems (GIS)

This technology is used to map terrorist incidents and is often referred to as 'crime mapping'. Not restricted to simply plotting incidents on maps, this software can be utilised to produce a wealth of information relating to hotspots, spatial patterns and trends in cyber terrorism. Boba (2001) notes that this software has the capacity to analyse trends, patterns and modify data. Plotting around city centres, referring also to the details of offences such as modus-operandi, time of incident or profiles of victims are all aspects that are invaluable. The most sophisticated GIS software has the capability to communicate internally between departments, externally with other partner agencies and enable the enhancement of an organisation's overall intellectual capital (Gottschalk and Tolloczko 2006).

Intelligent-Surveillance Systems (ISS)

Technological surveillance is becoming an increasing characteristic of twenty-first century policing. This system is concerned with crime analysis and surveillance. When operating on a global platform working in partnership with international crime and cyber terrorism fighting agencies such as INTERPOL or the FBI. It must have the capacity to communicate coherent, analytical insights and knowledge. An example of such a system would include the ORACLE system currently used by INTERPOL.

Expert Knowledge Systems (EKS)

The final and perhaps the most sophisticated approach is that of expert knowledge systems (EKS). Used to solve problems, the software uses an 'engine' of knowledge that can be applied to a specific scenario in an attempt to deploy existing expertise to configure an action plan. Often incorporating forms of artificial intelligence, the EKS will apply knowledge, reasoning and draw operational inferences based on programming to develop a real world strategy and appropriate action plans.

Conclusion

Clearly, for any government's cyber terrorist strategy to be implemented successfully, all policing and related agencies involved in combating cyber terrorism must adopt a coordinated approach in tackling this threat. Knowledge management offers a framework for all agencies both in the UK and abroad to work together, utilising and sharing intelligence which could result in improved decision-making and strategies thus resulting in improved national security. Prior to such application, the importance of understanding concepts such as intelligence and knowledge cannot be overstated. Individuals within an organisation must understand the reason why knowledge-management can improve the efficiency and effectiveness with which intelligence is used.

In conjunction with the theoretical background, its success will be determined by the ability to recognise issues such as organisational and human resistance to change and allegiance to such as a traditional work culture. Consultation and a thoughtfully planned and restructured management programme are ways to begin to overcome such obstacles. The importance of national security has recently been tested in the UK during the G20 summit (Edwards and Gammell 2009). Culture, resistance and knowledge-sharing issues must be overcome for any anti-terrorist strategy to be fully integrated. The police in the UK are only one example of an organisation that accesses the vast amount of intelligence in the form of computer records, forms, documents and community reports on a daily basis. The police and other security agencies must seek to engage with such knowledge efficiently, effectively and routinely. Successfully achieving this goal will enable the police and other agencies to utilise the available knowledge before making a decision to ensure the appropriate resources are targeted at the right location, on the right target and at the right time. This flow of information needs to be used to target potential terrorists and terrorist activity. In total this will enable senior officials and managers to direct resources effectively, prioritising tasking and utilising both criminal and community intelligence, revolutionising the way the security services analyse problems and deploy resources accordingly. If implemented correctly, it will improve the quality of service to all citizens by underpinning the success of any government anti-cyber terrorist strategy.

Further Reading

Dean, G. Gottschalk, P. 2007. *Knowledge Management in Policing and Law Enforcement: Foundations, Structures, Applications.* Oxford: Oxford University Press.

Gottschalk, P. 2009. *Knowledge Management in Policing: Enforcing Law on Criminal Business Enterprises.* New York: Hindawi Publishing Corporation.

References

Bichard, M. 2004. *The Bichard Inquiry: Report*. London: The Stationery Office.
Boba, R. 2001. *Introductory Guide to Crime Analysis and Mapping*. Washington: US Department of Justice.
Böhme, G. and Stehr, N. 1986. *The Knowledge Society: The Impact of Scientific Knowledge on Social Structures*. Dordrecht: Reidel.
Brodeur, J. and Dupont, B. 2008. *Introductory Essay: The Role of Knowledge and Networking in The Handbook of Knowledge Based Policing: Current Conceptions and Future Directions*. West Sussex: John Wiley & Sons.
Chan, H., Schroeder, J., Hauck, R., Ridgeway, L., Atabakhsh, H., Gupta, H., Boarman, C., Rasmussen, K. and Clements, A. 2002. COPLINK Connect: Information and Knowledge Management for Law Enforcement. *Decision Support Systems*, 34, 271–85.
Coliandris, G. and Rogers, C. 2008. The Governments Terrorism Strategy: Implications for Partnerships. *Safer Communities Journal*, 7 (3), 17–21.
Colarik, A. 2006. *Cyber Terrorism: Political and Economic Implications*. London: Idea Group Publishing.
Collier, P. 2001. Valuing Intellectual Capacity in the Police. *Accounting, Auditing & Accountability Journal*, 14 (4), 437–55.
Collier, P. 2006. Policing and the Intelligent Application of Knowledge. *Public Money and Management*, 26 (2), 109–16.
Collins English Dictionary. 1996. *Data*. London: Harper Collins Publishers.
Dalkir, K. 2005. *Knowledge Management in Theory and Practice*. Boston: Butterworth.
Davenport, T., Prusak, L. and Thomas, H. 1998. *Working Knowledge: How Organisations Manage What They Know*. Boston: Harvard Business School.
Dean, G. and Gottschalk, P. 2007. *Knowledge Management in Policing and Law Enforcement: Foundations, Structures, Applications*. Oxford: Oxford University Press.
De Lint, W. 2003. Keeping Open Windows: Police and Access Brokers. *British Journal of Criminology*, 43, 379–97.
Drucker, P. 1995. *The Post Capitalistic Executive: Management in a Time of Great Change*. New York: Penguin.
Edwards, R. and Gammell, C. 2009. G20 Summit: Britain's Biggest Ever Policing Operation Launched. [Online]. Available at: http://www.telegraph.co.uk/finance/g20-summit/5084250/G20-summit-Britains-biggest-ever-policing-operation-launched.html [accessed: 31 May 2011].
Ericson, R. and Haggerty, K. 1997. *Policing the Risk Society*. Toronto: University of Toronto Press.
FBI. 2009. Federal Bureau of Investigation: Career. [Online]. Available at: http://www.fbijobs.gov/111.asp [accessed: 9 September 2009].
Flanagan, R. 2007. *A Review of Policing – Final Report*. London: The Stationery Office.

Frappaola, C. 2006. *Knowledge Management*. Chichester: Capstone Publishing.

Gottschalk, P. and Tolloczko, P. 2006. Maturity Model for Mapping Crime in Law Enforcement. *Electronic Government: An International Journal*, 4 (1), 59–67.

Gravelle, J. and Rogers, C. 2009. Knowledge Management: a Key Ingredient in Tackling Terrorism. *Police Journal,* 82 (4), 289–314

Grieve, J., Harfield, C. and Macvean, A. 2007. *Policing*. London: SAGE.

Henderson, H. 2009. *Encyclopaedia of Commuter Science Technology*. New York: Facts on File Inc.

Home Office. 2001. *Diary of a Police Officer*. London: Stationery Office.

Home Office. 2006. *Countering International Terrorism: The United Kingdom's Strategy*. London: The Stationery Office.

Home Office. 2009. *Pursue, Prevent, Protect, Prepare: The United Kingdom's Strategy for Countering International Terrorism*. London: The Stationery Office.

Hyslop, M. 2007. *Critical Information Infrastructures: Resilience and Protection*. New York: Springer Publishing.

Ianni, E. and Ianni, F. 1983. *Two Cultures of Policing: Street Cop Management Cop*. USA: Transition Publishers.

James, J. and Forest, F. 2007. *Countering Terrorism and Insurgency in the 21st Century*. Abingdon: Greenwood Publishing Group.

Jashapara, A. 2004. *Knowledge Management: An Integrated Approach*. Essex: Pearson Education.

Luen, W. and Hawamdeh, S. 2001. Knowledge Management in the Public Sector: Principles and Practises in Police Work. *Journal of Information Science*, 27 (5), 311–8.

Makarenko, T. 2007. International Terrorism and the UK, in Wilkinson, T., *Homeland Security in the UK: Future Preparedness for Terrorist Attack since 9/11*. Abingdon: Routledge.

Meng, O. 2006. Cyber-Terrorism: An Emerging Security Threat of the New Millennium. [Online]. Available at: http://www.mindef.gov.sg/safti/pointer/back/journals/2002/Vol28_3/6.htm, [accessed: 31 May 2011].

Newburn, T. and Neyroud, P. 2008. *Dictionary of Policing*. Cullompton: Willan Publishing.

Ratcliffe, J. 2008. *Intelligence-Led Policing*, in Worthley, R., Mazerolle, L. and Rombouts, S. (eds), *Environmental Criminology and Crime Analysis*. Cullompton: Willan Publishing.

Reiner, R. 2010. *The Politics of the Police*. 4th Edition. London: Oxford University Press.

Rogers, C. 2008. Winning Hearts and Minds – The Government Terrorism Strategy. *Town and Country Planning*, 77 (5), 235–6.

Rumizen, M. 2002. *The Complete Idiot's Guide to Knowledge Management*. USA: Alpha Publishing.

Tiwana, A. 2008. *The Knowledge Management Toolkit*. USA: Pearson Education Ltd.

Van de Ven, A., Delbecq, A. and Koenig, R. 1976. Determinants of Coordination Models within Organisations. *American Sociological Review*, 41, 322–38.

Waddington, P.A.J. 1999. *Policing Citizens: Authority and Rights*. USA: Routledge.

Williamson, T. 2008. *The Handbook of Knowledge Based Policing: Current Conceptions and Future Directions*. West Sussex: John Wiley & Sons.

Chapter 8

Intelligence Gathering and Police Systems

Dr Colin Rogers

Introduction

Modern technology permits social relations across vast spaces. As transformations in information processing are accelerated, minimised and made cheaper, patterns of social control including the collection of information and intelligence will also be modified and reshaped. New labels such as cyber terrorism are now assigned as information becomes more electronic and digital (Manning 2000). This impacts upon the way in which social control such as policing is applied to such cyber communities. What is required is an idea of policing for this information age where national boundaries are less marked and clear and where information is a commodity and secrecy and security concerns are located in a large part in transnational information networks. The term policing is becoming increasingly diffuse within and between nation states (Jewkes and Yar 2010).

The rise of transnational policing is echoed in the growth of information policing function, including regulating the flow of information nationally and internationally. Communication policing, the ordering of cyberspace, is a growing facet of policing and depends upon the utilisation of good intelligence and information. Indeed intelligence can be said to underpin all aspects of counter terrorism work and is cast as its very lifeblood (Innes and Roberts 2008).

The need to counter the potential risk of the widespread damage of a cyber terrorist attack means policing agencies gravitate to a significant extent around the development of pre-emptive secret intelligence. Terrorism, cyber terrorism, transnational and organised crime all have a community basis and the inability to implement community interaction effectively may well jeopardise outcomes such as policing and tackling cyber terrorist activity (Tilley 2008)

Community policing approaches and engagement with all sections of society creates networks that aim to bind all sections of community together: reducing the supply of those who may otherwise be open to mobilisation for any form of terrorist activity, including cyber terrorism. This idea of engaging with communities at grass-roots level in order to provide information and intelligence for multi-level use has been strongly reinforced by government in the UK (Home Office 2006). The following chart illustrates the official approach of engagement with communities and how it should supply information and intelligence at different operational levels.

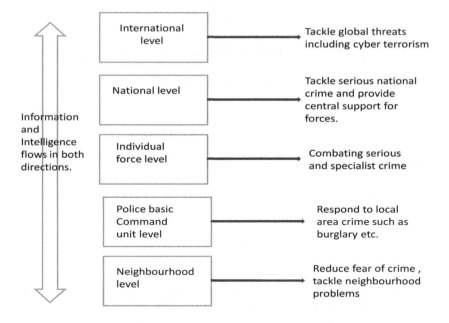

Figure 8.1   Levels of engagement for intelligence use

It is suggested that an attentive community trusting the authorities is more likely to pass on information that may allow these various acts at different levels to be pre-empted (Rogers 2008). Intelligence-led policing has the potential to provide a unifying theme embracing 'high' and 'low' paradigms that allows community forms of policing to grow and transform itself. 'Terror-oriented' policing, which includes cyber terrorism, introduces or propels the term 'intelligence' in 'intelligence-led' policing closer to its original meaning in special interest policing and stresses the growing importance of national security, once the stronghold of security services, to policing.

Government Response to Cyber Terrorism

The UK Government's response to the threat of cyber terrorist activity can be found in the Cabinet Office document entitled *Cyber Security Strategy of the United Kingdom* (Home Office 2009) and in the formation of a multi-agency Cyber Security Operations Centre (CSOC) based at Government Communications Headquarters (GCHQ) in Cheltenham, Gloucestershire. This document is discussed in more detail in Chapter 9. The main thrust of this strategy falls into three distinct areas, namely that of reduction of risk, exploiting opportunities in cyberspace and improving knowledge, and capabilities and decision-making. Amongst several approaches promoted, the following are specific to the implementation of these three strategic strands:

- reduce the threat of cyber operations by reducing an adversary's motivation and capability
- gather intelligence on threat actors
- intervene against adversaries
- improve knowledge and awareness

In order to achieve the objectives set out in this strategic document the gathering of information and intelligence by police and other security services is of paramount importance. Information from communities at all levels is therefore vital if this strategy is to be achieved. The following sections of this chapter examines some of the processes employed by police services in England and Wales for gathering intelligence that fits into the model shown in Figure 8.1 above including the intelligence cycle, the national intelligence model, as well as considering the impact of the Bichard enquiry and technological progress that underpins much police effort in gathering intelligence and information.

The Intelligence Cycle

For intelligence-gathering and application to be fully effective, the problems and deficiencies surrounding the intelligence cycle must be acknowledged and fully understood. The intelligence cycle shown in Figure 8.2 visualises the processes involved when dealing with intelligence.

This cycle always begins with 'direction' and is also known in some cycles as 'planning' the specific task once an issue is identified. Subsequently, it is the role of a knowledge-worker; in the case of the police service this could include investigators, officers or analysts to collate all surrounding data, information and knowledge on the particular issue previously identified (Ratcliffe 2008). Following the collection stage, analysts including senior strategic managers will evaluate and attempt to analyse the data, attaching reasoning and meaning. Finally the results, or a specific solution, are disseminated throughout the organisation. This will provide the police with a specific and targeted solution to effectively and efficiently deal with the issue identified at stage one (direction).The direction of intelligence gathering and use is often set by policy makers, which may include strategic tasking, coordinating groups and Community Safety Partnerships (CSPs). As a result, these groups will develop and feed into a force control strategy resulting in the publication of the force intelligence priorities (Thames Valley Police 2009). The different elements of the intelligence cycle are discussed below.

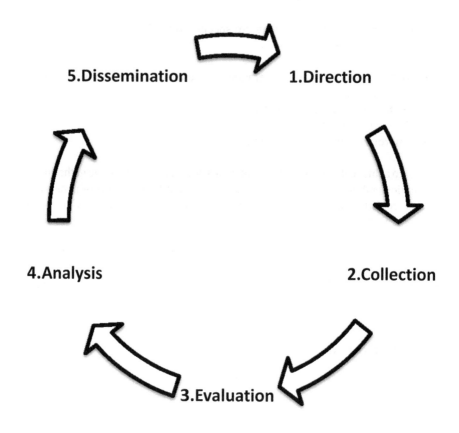

5.Dissemination   1.Direction

4.Analysis   2.Collection

3.Evaluation

Figure 8.2   The intelligence cycle

Direction

The first practical issue facing the intelligence cycle is the dichotomy between policy makers and intelligence managers. Although theoretically both policy makers and managers have clear distinctions in roles, with policy makers deciding where the focus should be in relation to intelligence resources and managers to effectively capture and analyse intelligence, in reality, the two roles often merge. This in part is due to global pressures that require intelligence managers to react and change priorities. In addition, policy makers often provide specific guidance to managers, where clearly it is the role of the intelligence manager to fill in intelligence gaps and dictate the direction of intelligence gathering on specific cases (Hulnick 2006). Ratcliffe (2004) adds that this first step in the cycle which encompasses setting the direction or focus of the intelligence gathering process is essential. Errors and oversights at this stage can affect the circular process, compounding the errors as each stage progresses. The consequences of any such errors could be catastrophic for both the organisation and the community which it serves.

Collection

Intelligence collection and the context in which it is collected will be fundamental to the end-to-end process of any investigation. Credibility and integrity of intelligence, including the methods used to capture intelligence, will undoubtedly come under intense scrutiny. Unfortunately the reality surrounding intelligence collection is that it often contains opinions, judgements and errors resulting in bias and impartiality. The skill for any investigator is to be detached, coherent, concise and critical (Ratcliffe 2004).

Evaluation/Analysis

The quality and validity of the output from the whole cycle can only be as good as the interpretation and evaluation at this stage. Analysts or local intelligence officers (LIOs) have the task of assessing the intelligence gathered. From previous research undertaken, local intelligence officers often receive no formal training and in some cases intelligence officers were neighbourhood or response police officers acting in the capacity of LIOs (Rogers and Martin 2007). Hulnick (2006) further concludes that often a full evaluation and analysis is not completed due to psychological barriers and a fear of discovering compromising sources of intelligence. This may include intelligence that challenges the current preferred hypothesis of the investigation team or the senior investigating officer (SIO).

Dissemination

Historically, the dissemination of intelligence has been an issue for all law enforcement agencies. The notion of mistrust and ownership has resulted in the fear of sharing intelligence both internally between departments and externally with other partner agencies (Hulnick 2006). In recent years, the importance of communication and the dissemination of intelligence has been recognised and there has been much work undertaken in the area to stimulate communication. For example, the introduction of the Crime and Disorder Act, (Home Office 1998a) places a statutory obligation on the police and its partners to work together and communicate. Although much progress has been made, the inherent stresses surrounding intelligence sharing still exist. The police services in the UK now use the National Intelligence Model (NIM) as a method of dealing with and disseminating intelligence inputs.

The National Intelligence Model (NIM)

Planning and preparing organisational responses and resources and the need to anticipate demand is an integral part of policing: this was facilitated by the introduction of the National Intelligence Model (NCIS 2000). Among many other definitions available, the national intelligence model can be defined as:

> the business process for policing in the UK. It provides a common basis for gathering and analysing information and for using this to adopt a problem-solving approach to reducing crime and disorder, to law enforcement and community reassurance. (Newburn and Neyroud 2008:173)

To be effective at tackling criminal activity the police need to be able to gather, process and retain large amounts of intelligence. It is for this reason the national intelligence model was introduced. David Philips, chairman of the crime committee, stated; 'Over the last few years, police activity has shifted from reactive investigation after events, towards targeting active criminals on the basis of intelligence' (NCIS 2000:4).

Supporting the idea of intelligence-led policing, Rogers (2006:189) describes the model as a 'business process' as it is seen to allow managers to allocate resources more efficiently and effectively in the long term, resulting in less crime, improved community safety and a reduction in the demand and reassurance gap. Waddington (2007) and Innes (2007) both indicate that the 'reassurance gap' is the difference between reality and perception of crime. Since the late 1980s, overall recorded crime has fallen; however the population is experiencing a rise in the fear of crime (Walker et al. 2009). Fear of crime can best be described as the rational or irrational state of alarm by an individual that is based on a belief that he or she will be victimised (McLaughlin and Muncie 2006). This difference between actual crime and fear of crime is therefore referred to as the 'reassurance gap'. The national intelligence model operates on three levels. Figure 8.3 below illustrates the model.

In practice the first level of implementation incorporates daily tasking, which relates to the local issues at basic command unit (BCU) level. Rogers (2006) notes, that volume crime would be calculated at this level. Increasing the scale of operations the second level considers the force itself, both from regional and cross-border approaches. Many different organisations are likely be involved in the sharing of intelligence at this point. The final level, which encompasses national tasking, is a level where combating serious and organised crime, including cyber terrorism, would operate. At the centre of this process tasking coordination groups (TCGs) operate. Their function as identified by Tilley (2003) is to meet and discuss how intelligence will be gathered and how intelligence will be used, both tactically and strategically. The four areas of concern include targeting offenders, managing hotspots, investigation and the application of preventative measures. Initial implementation of the national intelligence model took place

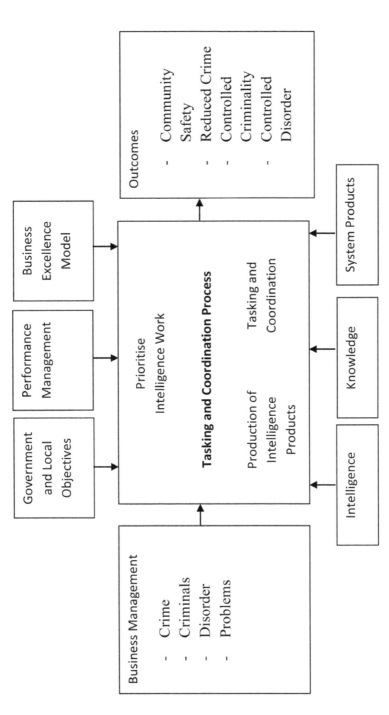

Figure 8.3 The national intelligence model (NIM) list of tables

across three force areas, namely Lancashire, Surrey and the West Midlands police services. Lancashire had adopted the model working under a problem-orientated policing approach, while the West Midlands relied on a community-focused approach, developing a community safety bureau and community support. Surrey had seen most change, with considerable restructuring as new dedicated teams and centres were created (John and Maguire 2004b). One positive advantage to the implementation of a national intelligence model is its ability to generate a picture of both local and national crime patterns: analysts are able to provide accurate useful data to police managers (John and Maguire 2004a). Tasking and coordination groups are then able to plan, prioritise, budget and target resources effectively at specific issues, thus in theory making police delivery more effective, efficient and economic (Rogers 2006). The national intelligence model offers a chance to continue the process of rationalisation and bureaucracy (Weber et al. 2005): demonstrated by the creation of the national intelligence model code of practice (Centrex 2004). Budgets and spending are a priority for managers and the model enables the premeditation and planning of long-term finances (NCIS 2000). Supporters of the NIM approach believe it allows the police to enlist the assistance of statutory partners, such as the local authority and others, to tackle the underlying causes of crime. It has long been recognised that policing is not exclusively a role performed by the police service (Rogers 2006), as policing as a concept is varied, covering many areas. The model is accredited with enabling police to tackle a wider, more diverse area of policing, focusing on areas such as anti-social behaviour and road safety at a local level (Gwent Police 2004), but being used to tackle high-level problems such as cyber terrorism. John and Maguire (2004a) identified several issues of concern, however, firstly, although the police have a statutory obligation to comply with the application of NIM; there are no Acts of Parliament which require a minimum participation and commitment between the police and its partner agencies. Secondly, John and Maguire (2004b) further established that the success of the implementation of the model depended greatly on the leadership and commitment of senior personnel, namely the tasking coordinator chair, BCU commanders and intelligence unit commanders. This has been a significant problem in some parts of the country. Closely linked to the above problem, John and Maguire (2004b) found that there was a general lack of understanding surrounding issues of ownership. To be effective, the model implementation relies on all its users to fully understand and comprehend its function. Due to a lack of consultation, training and preparation, officers of all ranks are failing to get to grips with the fundamental concepts and theoretical understanding behind the model. Whether cultural reasons or human/organisational resistance to change are responsible, many senior officers insist that junior officers need not know or understand the national intelligence model as part of their daily role. Ironically, one of the biggest drawbacks comes from not the model's design, but its name. Ratcliffe (2008), comments that the word 'intelligence' means so many different thinks to so many different people. The public attach words such as 'shady disposition' and 'moral ambiguity' to it (Ratcliffe 2008:213). Junior officers perceive the model as having 'little relevance' to their daily tasks, thus seeing the model as a specialist role using state-of-the-art technology, where senior officers see it as a tool for 'investigations' and not 'strategic decision-making'. Terms have evolved such as 'community intelligence' and 'criminal intelligence', which may further perplex an already confusing situation. The final issue to arise comes from the model's implementation objectives. Although the model is standard, the way in which BCUs collate and produce reports is not, consequently, resulting in incomparability between geographical areas. As stated previously, the national intelligence model is a business model and can be applied to all policing paradigms. The biggest preconception made is that the model is only applicable to intelligence-led policing and problem-orientated policing. The model can be particularly useful to a community or reassuring policing style. This is partially a result of the lack of understanding of the term 'intelligence': 'Association with "intelligence" prevented them from understanding its relevance to other favoured models of working, such as "community", "problem oriented", or "geographic" policing' (John and Maguire 2004a:18).

Although much advancement has been made in and around the use and implementation of intelligence, there are still many difficulties and deficiencies surrounding its use within policing exemplified by the results of the Bichard enquiry.

The Impact of the Bichard Enquiry

Although technology in itself can make the storing, retrieval and sharing process more efficient, there are often software limitations that are overlooked. In addition, technology must be designed, operated and maintained by people who can make user errors or omissions. The Soham murders and the subsequent Bichard enquiry (Bichard 2004) found information technology proved not only to be unsuccessful, but more importantly it instilled a false sense of security and safety which ultimately led to the murder of two young females. Prior to this particular murder it was believed that all individuals that work with young and vulnerable people were screened by cross-referencing their details with the criminal databases to ensure they were suitable to work with vulnerable people. As the murder investigation developed, it was found that Ian Huntley had been arrested some time previously in connection with sex offences involving young girls; unfortunately no charges could be brought against him. At the time of the murders, however, Huntley had moved away from his previous location where he was known to the police and as a result his background was not known to the investigating officers of the Soham murders. The BBC (2003) noted that this was in part due to the guidelines regarding the storing of information of offenders that had not been charged with any offences. Subsequently, it was concluded that vital information was not stored and made available on the database and that the data could only be accessed in Huntley's previous police force area. The data was not put on a force-wide database. This demonstrates that in this instance, information technology failed not by itself, but in conjunction with user errors and operational procedures. Bichard (2004) recorded following the enquiry that there had been 'systematic and corporate' failings on behalf of the primary investigating force Humberside Constabulary. Consequently it was found that police officers had little understanding of how the intelligence systems operated and demonstrated at best a vague understanding of the meaning of 'intelligence' which ultimately led to the loss of important information. Combined with the issues surrounding the Humberside intelligence database, it was further concluded that the relational databases such as the 'Child Protection Database' were also inadequate in their primary function (Bichard 2004). The Data Protection Act (Home Office 1998b) was believed to have contributed to the reluctance to record and share previous arrests and intelligence. The enquiry concluded that in fact the Act would have had no significant impact on the case. The issue with the Data Protection Act was found to be a lack of understanding and training surrounding the legislation. It must be noted that the Humberside Constabulary were not the only agency found to be at fault. Cambridgeshire Constabulary, Her Majesties Inspectorate for the Constabulary (HMIC) and the Association of Chief Police Officers (ACPO) were also found by the enquiry to be partly culpable for the failings of the investigation. Previous representation had been made to introduce an IT intelligence system across the whole of England and Wales to ensure standardisation and enable communication across police forces and different agencies such as the Criminal Records Bureau (CRB). Clearly from the Bichard Report, the failing consisted both of a technological and a human nature. Technological advances have expanded immeasurably in areas such as road policing, computer crime, paedophilia and terrorism. The affiliation between the police and information technology is a close one and in all probability is set to accelerate. For all agencies involved, the disadvantages surrounding technology and human limitations must be acknowledged. Although not a panacea to the issues surrounding such complex investigations, training and improving the understanding of systems and processes involved will go some way to improve economy, efficiency, effectiveness and performance.

Police Technological Developments

Technology

Information technology, databases and in a wider context 'technology' significantly impact on every aspect of policing including styles, technique and methods. Information technology (IT) can be defined as the 'Use of computers and electronic technology to store and communicate information (Collins 1996: 280) and database is defined as the 'Store of information that can be easily handled by a computer' (Collins 1996: 131). For these terms to have any significant meaning in the context of everyday policing, it is important to establish and evaluate the relationship between the police and technology including an assessment of the role which technology plays in the world of policing. Historically, there has been a strong investment by the police in technology, being especially true in relation to the Western world especially in Great Britain and America. The same, however, cannot be said of all countries, where developing countries experience a slower rate of development in comparison to the West. The expanding importance placed on technology within the domain of policing is partly due to the development of technology generally. Specifically, this would include communication via Internet, transnational communication and the way in which we travel. It is for the police service to develop and adapt in line with the new challenges created (Fleming and Wood 2007). No longer are British police forces responsible for policing their own jurisdictions alone. Many work as partner agencies across borders with neighbouring forces, with specialist forces such as the civil nuclear constabulary or with other forces overseas. The dynamics of crime have also steered the development of technology. Since the technical revolution in the 1960s–1970s, the types of crime the police have had to deal with have changed, becoming more sophisticated and hi-tech which would include such as Internet fraud and cyber threats, cyber hate and cyber terrorism, forcing the police to develop capabilities to deal with this problem (Nogala 1995). Serious and organised crime, with criminals travelling great distances, covering many police jurisdictions to commit serious and violent crimes again forced the police to find a way to deal with this, demonstrating the importance and reliance on technology (Nadelmann 2006). New and emerging terms such as 'Euro-crime' have been created, which refer to criminal activity that has 'transnational characteristics or tendencies', including offences such as terrorism, cyber terrorism, organised crime, drug-trafficking and money laundering (Anderson et al. 1995). Information technology has enabled the police service to develop new methods of policing which have been well established as styles of policing across the world. Such styles include problem-orientated policing, intelligence-led policing, zero-tolerance policing and community policing. These styles have become synonymous with Britain and other countries around the world (Maguire 2000). Central to the success of such policing paradigms is the wide and robust success and implementation of computerised databases.

Databases

Police work by its nature will accumulate almost an infinite number of reports, intelligence and conviction details. For this, the first police database was created called the Police National Computer or PNC in 1974 (BSSRS 1985). Its primary function was to hold offender fingerprints and vehicle details. Increasingly, there has been a greater emphasis on partnerships and inter-agency cooperation when dealing with crime. New technology, especially databases, has enabled organisations to store, sort, search, disseminate and share information resulting in improved communication, integration and efficiency (Williams 2000). Crime and criminality, both locally and globally, is becoming increasingly difficult for one agency to tackle independently, and increasingly the police rely on other agencies around the world to assist in the tracing and solving crime by efficiently utilising the resources and specific skill base of each organisation (Chester 1997). As criminals have become more dynamic, the police and other organisations have developed new and innovative ways to communicate using large databases (Ratcliffe 2008). The Police National Computer has the capacity to store millions of records: in 1999, the database held over 97 million items to which could be accessed 24 hours a day, 7 days a week from one of any of 25,000 terminals around the UK. The database now has links to several other databases involved in fighting crime, the Driving and Vehicle Licensing Agency (DVLA) and the deoxyribonucleic acid (DNA) databases are some typical examples, making its store of information even more valuable. The PNC has overcome and surpassed its original design as a simple data store as it now is an invaluable investigative tool, being able to manage queries and cross-tabulate items to match individuals with DNA, addresses and vehicles. The electronic database allows the searching and querying to be done quickly as hundreds of thousands of records are checked every second, far more quickly than a manual database. Other advantages include pattern analysis, the ability to build a picture of crime and predict and identify geographical hotspots, proving particularly useful when using a problem orientated or intelligence led policing approach.

Intelligence Databases

To support the current databases in place such as the Police National Computer (PNC), police intelligence databases have increasingly been utilised to direct resources and rationalise policing. Criminals take little regard to arbitrary police boundaries or jurisdictions that exist between police forces and as a consequence, crime is committed over wide geographical areas involving many different agencies. The requirement for agencies to communicate with each other and share intelligence has resulted in police intelligence databases becoming commonplace (Edwards 1999). It has become widely recognised that criminal intelligence should not exclusively be owned by one organisation, as the police have an obligation to share intelligence with statutory and voluntary agencies. Intelligence databases have enabled and standardised the way in which this is done. Each force has developed specific databases to meet the need of the force area and has worked to encourage officers to deposit any intelligence gathered through their operational duties by using community intelligence diaries or criminal intelligence databases. Police services in England and Wales have recently begun to combine the demand and management aspects of policing by amalgamating different databases. This knowledge management process is designed to facilitate and enhance the quality of service by improving the quality of information and knowledge available (Rogers and Martin, 2007).

Disadvantages of Databases

Limited funding and resources often diminishes the ability of technology to be wholly successful in achieving its aims and objectives. The annual running cost of the PNC in 2000 was, according to Her Majesty's Inspectorate for the Constabulary (HMIC), £17.6 million for England and Wales (HMIC 2000a:78). Another problem with any database is that it is impossible to fully eradicate human or user error. Although a database can alert the user that a 'field' has not been completed or that in some instances the data inputted is erroneous and the database cannot identify that this information is incorrect. This may have serious implications, with an individual being stopped in the street or arrested due to the incorrect information contained on the computer. This in some instances can be in contravention of the Human Rights Act (Home Office 2000) and the Data Protection Act (Home Office 1998b), which if breached could have profound consequences to the police service. Again the HMIC audit commission found that in England and Wales the error rate on the PNC was between 15 per cent and 65 per cent. From research conducted by HMIC (2000a), it has been concluded that a high percentage of error was due to the lack of formal training given to police officers, with only five days of training given to police officers in the use of the database, and reflects a basic misunderstanding of the models. The PNC is not the only database in use by the police and is reliant on other databases to operate efficiently. Examples include fingerprints (IDENT1), vehicle details (DVLA), the DNA database and automated fingerprint identification system (Public Service 2004). The same advantages and disadvantages with the Police National Computer are present and seem to be a common and recurring theme when evaluating computer databases. Databases have had a substantial effect on many areas within policing, including road and traffic policing, neighbourhood policing criminal investigations and security issues such as cyber terrorism.

Intelligence and its Influence on Policing Methods

The perceived inadequacies of the standard reactive police model, which has been labelled by Tilley (2003) as 'fire brigade policing 'are the focus on rapid response and deploying officers to respond to emergency calls, predominantly focused on enforcement (Weisburd and Eck 2004). In addition to the standard model, patrols were used alongside reactive policing to satisfy a rising demand for pro-activity'. Over time the inadequacies of this model were amplified by changes in technology, crimes and overall demand (Ratcliffe 2008). Random proactive patrols in areas were not having the desired effect and it was concluded that simply increasing the number of officers on a beat, or committing to operate more patrol beats, did not have any significant impact on levels of crime (Kelling et al. 1974). Crime complexity added to the model's inadequacies, as it failed to deal with the rise in organised crime, especially as criminality become more coordinated, complex and transnational and the increase in international terrorism. The final driver for change to a 'perceived' better model of policing arose due to the rise in demand for policing services. The 'demand gap' became more apparent as the public began to report more crime (Ratcliffe 2008). Since 1970, demand for policing services has risen by 250 per cent, where policing numbers have only managed a 50 per cent increase (Ratcliffe 2008). As a consequence of these changes, many senior police officers and other professionals began to notice how police officers had become detached from the public whom they served, which led to the emergence of a community-policing model by the 1980s (Morgan and Newburn 1997). The aim of the community policing model was predominantly to realign the police and the public with an emphasis on partnerships, both between the police and other organisations engaging with the general public. This new style aimed to improve public confidence in the police by improving legitimacy and transparency (Ratcliffe 2008). The most recent examples of this public engagement and consultation have been the use of Partner and Communities Together meetings (PACT) and surgeries where the public have an opportunity to influence police priorities (Home Office, 2005). Unfortunately, some academics now believe that the term 'community policing' has become a catch-all phrase to accommodate far too many ideas, philosophies and concepts, making it ambiguous and open-ended (Mastrofski 2006, Bayley 1994b). More recently, using the community model as bedrock, police managers have begun to adopt a problem orientated approach to solving policing issues. Developed and researched by Goldstein (1990), the problem-orientated approach consists of using a critical and analytical approach to solving specific problems which applied to both crime and non-crime issues. By setting the solution around an evidence-based approach, police managers are able to deal with recurring issues. Problem-orientated policing (POP) is often utilised through a partnership approach to problem-solving, which includes consultation with the crime-reduction partnerships and the public (Bullock et al. 2006, Rogers 2006). Inevitably, as with all policing styles, there are disadvantages. Firstly, although the principles of the style are clearly defined by Goldstein (1990) the question remains as to whether or not police officers are carrying out a comprehensive analysis of the problem (Weisburd 2004). Other difficulties have been found at the implementation stage of this style: a lack of understanding, officers in the habit of just responding to calls and not considering the reason for the calls, culture, resistance and cynicism (Bullock et al. 2006). In addition, the HMIC (2000b) reports found there were issues regarding the analysis, quality of data, problem-solving and evaluation of cases. Read and Tilley (2000) note that police are preoccupied with law enforcement and it will be difficult to implement problem-orientated policing successfully. Many police forces have implemented a problem-orientated approach, with Surrey Constabulary attempting to remain closely aligned with Goldstein's theories. In 1992 following consultation, areas within the borough were divided into locally recognised areas. Increased resources at peak demand times and call-grading enabled the local teams to respond personally to calls, reinforcing the notion of neighbourhoods. This enabled police to identify and analyse specific problems, resulting in detailed action plan being developed. Surrey introduced the 'policing menu', giving each officer a list of community problems which need to be addressed at the beginning of each shift. Each of the stages increased accountability and improved public relations by addressing issues deemed important by the community (Leigh et al. 1996). Community policing and problem-orientated policing have been styles used by Britain's police service for some time (Bullock et al. 2006). Since community policing was introduced, there has been a plethora of different policing paradigms being advertised and driven centrally from government, which include neighbourhood policing, reassurance policing and perhaps most recently citizen-focused policing. The Home Office publication 'Neighbourhood Policing: Your Police, Your Community our Commitment' (Home Office 2005) details dedicated resources for specific areas, including police, special constables, police community safety officers, wardens and other partners. This is a strategy of embedding dedicated neighbourhood teams into communities, working to improve relations, gathering intelligence and working conterminously within the intelligence-led policing (ILP) model (see below). Slightly different to community policing, this neighbourhood policing style will involve the use of intelligence and a wider inclusion of the local authority. In particular, neighbourhood policing will use the national intelligence model in line with crime reduction partnerships (Grieve et al. 2007). This policing style is citizen-focused, which revolves around policing in a manner that meets the needs of the community (Wakefield and Fleming 2009), attempting to make police officers more accessible, accountable and their actions transparent to the public. Neighbourhood policing goes further than community policing in a sense that it aspires to work by public cooperation and not just simple consent (Home Office 2005). There are, however, problems with this approach. Bullock et al. (2006) conclude that to ensure maximum effectiveness, a multi-agency approach must be undertaken which is often not under the direct control of the police. It has also been noted that although in principle neighbourhood policing is sound, it has yet to be seen to have introduced any real change in practice on the ground (Bullock et al. 2006). Reassurance policing was developed to primarily address the public's fear of crime and simply to reassure. Innes (2007), in partnership with Surry police and the University of Surrey identified an important concept, that of 'signal crimes'. These signal certain types of crimes as are perceived by the public as more important than others and consequently the police need to target these to re-legitimise themselves. This theory is linked with neighbourhood insecurities and concerns and identifies how certain types of anti-social behaviour and other crimes can lead to the population feeling anxiety, thinking the area is degenerating and stigmatising groups such as young people. By taking on board public opinion and dealing with crimes the public see as important, the police gain public confidence, closing the reassurance gap. National reassurance policing programmes (NRPPs) are now beginning to be implemented within force areas. Some have argued that reassurance policing has been an elaborate public relations exercise: Milie and Herrington (2004) pose that if reassurance policing is merely community policing repackaged, this may result in the credibility of reassurance policing being undermined. There appears to have been a drive from central government, for example, in the form of the Crime and Disorder Act 1998 (Home Office 1998), to introduce intelligence-led policing. The development and introduction of ILP perhaps alludes to the expansion of the performance culture that exists within the police service. This model enables police managers to contextualise intelligence, attaching processes and methods. The 'linear method', in terms of the end-to-end process aims to produce key operational and strategic outcomes in order to create key objectives for officers and the wider force (Ratcliffe 2008). For knowledge-management to have any measurable impact on an organisation, the processes in which knowledge can be harvested and used are crucial. For example, there is a clear need for understanding such issues as the intelligence management cycle and its component parts, discussed in some depth in Chapter 7 of this book. The paradigm of intelligence-led policing is argued by some to have been part of the policing method in the UK for over 150 years. However, Ratcliffe (2008) argues that this has been mistaken as investigation led intelligence and not ILP. Policing has clearly become more innovative (Weisburd and Eck 2004). Advances in technology allowed mass storage of data and the ability to manipulate that into information allowing the police to use intelligence more efficiently. New public management and the drive to make policing more professional ensured senior management would need to close this demand 'gap'. Finally the dynamics of crime itself changed, with police now facing more serious and organised crime than ever before, especially international forms including cyber terrorism. The modern criminal and terrorist would be far more difficult to detect using conventional methods which also fuelled the introduction of intelligence-led policing. Tilley (2003) defines ILP simply as 'a way of doing police business' (Newburn 2003:321). However, this may be construed as too simplistic a view on what is clearly a complex set of interactions and intentions. Ratcliffe (2008) provides a more in-depth definition 'a business model and managerial philosophy where data analysis and crime intelligence are pivotal to an objective, decision-making framework that facilitates crime and problem reduction, disruption and prevention through both strategic management and effective enforcement strategies that target prolific and serious offenders'(Ratcliffe 2008:182). Radcliffe's definition therefore provides us with an understanding of how complex this approach can be. Even though the concept of ILP is unique in terms of its processes, the styles often overlap. Newburn (2003) and Reiner (2010) suggest problem-orientated policing and ILP both focus on crime patterns, statistical data and a reduction in crime overall. Underpinning these approaches is the use of information technology and intelligence which is pivotal (Maguire et al. 2007). It appears that policing in Britain has adopted not one but all of the different paradigms of policing in its attempt to combat different forms of crime both locally and globally. Recent events such as the terrorist attacks on the UK and US ensure that intelligence is continually being gathered and utilised. Tilley (2003) suggests that by collecting and collating all criminal and community intelligence together and carrying out a detailed evaluation will enable the police and its partner agencies to be better informed about all forms of crime, thus enabling a more directed and potent approach to enforcement and disruption 'Intelligence-led policing involves developing and managing a detailed and up-to-date picture of patterns of crime and criminality in order to intervene in it most effectively to disrupt networks and remove prolific offenders' (Newburn 2003:231–2).

Conclusion

Clearly for cyber threats, cyber hate, cyber terrorism and other forms of criminality, both local and global, to be dealt with effectively official agencies such as the police and security services must rely heavily on information and intelligence. Much of this is provided by communities and individuals within communities and the intelligence led approach has been utilised by the police for some time in an effort to deliver effective services. Therefore, in order to ensure that communities and individuals engage with the police there must be a process of actively encouraging engagement from official bodies. Once this trust has been established, and information and intelligence provided, there has to be a robust process of evaluation and dissemination to all levels that require intelligence in order to combat potential or real threats. The current process and use of the national intelligence model appears to be an adequate vehicle for this to be achieved effectively, although there are some problems with its implementation. The police have made great strides in the past decade to ensure that their ability to gather information and intelligence has been enhanced. It is only by understanding the intelligence cycle, how information is gathered and disseminated, whilst continuing to engage with communities at all levels, that an effective response can be formulated to global problems such as cyber terrorism.

References

Anderson, M., Boer, M., Cullen, M., Gilmore, W., Raab, C., Walker, N. 1995. *Policing the European Union*, Oxford: Oxford University Press.

Bayley, D. 1994. International Differences in Community Policing, in Rosenbaum, D., *The Challenge of Community Policing: Testing the Promises*, California: Sage.

BBC News. 2003. Police Wipes Huntley Rape Charge. [Online]. Available at: http://news.bbc.co.uk/1/hi/uk/3528135.stm [accessed: 7 July 2011].

Bichard, M. 2004. *The Bichard Inquiry: Report*, London: The Stationery Office.

BSSRS. 1985. *Techno Cop – New Policing Technologies*, London: Free Association Books.

Bullock, K., Erol, R., Tilley, N. 2006. *Problem Orientated Policing and Partnerships*, Cullompton: Willan Publishing.

Centrex. 2004. *Code of Practice: National Intelligence Model*, London: HMSO.

Chester, C. 1997. Digitising the Beat: Police Databases and Incorporeal Transformations, *Journal of Research into New Media Technologies*, 3(2), 72–81.

Collins English Dictionary. 1996. *Data*, London: Harper Collins Publishers.

Edwards, C. 1999. *Changing Policing Theories for 21st Century Societies*, London: The Federation Press.

Fleming, J. and Wood, J. 2007. *Fighting Crime Together: The Challenges of Policing and Security Networks*, Sydney: UNSW Press.

Goldstein, H. 1990. *Problem-Orientated Policing*, USA: McGraw-Hill, Inc.

Grieve, J., Harfield, C., Mcvean, A. 2007. *Policing*, London: Sage.

Gwent Police. 2004. *Policy: National Intelligence Model Implementation of the Tasking & Coordination Process*, Gwent: Gwent Constabulary.

Harfield, C. and Harfield, K. 2008. *Intelligence: Investigation, Community and Partnership*, Oxford: Oxford University Press.

HMIC. 2000a. *On the Record: Thematic Inspection Report on the Police Crime Recording, the Police National Computer and the Phoenix Intelligence System Data Quality*, London: HMIC.

HMIC. 2000b. *Calling Time on Crime: HMIC Thematic Report*, London: HMIC.

Home Office. 1998a. *Crime and Disorder Act 1998*, London: Stationery Office.

Home Office. 1998b. *Data Protection Act 1998*, London: Stationery Office.

Home Office. 2000. *The Human Rights Act 2000*, London: Stationery Office.

Home Office. 2005. *Neighbourhood Policing: Your Police, Your Community, Our Commitment*, London: Stationery Office.

Home Office. 2006. *From Policing the Local Beat to Disrupting Global Crime Networks: Reforming the Structure of Policing in the 21st Century*, London: Stationery Office.

Home Office. 2009. *Cyber Strategy of the United Kingdom*, London: Stationery Office.

Hulnick, A., 2006.What's Wrong with the Intelligence Cycle?, *Intelligence and National Security*, 1743–9019, 21 (6), 959–79.

Innes, M. 2007. The Reassurance Function, *Policing: A Journal of Policy and Practice*, 1, (2), 129–31.

Innes, M. and Roberts, C. 2008. Reassurance Policing, Community Intelligence and the Co-Production of Neighbourhood Order, in Williamson, T. (ed.), *The Handbook of Knowledge-Based Policing*, Chichester: Wiley.

Jewkes, Y. and Yar, M., 2010. Introduction: the Internet, Cybercrime, and the Challenges of the 21st Century, in Jewkes, Y. and Yar, M., *The Handbook of Internet Crime*, Cullompton: Willan.

John, T. and Maguire, M. 2004a. *The National Intelligence Model – Key Lessons from Early Research*, London: Home Office.

John, T. and Maguire, M. 2004b. *The National Intelligence Model: Early Implementation Experiences in Three Police Force Areas*, Cardiff, Wales: School for Social Science, University of Cardiff.

Kelling, G., Pate, T., Dieckman, D., Brown, C. 1974. *The Kansas City Preventative Patrol Experiment: A* Summary Report, Washington, DC: Police Foundation.

Leigh, A., Read, T., Tilley, N. 1996. *Problem-Orientated Policing: Brit Pop*, Crime Detection and Prevention series 75, London: Home Office, Stationery Office.

Mike Maguire (2000): *Policing by risks and targets: Some dimensions and implications of intelligence-led crime control*, Policing and Society: An International Journal of Research and Policy, 9:4, 315-336.

Maguire, M., Morgan, R., Reiner, R. 2007.*The Handbook of Criminology*, 4th Edition, Oxford: Oxford University Press.

Morgan, R., and Newburn, T. 1997. *The Future of Policing*, Oxford: Oxford University Press.

Manning, P.K. 2000. Policing New Social Spaces, in Sheptycki, J.W.E. (ed.), *Issues in Transnational Policing*, London: Routledge.

Mastrofski, S. 2006. Community Policing: A Sceptical View, in Weisburd, D., Braga, A. (eds), *Police Innovation: Contrasting Perspectives*, Chicago: Cambridge University Press, 44–73.

McLaughlin, E. and Muncie, J. 2006. *The Sage Dictionary of Criminology*, 2nd Edition, London: Sage Publications.

Milie, A., and Herrington, V. 2004. *Reassurance Policing in Practice: Views from the Shop Floor*, Wolverhampton: University of Wolverhampton.

Nadelmann, E. 2006. *Policing the Globe: Criminalisation and Crime Control in International Relations*, Oxford: Oxford University Press.

NCIS (National Criminal Intelligence Service). 2000. *The National Intelligence Model*, London: NCIS.

Newburn, T. 2003. *Handbook of Policing*, Cullompton: Willan Publishing.

Newburn, T. 2007. *Criminology*, Cullompton: Willan Publishing.

Newburn, T. and Neyroud, P. 2008. *Dictionary of Policing*, Cullompton: Willan Publishing.

Nogala, D. 1995. *The Future Role of Technology in Policing*, Aldershot: Avebury.

Public Service. 2004. Taking Police into the Future. [Online]. Available at: http://www.publicservice.co.uk/feature_story.asp?id=3435 [accessed: 7 July 2011].

Ratcliffe, J. 2004. *Strategic Thinking in Criminal Intelligence*, Sidney; The Federation Press.

Ratcliffe, J. 2008. Intelligence-led Policing, In; Worthley, R,. Mazerolle, L,. Rombouts, S., (Eds) *Environmental Criminology and Crime Analysis*, Cullompton: Willan Publishing.

Read, T., and Tilley, N. 2000. *Not Rocket Science: Problem-solving and Crime Reduction*, Crime Reduction Research Series 6, London: Home Office.

Reiner, R. 2010. *The Politics of the Police*, 4th Edition, London: Oxford University Press.

Rogers, C. 2006. *Crime Reduction Partnerships*, Oxford: Oxford University Press.

Rogers, C. 2008. *Leadership Skills in Policing*, Oxford: Oxford University Press.

Rogers, C. 2008b. Winning Hearts and Minds, – The Government Terrorism Strategy, UK, *Town and Country Planning*, 77 (5), 235–6.

Rogers, C., and Martin, H. 2007. Managing Customer Demand, *Policing Today*, 14 (3), 33–4.

Rumizen, M. 2002. *The Complete Idiots Guide to Knowledge Management*, USA: Alpha Publishing.

Thames Valley Police. 2009. Force Control Strategy. [Online]. Available at: http://www.thamesvalley.police.uk/aboutus-stplan-fcstrat [accessed: 8 July 2011].

Tilley, N. 2003. Community Policing, Problem-Orientated Policing and Intelligence-Led Policing, in Newburn, T (ed.), *Handbook of Policing*, Cullompton: Willan Publishing.

Tilley, N. 2008. The Development of Community Policing in England: Networks, Knowledge and Neighbourhoods, in Williamson, T. *The Handbook of Knowledge-Based Policing*, Chichester: Wiley.

Wakefield., A. and Fleming, J. 2009. *The* Sage *Dictionary of Policing*, London: Sage Publishing.

Waddington, P.A.J. 2007. *Community Policing*, Policing: A Journal of Policy and Practice, 1, (2): 129–31.

Walker, A., Flatley, J., Kershaw, K., Moon, D. 2009. *Crime in England and Wales 2008/9: Volume 1: Findings from British Crime Survey and Police Recorded Crime*, London: Statutory Office.

Weber, M., Gerth, H., Mills, C, Turner, B. 2005. *From Max Weber: Essays in Sociology*, Abingdon: Routledge.

Weisburd, D., Eck, J. 2004. What Can Police do to Reduce Crime, Disorder and Fear?, *Annals of the American Academy of Political and Social Science*, 593 (1).

Williams, G. 2000. *Handbook for Information Communication Technology*, 4th Edition, Cambridge: Pearson Publishing.

Chapter 9

National and International Cyber Security Strategies

Tim Read

Introduction

This chapter will consider the extent to which issues of cyber security and cyber terrorism have been considered in existing policy guidance in the UK and abroad. As a starting point it will examine the 2009 Cyber Security Strategy (Cabinet Office) and the 2010 Home Office Cyber Crime Strategy. Analysis will focus upon the definitions of cyber crime provided in the documents, their descriptions of the nature of cyber crime, and the responses to cyber crime suggested in these documents.

A number of the documents that are examined in this chapter are not concerned specifically with cyber terror but more generally with cyber crime or cyber security. They are examined for a variety of reasons; because cyber terror is sometimes considered under these broader headings or because issues that are of concern in relation to cyber security or cyber crime apply equally to cyber terror (the globalised nature of the problem, for example, and the transnational responses proposed).

The adequacy of existing policy will be considered specifically in the light of recent concerns expressed by the director of GCHQ, Iain Lobban, that cyber terrorism presented a 'real and credible' threat to the UK's critical services (Lobban 2010: 14). Lobban has suggested that while GCHQ provides expert advice and incident response to critical infrastructure providers, it needs to be quicker in its response to try to match 'the speed at which cyber events happen' (Lobban 2010: 15). 'For me this points to a different sort of partnership between the national security agencies and the key industry players. Our systems will need to be more interconnected. And we may need to establish different financial models to underpin a national capability which will be both public and private' (Lobban 2010: 15).

In a situation where 80 per cent of the critical infrastructure is privately owned and does not belong to the government or military, policy increasingly needs to be concerned with the protection of the civilian critical infrastructure (as illustrated by the characteristics of the botnet attacks against Estonia in 2007), and a number of governments are already working on dialogue with the private sector. The response to the Estonian attack also illustrates the need for international cooperation. In the words of an adviser to the Estonian Ministry of Defence 'the good news for the state people and the policymakers is that the nation state is still the prime international actor that has the responsibility to draft the policies and to carry them out', but stresses that there is a need to develop international mechanisms, as well as the national strategies that have been drafted. Consequently, the chapter will also examine the existing international instruments that exist to tackle cyber crime, and consider their effectiveness; for example, the Council of Europe Convention on Cybercrime, the European Union Critical Infrastructure Protection policy and the NATO cyber defence policies (see Chapter 6 of this book for further information on international agreements).

The Context for the UK Cyber Crime Strategy

Contest

The Contest strategy (originally launched in 2003, published in 2006, revised in 2009) is the UK government's counter-terrorism strategy. Perhaps surprisingly there is little in the document about cyber terrorism. Contest is split into 4 themes: pursue, prevent, protect and prepare. The only direct reference to cyber terrorism in the document is in part 2, under a section dealing with 'future challenges' to the protect element of the strategy. This states that 'the Government will continue to monitor and assess the risk of "cyber terrorism" – an electronic attack by terrorists on our information and communications infrastructure. Currently that threat is not assessed to be great. But this may change' (HM Government 2009: 116).

Obviously, there are sections of Contest that discuss issues where cyber terrorism might be thought relevant (the importance of protecting critical national infrastructure, the work of the Centre for the Protection of National Infrastructure (CPNI), and its work with the private sector (pages 106, 111 and 116 of the document) but specific mention is limited to the single paragraph above. In comparison, there is an entire section of the report given over to the threat posed by chemical, biological, radiological and nuclear weapons and explosives. Interestingly too, in the cyber crime strategy produced by the Home Office in 2010 the use of the Internet by terrorists is described as being beyond the scope of that document, but as being covered within the Contest strategy (Home Office 2010:14).

The CPNI, established in 2007, 'delivers advice that aims to reduce the vulnerability of organisations in the national infrastructure to terrorism and other threats such as espionage, including those from cyber-space' (Cabinet Office 2009: 11). Also established in 2007 was the Research, Information and Communications Unit (RICU) staffed and directed by the Department of Communities and Local Government, Foreign and Commonwealth Office and the Home Office (and which now forms part of the OSCT). Described in 2009 as being 'at the centre of the Government's efforts to communicate the Government's counter-terrorism strategy', RICU's roles included:

- 'advising CONTEST partners on their counter-terrorism related communications
- exposing the weaknesses of violent extremist ideologies and brands, and
- supporting credible alternatives to violent extremism using communications' (HM Government 2009: 153).

While the National Information Assurance Strategy (2003, 2007) 'outlined the first steps for the UK in assuring the integrity, availability and confidentiality of Information and Communications Technology systems and the information they handle' (Cabinet Office 2009: 11), more detailed policy on cyber crime was contained in two documents; one produced in 2009, the other 2010. The first is the UK's Cyber Security Strategy, published by the Cabinet Office, the second the Home Office's Cyber Crime Strategy, produced as a response to the 2009 document.

Cyber Security Strategy (2009)

The vision for the UK government's 2009 Cyber Security Strategy was that:

> citizens, business and government can enjoy the full benefits of a safe, secure and resilient cyber space: working together, at home and overseas, to understand and address the risks, to reduce the benefits to criminals and terrorists, and to seize opportunities in cyber space to enhance the UK's overall security and resilience. (Cabinet Office 2009: 3)

The strategy intended 'to provide a strategic enabling framework through which to examine the challenges and opportunities' faced (Cabinet Office 2009: 7). Cyber security was understood to mean 'both the protection of UK interests in cyber space and also the pursuit of wider UK security through exploitation of the many opportunities that cyber space offers' (Cabinet Office 2009: 9). Amongst the rather varied 'principles' identified as guiding the 2009 strategy were:

- consistency with the overarching principles of the National Security strategy
- adherence to 'a set of core values, including; human rights, the rule of law, legitimate and accountable government, justice, freedom, tolerance and opportunity for all'

the presumption of:
- a partnership approach at home
- a multilateral approach overseas
- a more integrated approach within government

- a 'hard-headed' approach to the UK's risks, aims and capabilities
- the retention of 'strong, balanced and flexible capabilities'
- where possible, the early tackling of security challenges
- continued strengthening of the UK's security through investment, learning and improvement.

(Cabinet Office 2009:10)

The 2009 strategy was intended to establish a 'strategic enabling framework' to help coordinate existing cyber security efforts across government, prioritising the 'development and growth of critical skills and additional funding for the development of innovative future technologies to protect the UK network' (Downing 2011:8). Perhaps most importantly the strategy established the Office of Cyber Security (now called the Office of Cyber Security and Information Assurance – OCSIA) to coordinate policy across government and pool intelligence from police and security services, and the Cyber Security Operations Centre in GCHQ Cheltenham to coordinate the protection of the country's major IT systems (also discussed in Chapter 6) (Downing 2011:8).

According to the Cabinet Office website, the two organisations 'work with lead government departments and agencies'; the Home Office, Ministry of Defence (MoD), Government Communications Headquarters (GCHQ – including Communications-Electronics Security Group (CESG)), the Centre for the Protection of National Infrastructure (CPNI) and the Department for Business, Innovation and Skills (BIS) in 'driving forward the cyber security programme for UK government and give the UK the balance of advantage in cyberspace' (Cabinet Office website).

The OCSIA has responsibility for implementing a number of cross cutting agendas including:

- providing a strategic direction on cyber security and information assurance for the UK including e-crime;
- supporting education, awareness, training and education;
- working with private sector partners on exchanging information and promoting best practice;
- ensuring that the UK's information and cyber security technical capability and operational architecture is improved and maintained;
- working with the Office of the Government Chief Information Office (OGCIO) to ensuring the resilience and security of government ICT infrastructures;
- engaging with international partners in improving the security of cyberspace and information security (Cabinet Office website).

2010 Cyber Crime Strategy

There had been mention of the importance of cyber crime and cyber terrorism in the Home Office's 'Science and Innovation Strategy 2009 –12' published in 2009. Cyber crime had been identified as one of two 'cross-cutting priorities' where there had been 'recent rapid and significant changes in the capability of new technologies' (Home Office 2009: 7). The document went on to say that there were 'three types of crime conducted via the Internet' that would be considered:

- 'traditional crime now conducted using the Internet (for example, deception, fraud, illegal pornography);
- new forms of Internet-enabled crime (for example, online 'life crimes', computer misuse, viruses);
- cyber terrorism'.

(Home Office 2009: 7)

Research in the area needed to concentrate on understanding where individuals (presumably criminal, although this is not specified) were located, using patterns of activity, building networks of association and recovering data from seized computers to pursue those using the Internet for criminal purposes; improved data on how to use the Internet to influence and promote positive messages about helpful and safe behaviour; and, because cyber crime was not limited by geography, better understand the 'potential tension' between local crimes and crimes that cut across borders and areas. 'We are planning new research in this area, coordinated centrally and funded from across the department. To start with we will look at what research is currently being carried out in this area, both in the private and public sector' (Home Office 2009: 7).

A more comprehensive statement of Home Office aims was contained in the 2010 Cyber Crime Strategy, which set out how the department would coordinate and deliver policies to counter cyber crime, as required by the 2009 Cyber Security Strategy. Much of the 2010 document is concerned with definitions of cyber crime; its nature, the means by which it is carried out, its scale and international dimensions. Using the 'vision' provided by the 2009 Cyber Security Strategy, the Home Office document says that it will achieve this:

- 'Coordinate activity across Government to tackle crime and address security on the Internet in line with the strategic objectives laid out in the UK Cyber Security Strategy.
- Reduce the direct harms by making the Internet a hostile environment for financial criminals and child sexual predators, and ensuring that they are unable to operate effectively through work to disrupt crime and prosecute offenders.
- Raise public confidence in the safety and security of the Internet, not only through tackling crime and abuse, but through the provision of accurate

and easy-to-understand information to the public on the threats.
- Support industry leadership to tackle cyber crime, and work with industry to consider how products and online services can be made safer and security products easy to use.
- Work with international partners to tackle the problem collectively'.

(Home Office 2010:17)

Overall one author described the 2010 strategy as a 'modest revamp' (Leyden 2010), re-affirming the Office for Cyber Security at the centre of efforts to tackle cybercrime.

> The policy itself is largely an extension of previously announced policies and largely uncontroversial. The devil is in the detail, such as how much resources get allocated to the Police Central eCrime Unit or how seriously banks will take frauds reported to them through action fraud. (Leyden 2010)

Bearing in mind the quote above, the strategy is striking in the lack of detail it provides, and for the number of 'apple-pie and motherhood' statements it contains. For example, in the section of the report that develops the need to work with the private sector the Home Office asserts that it will:

- 'Work with the Internet industry and commercial business to ensure that safety and security are factors in designing services and that criminals are deterred from exploiting the online environment.
- Ensure that there is successful liaison between all groups working to protect the public'.

Similarly, in tackling crime internationally, it will:

- 'Work internationally to tackle cyber crime, including through effective collaboration with countries that have a well-developed understanding and capacity' (Home Office 2010:18).

The statements in relation to working with the private sector are particularly interesting in the light of comments made at the same time by the House of Lord's European Union Committee in their report 'Protecting Europe against large-scale cyber attacks', a response to the Commission to the European Parliament's 2009 communication of the same name (discussed in greater detail below). In their inquiry the committee discussed the public private partnership model operating in the UK and had hoped to test the claims that the model had proved successful in 'enhancing the resilience of the communications sector', as a result of the government maintaining 'a close working relationship with industry on a voluntary basis' (House of Lords, 2010: 24). They were forced to conclude:

We would be better placed to assess the extent of the problem if we had received evidence from United Kingdom ISPs, but the only ISP which replied to our call for evidence was XS4ALL, a Dutch company. With the single exception of JANET(UK), the United Kingdom's networking companies, Internet trade bodies and Internet exchange points showed a similar lack of interest.

We regret that United Kingdom Internet Service Providers and the rest of the commercial United Kingdom Internet industry should not have shown more interest in submitting evidence to this inquiry. This may be a reflection of their view that the Commission Communication will have little effect on them. (House of Lords 2010:24 emphasis in original document)

These conclusions would have been dispiriting enough, but the government might have consoled itself that they applied largely to the level of cooperation with the Lord's Committee. However, the report went further:

It is clear to us that, despite good intentions, the involvement of Internet entrepreneurs in the formulation of Government policy is as yet at best superficial. Both the Government and the Commission seem to think that it is for the private sector to come forward. We think that, on the contrary, it is for the public sector to take the initiative and to offer to experienced Internet entrepreneurs a real say in how public private partnerships are best developed. (House of Lords 2010:25 emphasis in original document)

It is noticeable too that there is a commitment (on page 4 of the 2010 strategy) that the Home Office will review the cyber crime strategy on a six-monthly basis, to ensure that it is consistent with the National Security Strategy and the UK Cyber Security Strategy. However, at the time of writing (summer 2011) this review had not been published, having been postponed twice, in autumn 2010 and again in the spring of 2011.

The 2010 National Security Strategy

The UK's 2010 National Security Strategy (NSS) (HM Government 2010b) stated that the National Security Council had identified four risks as being the highest priority (tier one) for UK national security 'taking account of both likelihood and impact' (HM Government 2010b: 27). These were:

- international terrorism affecting the UK or its interests
- a major accident or natural hazard requiring a national response
- an international military crisis between states drawing in the UK
- 'hostile attacks upon UK cyber space by other states and large scale cyber crime'.

(HM Government 2010b:27).

The strategy went on to say that cyber attack was 'not simply a risk for the future. Government, the private sector and citizens are under sustained cyber attack today, from both hostile states and criminals' (HM Government 2010b: 29). It added that 'the Internet provides great benefits for UK's industry, government and general populace, but as our dependency on it increases so do the risks and threats we face online' (HM Government 2010b:29); threats specifically mentioned were to the UK's national infrastructure, government and business, as it became more dependent on the Internet, cyber crime, the Olympics, and attacks in cyberspace, including terrorism.

Strategic Defence and Strategy Review 2010 (SDSR)

The 2010 SDSR set out the 'ways and means' to deliver the ends identified in the NSS (HM Government 2010a: 9). Because one of the highest priority risks identified in the NSS was cyber security, the government made a commitment to 'develop a transformative programme for cyber security, which addresses threats from states, criminals and terrorists, and seizes the opportunities which cyber space provides for our future prosperity and for advancing our security interests' (HM Government 2010a: 10). This National Cyber Security Programme would be 'supported by £650 million of new investment over the next four years, working to one national programme of activity with supporting strategies in other departments' (HM Government 2010a: 47).

The important role of the private sector and academia was again stressed in terms of leveraging the knowledge and resources necessary to co-design credible policy, achieve buy-in from those that own and operate large elements of the critical cyber infrastructure and to obtain value for money. The lead minister for cyber security would be the Security Minister in the Home Office, working with the Director of Cyber Security and the National Security Secretariat both in the Cabinet Office (Downing 2011:9).

The aims of the programme were to:

- 'Overhaul the UK's approach to tackling cybercrime' by creating a single point of contact for businesses and the public to report cyber crime. Introduce a 'new programme of skill development, to ensure that those involved in combating cyber crime have the knowledge required to identify, understand and tackle the threat' (HM Government 2010a: 47).
- Address deficiencies in the UK's ability to detect and defend itself against cyber attack (from terrorists, states or 'other hostile actors'). Two elements are identified: (1) improving the ability to deliver cyber products and services and (2) enhancing investment in national intelligence capabilities 'focusing on the UK's centre for cyber security operations at GCHQ, working in cooperation with other government departments and agencies' (HO Government 2010a: 47).
- Create a new organisation 'to mainstream cyber security throughout the

MOD and ensure the coherent integration of cyber activities across the spectrum of defence operations' (HO Gov 2010a: 47) – the UK Defence Cyber Operations Group.

- Address shortcomings in the UK's cyber infra-structure 'both to tackle immediate weaknesses in security and to ensure that we maintain access to a trusted industrial base'. 'Strategic leadership and regulatory oversight' in this respect would be provided by a newly established Cyber Infrastructure Team in the Department for Business, Innovation and Skills (BIS) (HO Government 2010a: 47).
- Introduce a new programme of cyber security education and skills 'in order to foster a more preventative approach to cyber security throughout the UK. Simple, common sense security measures available to ordinary citizens and businesses' (HO Government 2010a: 48).
- Sponsor long-term cyber security research, working closely with the research councils, the private sector and others.
- Continue to build cyber security alliances (see below).
- Establish a programme management office within the Office of Cyber Security and Information Assurance in the Cabinet Office to 'oversee, prioritise and coordinate the centralised funding and implementation of the National Cyber Security Programme'.

(HO Government 2010a: 49).

Part 5 of the SDSR also stressed the importance of 'alliances and partnerships', both bilateral and multilateral, as a 'fundamental part of our approach to defence and security', something which is referred to in greater detail subsequently in this chapter (HO Government 2010a: 59). The review referred to the 'pre-eminent' security and defence relationship with the US, 'as part of our ongoing commitment to working with our US at all levels, we will strengthen our joint efforts in priority areas' – cyber is one of the six mentioned. Part of this would be the future development of a Cyber Operations Memorandum of Understanding between the two.

On 25 May 2011 the United Kingdom and the United States signed a cyber communiqué which reaffirmed the two governments' desire to:

> preserve peace and stability, empower innovation and prosperity, and protect and promote the democratic rights and responsibilities of citizens around the world … President Obama and I agree on a shared vision for cyberspace which places at its heart fundamental freedoms, privacy and the free flow of information in a secure and reliable manner. (Cabinet Office website)

The communiqué involved the two governments promoting accession to, and implementation of, the Budapest Convention on Cybercrime 'to which the UK acceded today, joining the United States and 30 other states as parties to the world's foremost treaty to combat cybercrime internationally'; working more closely with private sector and business partners; establishing regular collaboration between the US and UK on Information and Communications Technology (ICT) development; coordinating efforts for research and development to improve cyber security, and generally developing further 'our ability and the ability of our allies to prevent, detect, defend against and recover from the full range of national security threats we face in cyberspace' (Cabinet Office website).

UK Defence Cyber Operations Group

In large part the 'transformative' commitment by the government contained in the 2010 SDSR appears to rely on the establishment of the UK Defence Cyber Operations Group. This group aim to provide 'a cadre of experts to support our own and allied cyber operations to secure our vital networks and to guide the development of new cyber capabilities' (HM Government 2010a: 27), bringing together existing expertise from across defence, including the armed forces and the science and technology community. 'It will ensure we plan, train, exercise and operate in a way which integrates our activities in both cyber and physical space; and be responsible for developing, testing and validating cyber capabilities as a complement to traditional military capabilities' (HM Government 2010a: 27).

Standards and Skills

However, as Downing identifies, there is nothing in the new programme about initiatives relating to security standards (Downing 2011:12), contrasting this with a 2011 OECD report on cyber security risks which suggested that one of the key actions for governments to take in tackling cyber security should be to 'use procurement power, standards-setting and licensing to influence computer industry suppliers to provide properly tested hardware and software' (Sommer and Brown, cited in Downing 2011:12). Downing goes on to identify that there are a number of standards for cyber security and national security which organisations can choose (compliance with ISO 27001, for example) and that it would be helpful for the government to undertake rationalisation of the cyber security standards used in the UK, although other research has commented on the array of standards used across government departments themselves (Intellect, 2010). In addition the government has tried to overcome a potential shortage of cyber security skills by launching, in July 2010, the Cyber Security Challenge. Based on a US model, this is a series of national online games and competitions to 'identify and nurture' the UK's future cyber security workforce run by a management consortium of cyber security professionals across the public and private sectors and academia (Downing 2011: 13).

The International Context

The importance of international, indeed global, efforts to tackle cyber terrorism and cyber crime is something that is widely recognised, and widely referred to. A UN paper produced in 2010 stressed the transnational nature of cyber crime – 'as a consequence of its underlying architecture and the global availability of services, cyber crime often has an international dimension'. From this 'the challenges that the transnational element poses for investigating cyber crime are similar to those involved in other transnational offences. As a result of the fundamental principle of national sovereignty, according to which investigations in foreign territories cannot be carried out without the permission of local authorities, close cooperation between the States involved is crucial in cyber crime investigations'. Another major challenge relates to the short time available to carry out investigations into cyber crime. 'Timely and effective cooperation between authorities in different countries is also crucial because in cases of cyber crime the evidence is often deleted automatically and within short time frames. Protracted formal procedures can seriously hinder investigations' (UN 2010: 4).

As the UK material previously described in this chapter demonstrates, there is widespread recognition of the importance of agreement and cooperation between states in determining the success of efforts to ensure cyber security. Yet, writing in 2010, Harley stated that 'despite the clear need for international cooperation on cybercrime, there is as yet no genuinely global multilateral treaty (convention) dealing with the issue' (2010).

This fact had been explicitly recognised at the 12th United Nations Congress of Crime Prevention and Criminal Justice in April 2010, where a paper produced by the secretariat of the UN Office on Drugs and Crime (UNODC) stated that 'a large number of existing mutual legal assistance agreements are still based on formal, complex and often time-consuming procedures. The establishment of procedures for quick responses to incidents and requests for international cooperation is therefore considered vital' (UN 2010:4). It concluded that 'the development of a global convention against cybercrime should be given careful and favourable consideration' (UN 2010: 15). However, UNODC's identification in the final paragraph of the report of its aims in period before this eventual global objective was achieved gives some indication of the size of the task:

> Specifically, UNODC will aim to do the following: assist Member States in adopting legislation for effectively investigating computer-related crimes and prosecuting offenders; build the operational and technical knowledge of judges, prosecutors and law enforcement officers on issues pertaining to cybercrime, through training, the adaptation/development of training materials on investigation and prosecution of computer-related crime etc.; train law enforcement authorities to effectively use international cooperation mechanisms to combat cybercrime; raise the awareness of civil society and create momentum among decision-makers to coalesce efforts to prevent and address cybercrime;

and identify and disseminate good practices and promote public-private partnerships in preventing and combating cybercrime. (UN 2010: 16)

The Convention on Cybercrime (ETS No. 185)

There have been a number of efforts to harmonise cyber crime legislation. The most successful, in terms of the extent of its adoption, has been the Council of Europe's Convention of Cyber crime, introduced in 2001 (Council of Europe 2001). In 2003 an Additional Protocol to the Convention was introduced, dealing with the criminalisation of racist or xenophobic acts committed through computer systems, and in 2007 the Council of Europe Convention on the Protection of Children against Sexual Exploitation and Sexual Abuse was introduced for signature. As at December 2009 the latter had been signed by 38 states, three of which had ratified it (Council of Europe website, UN 2010: 7)). Although the UK was a signatory of the 2001 Convention, it did not ratify it until 2011 as part of the cybercrime communiqué it signed with the United States.

The 2001 Convention was the first international treaty on crimes committed via the Internet and other computer networks, dealing particularly with infringements of copyright, computer-related fraud, child pornography and violations of network security. It also contained a series of powers and procedures such as the search of computer networks and interception. Its main objective was to pursue a common criminal policy aimed at the protection of society against cyber crime, especially by adopting appropriate legislation and fostering international cooperation (Council of Europe website). The Convention may be acceded to by any state that is not a member of the Council; indeed four non-member states (Canada, Japan, South Africa and the United States) were involved in the negotiation of the Convention.

However, while it has the widest coverage of any international agreement dealing with cybercrime, estimated by Harley in 2010 to cover about one third of Internet users, the Convention has been the subject of a number of criticisms. It has been criticised as outdated and for being drafted largely by and for European states; in the nine years since 2001 when the first 30 states signed the convention only 16 additional states had become signatories, and no non-member of the Council of Europe had acceded to the Convention, despite five being invited to do so. 'The pace of ratification has been similarly slow' (UN 2010: 11). Russia has not signed the Convention (despite being a member of the European Council), neither has Brazil, which considered signing but then declined, voicing reservations about the provisions relating to the criminalisation of intellectual property infringements. In addition, the ratification of the Convention by the US in 2007 led to domestic criticisms that it might lead to the US government having to monitor political dissidents or enforce foreign laws curbing free speech. There are also questions about whether states such as China and Russia, widely suspected of sponsoring cyber attacks, will agree to the levels of international cooperation in investigating and prosecuting cyber crime required by the Convention (the utility of a Convention that did not include these two states led one author to use the sub-heading 'No Russia + No China = No point' in an article about the UK's ratification of the Convention (Leyden 2011)). Overall, Harley concludes that 'globally there is clearly a divergence of views regarding the appropriate global standards' (Harley 2010).

European Critical Infrastructure Protection

Much of the guidance and direction about cybercrime in Europe and elsewhere has been connected with the safeguarding of states' critical infrastructure.[1] Although a number of organisations have produced guidance on critical infrastructure protection (The OECD's Recommendation on the Protection of Critical Information Infrastructures, G8's principles on CIIP, and the UN. General Assembly Resolution 58/199 'Creation of a global culture of cyber security and the protection of critical information infrastructures') the most relevant guidance for the UK is the European Programme for Critical Infrastructure Protection (EPCIP).

Following the Madrid Terror attacks in 2004 the European Council asked for the preparation of an overall strategy to protect critical infrastructures in the region. This resulted in a proposal in late 2005 for the establishment of EPCIP, giving priority to the threat of terrorism. In April 2007 the Council adopted EPCIP's conclusions that it was the ultimate responsibility of Member States to manage arrangements for the protection of critical infrastructures within their national borders, but that the European Commission would work to develop a European procedure for the identification and designation of ECIs and assess the need to improve their protection (European Council 2008a: section 4). In 2008 the European Council produced a directive (2008/114/EC) requiring member states to identify and designate ECIs, assess the need to improve their protection, nominate Security Liasion Officers for all designated ECIs, and to enter into bilateral or multilateral discussions with any other Member State which might be significantly affected by the ECI (European Council 2008a).

However, a subsequent European Commission document ('Protecting Europe from large scale cyber attacks and disruptions: enhancing preparedness, security and resilience') in 2009 identified limitations in the existing programme and the need for a new European Governance model for critical Information Infrastructures (CIIs). Amongst the 'challenges' existing in Europe was the fact that 'measures and regimes to ensure the security and resilience of CIIs, as well as the level of expertise and preparedness, differ across member states' (Commission of the European Communities 2009: 5). In addition there was limited European early warning and

---

1 Critical infrastructure is 'an asset, system or part thereof ... which is essential for the maintenance of vital social functions, health, safety, security or economic well-being of people, and the disruption or destruction of which would have a significant impact in a Member State'. 'European critical infrastructure' (ECI) means critical infrastructure in Member States the disruption/destruction of which would have a significant impact on at least two Member States (Europa website).

incident response capability (again, this varied in quality across member states). 'While Member States remain ultimately responsible for defining CII-related policies, their implementation depends on the involvement of the private sector, which owns or controls a large number of CIIs. On the other hand, markets do not always provide sufficient incentives for the private sector to invest in the protection of CIIs at the level that governments would normally demand. To address this governance problem public–private partnerships (PPPs) have emerged at the national level as the reference model. However, despite the consensus that PPPs would also be desirable on a European level, European PPPs have not materialised so far' (Commission of the European Communities 2009: 5–6).

Yet again, what this pointed to, in the opinion of the Commission of the European Communities, was the need for an 'integrated EU approach to enhance the security and resilience of CIIs which would 'complement and add value to national programmes as well as to the existing bilateral and multilateral cooperation schemes between member states' (Commission of the European Communities 2009: 7). 'A multi-stakeholder, multi-level approach is essential, taking place at the European level while fully respecting and complementing national responsibilities'. This approach was to be based around 'five pillars':

1. 'Preparedness and prevention: to ensure preparedness at all levels' (achieved via the definition of a minimum level of capabilities and services for national/governmental CERTs by the end of 2010, CERTs established in all member states by the end of 2011; foster cooperation between public and private sector through EP3R; establishment of a European Forum by the end of 2009).
2. 'Detection and response: to provide adequate early warning mechanisms' (largely through the development of the European Information Sharing and Alert System (EISAS)).
3. 'Mitigation and recovery: to reinforce EU defence mechanisms for CII' (by the end of 2010 at least one national exercise to have been run in every member state to demonstrate the development of national contingency plans, to have planned and run a pan-European exercise by the end of the same year).
4. 'International cooperation: to promote EU priorities internationally' (production of European 'roadmaps' providing guidelines/principles for international cooperation on critical Internet components, and international cooperation).
5. 'Criteria for the ICT sector (support the implementation of the Directive on the Identification and Designation of European Critical Infrastructures)' .

(Commission of the European Communities 2009: 7–10).

Even at the point that the 2009 report was produced there was some scepticism about the extent to which a number of the targets supporting these five pillars were achievable. The House of Lord's committee considering the report in 2010 described it as being 'fine as far as it went, but that it did not go very far' (House of Lords 2010: 20). In particular the communication was criticised for saying little about the role of the EU in a global context, for suggesting that all member states set up a national CERT (the Lords' Committee felt that the UK's network of CERTs worked satisfactorily), for its lack of consideration of the role of NATO, and for having unrealistic expectations about the timescale for resilience exercises (national and pan-European) 'it is not only in the case of resilience exercises that our witnesses thought many of the Commission's target dates over-ambitious. We hope the Commission will accept that changes that are meticulously prepared will be more valuable than any designed only to meet artificial deadlines' (House of Lords 2010: 29).

EU security strategy

In February 2010 ministers adopted the European Union's Internal Security Strategy which set out plans for a European security model, integrating action on law enforcement and judicial cooperation, border management and civil protection (Consilium website). The strategy set out the main threats and challenges the EU faces. The common threats identified were 'terrorism, in any form', serious and organised crime, cross border crime, violence and cyber crime ('a global, technical, cross-border, anonymous threat to our information systems and because of that, it poses many additional challenges for law-enforcement agencies' Council of the European Union, 2010: 6). It identified 10 broad guidelines for action 'in order to guarantee the EU's internal security over the coming years':

1. A wide and comprehensive approach to internal security
   – comprises both horizontal (involvement of law-enforcement and border-management authorities, judicial cooperation, civil protection agencies and also the political, economic, financial, social and private sectors, including non-governmental organisations) and vertical dimensions (international cooperation, EU-level security policies and initiatives, regional cooperation between Member States and Member States' own national, regional and local policies).
2. Ensuring the effective democratic and judicial supervision of security activities
3. Prevention and anticipation: a proactive, intelligence-led approach
4. Development of a comprehensive model for information exchange
5. Operational cooperation
6. Judicial cooperation in criminal matters
7. Integrated border management
8. A commitment to innovation and training
9. External dimension of internal security/cooperation with third countries
   – 'International cooperation by the EU and its Member States, both bilaterally and multilaterally, is essential in order to guarantee security

and protect the rights of our citizens and to promote security and respect for rights abroad'. 'Special attention will have to be paid to 'weak and failed States' so that they do not become hubs of organised crime or terrorism'.

10. Flexibility to adapt to future challenges.

(Council of the European Union, 2010: 6).

A subsequent communication – the EU Internal Security Strategy in Action – built on what Member States and EU institutions had already agreed, proposed how EU members should work together on five 'strategic objectives and specific actions for 2011–2014 which, alongside ongoing efforts and initiatives, will help make the EU more secure'. The five objectives identified were:

- Serious and organised crime.
- Border security.
- Natural and man-made disasters in Europe and in its immediate neighbourhood.
- Terrorism: 'our societies remain vulnerable to the sorts of attacks suffered with the bombings of public transport in Madrid in 2004 and in London in 2005. We must work harder and more closely to prevent new attacks recurring'.
- 'Another growing threat is cybercrime. Europe is a key target for cybercrime because of its advanced Internet infrastructure, the high number of users, and its Internet-mediated economies and payment systems. Citizens, businesses, governments and critical infrastructure must be better protected from criminals who take advantage of modern technologies'.

(European Commission 2010a: 4).

Under the terrorism objective ('prevent terrorism and address radicalisation and recruitment'), three areas of action were identified:

1. Empower communities to prevent radicalisation and recruitment. This encompassed; the creation by 2011 of an EU radicalisation-awareness network; the organisation in 2012 of a ministerial conference on the prevention of radicalisation and recruitment 'at which Member States will have the opportunity to present examples of successful action to counter extremist ideology', and the production of a handbook of actions and experiences to support Member States' efforts.
2. Cut off terrorists' access to funding and materials and follow their transactions. A commitment that in 2011 the Commission would develop a policy for the EU to extract and analyse financial messaging data held on its own territory, following the signature of the Terrorist Financing Tracking Programme agreement with the United States.
3. Protect transport.

The strategy also identified a number of actions that would be required to be undertaken by member states in order to 'raise levels of security for citizens and businesses in cyber space' (European Commission 2010a: 9).

Action 1: Build capacity in law enforcement and the judiciary:

- By 2013 the EU would have established a cybercrime centre 'the focal point in Europe's fight against cybercrime'. This centre would improve the evaluation and monitoring of existing preventive and investigative measures, support the development of training and awareness-raising for law enforcement and judiciary, cooperate with ENISA,[2] and liaise with national/governmental CERTs.[3]
- Nationally, Member States should ensure common standards among police, judges, prosecutors and forensic investigators in investigating and prosecuting cybercrime offences (European Commission 2010a: 9).
- Before 2013 member states should develop national cybercrime awareness and training capabilities, and set up centres of excellence at national level or in partnership with other Member States – 'these centres should work closely with academia and industry'.

(European Commission 2010a:10).

Action 2: Work with industry to empower and protect citizens:

- All Member States should ensure that people could easily report cybercrime incidents.
- Member States should ensure that citizens had easy access to guidance on cyber threats and the basic precautions that need to be taken.
- By 2013 the Commission undertook to 'set up a real-time central pool of shared resources and best practices among Member States and the industry'.
- Strengthen cooperation between the public and private sector on a European level through the European Public–Private Partnership for Resilience (EP3R).[4] It should further develop innovative measures and instruments to improve security, including that of critical infrastructure, and resilience of network and information infrastructure. EP3R should also engage with international partners to strengthen the global risk management of IT networks.

---

2   ENISA – European Network and Information Security Agency. 'ENISA is helping the European Commission, the Member States and the business community to address, respond and especially to prevent Network and Information Security problems' (ENISA website).

3   CERT (Computer Emergency Response Team) is the name given to expert groups that handle computer security incidents.

4   EP3R – European Public Private Partnership for Resilience.

- By 2011 the Commission, in conjunction with Internet service providers, law enforcement authorities and non-profit organisations, would develop guidelines on the handling of illegal Internet content – including incitement to terrorism.

Action 3: Improve capability for dealing with cyber attacks:

The document requires that:
- Every Member State, and EU institutions themselves, should have, by 2012, a well-functioning CERT, and that, once established, these should cooperate with law enforcement authorities cooperate in prevention and response.
- Member States should network together their national/governmental CERTs by 2012 to enhance Europe's preparedness, allowing the development of a European Information Sharing and Alert System (EISAS) to the wider public by 2013, and establish a network of contact points between relevant bodies and Member States.
- Member States should develop national contingency plans and undertake regular national and European exercises in incident response and disaster recovery.

(European Commission 2010a: 10).

Role of NATO

A further organisation that currently plays a major role in coordinating responses to cybercrime is NATO (the North Atlantic Treaty Organisation). In April 2008 NATO launched its Policy on Cyber Defence which allowed for extended cyber defence if requested from NATO Member States. The new policy envisaged a common coordinated approach to cyber defence and any response to cyber attacks. However, it did not allow for pre-emptive operations, but reflected an understanding that militarised cyber war was inherently escalatory. Through its Cyber Defence Management Authority (CDMA) established by the policy, NATO has the authority to respond immediately to cyber attacks on its members and to deploy support teams – also holding what are called annual 'red team' exercises 'aimed at engendering cooperation and awareness across the NATO community. NATO evidently hopes that its operations can provide a model of best practice that can filter down to national levels' (House of Lords 2010: 25).

Following the Lisbon Summit, a revised NATO policy on Cyber Defence was adopted in June 2011. According to the NATO website the 'policy sets out a clear vision on NATO's efforts in cyber defence throughout the Alliance', offering a 'coordinated approach to cyber defence across the Alliance with a focus on preventing cyber threats and building resilience. All NATO structures will be brought under centralised protection, and new cyber defence requirements will be applied' (NATO website). The policy also sets the principles on NATO's cyber defence cooperation with partner countries, international organisations, the private sector and academia. In parallel to the policy, a cyber defence Action Plan has been agreed' (NATO website).

However, in 2010 the House of Lords committee had identified the 'considerable overlap' in the membership of the European Union and NATO, and mentioned existing research which referred to inadequate cooperation and coordination between the two bodies, 'so that the work of each tends too often to duplicate the work of the other, rather than complementing it' (House of Lords 2010:25). Witnesses to the committee commented also that, although it was 'perhaps natural' that NATO should see itself as having a significant part to play where attacks had occurred against members, it had struggled to get agreement between member states on technical standards, and making NATO the lead agency for the coordination of cybercrime policy made cooperation with Russia, in particular, much harder. Overall the Lord's committee concluded 'the EU and NATO should urgently develop their thinking on working together, and the [UK] Government should encourage this to happen, to achieve cooperation rather than duplication. Just as with other aspects of civil protection, there is considerable overlap between the roles of the EU and NATO in relation to cyber attacks, and cooperation between them should be put on a more formal basis' (House of Lords, 2010:26, emphasis in original).

Conclusion

As the preceding chapter has demonstrated, both domestically and abroad there is a plethora of directives, communications and guidance about how cyber crime, cyber terror and cyber security should be addressed. Certain key themes emerge from this material consistently and continually; the need for an international perspective, the need for a partnership approach between the private and public sectors, and the importance of ensuring that the weakest element in the chain is strengthened in the interests of all. As one of the witnesses to the 2010 House of Lords Committee stated 'There is no one way to protect the Internet; many organisations have a role to play in this and clearly NATO has a role itself in protecting certain networks, the EU has a role and national bodies have a role as well' (House of Lords 2010:25).

The problem at the moment is that, while everyone is convinced that the solution to the problems of cyber security and cyber terror is global, nobody seems entirely clear how this might be achieved – particularly in the light of the unwillingness of certain key players (notably Russia and China) to adopt any of the existing standards. As the UN identified in 2010 'the global impact of the regional approaches that have been adopted by the Commonwealth, the Economic Community Of West African States (ECOWAS), the European Union and the Council of Europe – is limited as the approaches adopted are applicable only to the

States members of the respective organisation' (United Nations 2010: 10). Similar difficulties emerge with respect to the much vaunted public–private partnership model on which European cyber policy appears to be predicated.

In addition, the picture is confused by the multiplicity of bodies at both a domestic and international level that have identified a role for themselves around the determination of cyber security policy. Internationally this encompasses the Commonwealth, ECOWAS, the European Council, European Union, NATO and the United Nations, to name a few. On the domestic front, a practical illustration is provided by Downing, who, in early 2010 produced a tabular overview of 'current government responsibilities' (role, responsible body and remit) for cyber security in the UK. Under the heading 'Policy Coordination' she identified the Office of Cyber Security and Information Assurance (OCSI) based in the Cabinet Office. 'Strategic analysis' was the responsibility of the Cyber Security Operations Centre (CSOC) in GCHQ. 'Response and analysis' was the responsibility of three bodies; for the public sector it was provided by the UK's Government Computer Emergency Response Team (Gov Cert UK), for the MoD by the MoD Computer Emergency Response Teams and thirdly, the Combined Security Incident Response Team (CSIRTUK) provided response and analysis for critical infrastructure providers. Finally, under the heading of 'advice and guidance' she identified two bodies; the Centre for Protection of National Infrastructure (CPNI) and the National Technical Authority for Information Assurance, both providing advice to government departments and critical infrastructure providers on cyber attack (Downing 2011: 16). Obviously the description she provided has subsequently been supplemented by the introduction of the UK Defence Cyber Operations Group in 2011.

Further Reading

A useful summary of the development of UK cyber security policy is contained in Downing's 2011 overview. Detailed (if rather generic) guidance on the current direction of government policy is contained in the Cabinet Office's 'Cyber Security Strategy of the United Kingdom' (2009), the National Security Strategy (2010) and the Home Office's 'Cyber Crime Strategy' of the same year. Clearly, too, the revised Home Office cyber crime strategy, when (if?) it becomes available, will be essential reading. Details of European policy are to be found in the following European Commission publications: 'The EU Internal Security Strategy', 'The EU Internal Security Strategy in Action: Five steps towards a more secure Europe' and 'A digital agenda for Europe', all published in 2010.

References

Cabinet Office. 2009. *Cyber Security Strategy of the United Kingdom.* [Online]. Available at: http://www.official-documents.gov.uk/document/cm76/7642/7642.pdf [accessed: 24 June 2011].

Cabinet Office Website. *Cyber Security.* [Online]. Available at: http://www.cabinetoffice.gov.uk/content/cyber-security [accessed: 5 March 2011].

Cabinet Office Website. *OCSIA.* [Online]. Available at: http://www.cabinetoffice.gov.uk/content/office-cyber-security-and-information-assurance-ocsia [accessed: 24 June 2011].

Cabinet Office Website. *Cost of Cyber Crime* (posted 17th February 2011). [Online]. Available at: http://www.cabinetoffice.gov.uk/resource-library/cost-of-cyber-crime [accessed: 24 June 2011].

Cabinet Office Website. *US/UK Cyber-Communiqué* (posted 25/5/2011). [Online]. Available at: https://update.cabinetoffice.gov.uk/sites/default/files/resources/CyberCommunique-Final.pdf [accessed: 10 June 2011].

Consilium website. (nd). *Making the Lives of EU Citizens Safer.* [Online]. Available at: http://www.consilium.europa.eu/showFocus.aspx?lang=EN&focusID=447 [accessed: 27 June 2011].

Commission of the European Communities. 2009. *Protecting Europe from Large-Scale Cyber-Attacks and Disruption: Enhancing Preparedness, Security and Resilience.* [Online]. Available at: http://ec.europa.eu/information_society/policy/nis/docs/comm_ciip/comm_en.pdf [accessed: 5 July 2011].

Council of Europe. (nd). *Explanatory Report to the Convention on Cybercrime (ETS. No. 185). Council of Europe website.* [Online]. Available at: http://conventions.coe.int/Treaty/en/Reports/Html/185.htm [accessed: 21 June 2011].

Council of Europe. 2001. *European Treaty Series 185 Commission on Cybercrime: Budapest.* [Online]. Available at: http://conventions.coe.int/Treaty/Commun/QueVoulezVous.asp?NT=185andCM=8andDF=02/06/2010andCL=ENG [accessed: 10 June 2011].

CPNI. 2010. *Protecting against Terrorism (3rd edition).* [Online]. Available at:http://www.cpni.gov.uk/documents/publications/2010/2010002-protecting_against_terrorism_3rd_edition.pdf [accessed: 23 June 2011].

Downing, E. 2011. *Cyber Security: A New National Programme Standard Note SN/SC/5832 House of Commons Library.* [Online]. Available at: www.parliament.uk/briefing-papers/SN05832.pdf [accessed: 24 June 2011].

ENISA website. [Online]. Available at: http://www.enisa.europa.eu/about-enisa [accessed: 8 July 2011].

Europa website. *Commission to Boost Europe's Defences against Cyber Attacks* (posted 30th September 2010). [Online]. Available at: http://europa.eu/rapid/pressReleasesAction.do?reference=IP/10/1239andformat=HTMLandaged=1andlanguage=ENandguiLanguage=en [accessed: 24 June 2011].

European Programme for Critical Infrastructure Protection. [Online]. Available at: http://europa.eu/legislation_summaries/justice_freedom_security/fight_ against_terrorism/l33260_en.htm [accessed: 5 July 2011].

Council of the European Union. 2010. *The EU. Internal Security Strategy*. [Online]. Available at: http://register.consilium.europa.eu/pdf/en/10/st05/st05842-re02. en10.pdf [accessed: 27 June 2010].

European Commission. 2010a. *The EU Internal Security Strategy in Action: Five Steps Towards a More Secure Europe.* [Online]. Available at: http://ec.europa. eu/commission_2010–2014/malmstrom/archive/internal_security_strategy_ in_action_en.pdf [accessed: 24 June 2011].

European Commission. 2010b. *A Digital Agenda for Europe.* [Online]. Available at: http://ec.europa.eu/information_society/digital-agenda/documents/digital-agenda-communication-en.pdf [accessed: 27 June 2011].

European Council. 2008a. *Council Directive 20087/114/EC of 8 December 2008 on the Identification and Designation of European Critical Infrastructures and the Assessment of the Need to Improve their Protection.* [Online]. Available at: http://eur-lex.europa.eu/LexUriServ/LexUriServ.do?uri=OJ:L:2008:345:0075 :0082:EN:PDF [accessed: 8 July 2011].

EU. Council .2008b. *Fact Sheet: European Critical Infrastructure.* [Online]. Available at: http://www.eurunion.org/partner/euusterror/EUCritInfrastruct-Factsheet-6–5-08.pdf [accessed: 5 July 2011].

Harley, B. 2010. A Global Convention on Cybercrime? *The Columbia Science and Technology Law Review.* [Online]. Available at: http://www.stlr.org/2010/03/a-global-convention-on-cybercrime/ [accessed: 10 June 2011].

HM Government. 2009. *Pursue Prevent Protect Prepare: The United Kingdom's Strategy for Countering International Terrorism.* [Online]. Available at: http://tna.europarchive.org/20100419081706/http:/security.homeoffice.gov. uk/news-publications/publication-search/contest/contest-strategy/contest-strategy-2009?view=Binary [accessed: 23 June 2011].

HM Government. 2010a. *Securing Britain in an Age of Uncertainty: The Strategic Defence and Security Review.* [Online]. Available at: http://www.direct.gov.uk/ prod_consum_dg/groups/dg_digitalassets/@dg/@en/documents/digitalasset/ dg_191634.pdf?CID=PDFandPLA=furlandCRE=sdsr [accessed: 24 June 2011].

HM Government. 2010b. *A Strong Britain in an Age of Uncertainty: The National Security Strategy.* [Online]. Available at: http://www.direct.gov.uk/ prod_consum_dg/groups/dg_digitalassets/@dg/@en/documents/digitalasset/ dg_191639.pdf?CID=PDFandPLA=furlandCRE=nationalsecuritystrategy [accessed: 24 June 2011].

Home Office. 2009 *Science and Innovation Strategy.* [Online]. Available at: http://webarchive.nationalarchives.gov.uk/+/http://www.homeoffice.gov.uk/ documents/science-strategy2835.pdf?view=Binary [accessed: 4 July 2011].

Home Office. 2010. *Cyber Crime Strategy. The Stationery Office.* [Online]. Available at: http://www.official-documents.gov.uk/document/cm78/7842/7842. pdf [accessed: 24 June 2011].

Home Office website. *New National Crime Fighting Agency to Transform the Fight against Serious and Organised Crime* (posted 8th June 2011). [Online]. Available   at: http://www.homeoffice.gov.uk/media-centre/press-releases/ national-crime-agency [accessed: 24 June 2011].

House of Lords, European Union Committee. 2010. *Protecting Europe against Large-Scale Cyber Attacks. HL Paper 68.* The Stationery Office Limited: London. [Online]. Available at: http://www.publications.parliament.uk/pa/ ld200910/ldselect/ldeucom/68/68.pdf [accessed: 24 June 2011].

Intellect. 2010. *Improving Cyber-Security Partnerships: Government-Industry Information Sharing Mechanisms on Cyber Threats.* [Online]. Available at: http://www.intellectuk.org/component/content/article/136/6446-improving-cyber-security-partnerships [accessed: 21 June 2011].

Leyden, J. 2011. *UK finally Ratifies Cybercrime Convention during Obama Visit* (posted 25 May 2011). The Register. [Online]. Available at: http://www. theregister.co.uk/2011/05/25/uk_ratifies_cybercrime_convention/ [accessed: 10 June 2011].

Lobban, I. 2010. *Cyber: Threats and Security. International Institute for Strategic Studies website.* [Online]. Available at: http://www.iiss.org/recent-key-addresses/iain-lobban-address/ [accessed: 11 July 2011].

NATO website. *NATO Defence Ministers Adopt New Cyber Defence Policy* (posted 8/6/2011). [Online]. Available at: http://www.nato.int/cps/en/natolive/ news_75195.htm [accessed: 27 June 2011].

NATO website. *Cyber Defence: Next Steps* (posted 10/6/2011). [Online]. Available at: http://www.nato.int/cps/en/natolive/news_75358.htm?selectedLocale=en [accessed: 27 June 2010].

Sommer, P. and Brown, I. 2011. *Reducing Systemic Cyber Security Risk: OECD.* [Online].   Available   at: http://www.oecd.org/dataoecd/3/42/46894657.pdf [accessed: 21 June 2011].

United Nations. 2010. Recent Developments in the Use of Science and Technology by Offenders and by Competent Authorities in Fighting Crime, Including the Case of Cyber Crime. *Paper prepared for Twelfth United Nations Congress on Crime Prevention and Criminal Justice.* [Online]. Available at: http://www. unodc.org/documents/crime-congress/12th-Crime-Congress/Documents/A_ CONF.213_9/V1050382e.pdf [accessed: 5 July 2011].

Chapter 10

Policing Cyber Hate, Cyber Threats and Cyber Terrorism

Imran Awan and Brian Blakemore

Cyberspace is expanding and producing an ever increasing loss of reality as we move to living virtually. Soon arguably the distinction between the two states will no longer exist which coupled to a move to a culture of instant gratification and sound bites where the masses have little depth of analysis or contextualisation (Osborne 2002) is easing the work of the terrorist propaganda machine. Smith, cited in Pilkington (2011), has questioned if 'social networking is creating a generation of People 2.0'? Terrorism aims to deliver a narrative and not only is deception harder to identify online but also anonymous groups are stronger than face-to-face groups in recruiting, involving and committing their members to adhere to group norms and actions (see Chapter 3). Many countries have their own jurisdictions that define cyber terrorism but many jurisdictions would argue that their cyber terrorists are *virtual freedom fighters*, for example Muslim countries and Jihadists. The concern is that the discourse on cyber terrorism might actually alienate such communities and countries exacerbating the potential for perceived bias hence hindering needed relevant international agreements.

The authorities have been slow to realise the extent of virtual living and that ICT does not automatically work for freedom and democracy: Morozov states 'Because of cyber-utopian ideas, for the past 10 years the west has failed to think about how to use the Internet to its best advantage' (Pilkington 2011). This has recently been taken up in Britain with an increased emphasis on countering cyber crime and cyber terrorism (BBC News 2011a). However, the public is not sufficiently security conscious to the threat of cyber attack. Robinson (2011) cites research that found half of employees are less diligent regarding security on work ICT systems than with their home computers. Governments are not using their 'procurement power' to ensure the use of common standards to provide properly tested hardware and software (Sommer and Brown, 2011:12). Furthermore, governments need to rationalise cyber security standards used not only within a country but across national boundaries.

The threat from cyber terrorism is real and present and so this is an area that requires deeper discussion and critique from academics, the security and law enforcement agencies and governments (Yar 2006). However, the terminology (see Chapter 2) of what cyber terrorism is has remained problematic. There is no universal definition of cyber terrorism: Collin argued that the term meant the convergence of the physical and cyber world (1997). For Verton (2003), however, cyber terrorism is the execution of a surprise attack by terrorist groups that use computers and the Internet to cripple a nation's infrastructure. Furthermore, there are numerous conflicting interpretations of the term, as highlighted by Denning (2000) who argued that cyber terrorism is an attack which uses the computer as a weapon of warfare. In contrast Weimann (2005) argues that cyber terrorism is used for recruitment, propaganda purposes and gathering support through websites (see Chapter 2).

Tsfati and Weimann (2002) found terrorist groups do use the Internet to groom vulnerable individuals by justifying violence as a last resort option. They further noted that the groups use well-designed websites that contain content which is appealing to audiences for indoctrination purposes.

The debate over what the term cyber terrorism means has become a major legal, political and criminological issue. Notwithstanding the serious threat posed by cyber terrorism critics have argued cyber terrorism is nothing more than sensationalised fear-mongering (Wykes and Harcus 2010). The authors take the view that there are many forms of cyber hate, cyber threat and cyber terrorism and support the adoption of such a wide spectrum approach to defining cyber terrorism akin to that proposed by Weimann (2005:131) 'terrorists use of computers as a facilitator of their activities, whether for propaganda, recruitment, defaming communication or other purposes'. International agreement on the definition of cyber terrorism is needed as a precursor to developing meaningful, complete and holistic legislation protocols and agreements for dealing with this global phenomenon.

Fear of Cyber Terrorism

Terrorism is the use of violence and other activities to instil fear in the targeted public. There are very few studies in relation to the specific fear of cyber terrorism, as much of the literature focuses on the fear of cyber crime, yet these studies do provide an insight into criminological discourse on fear and terrorist use of the Internet. Stohl (2007) argues that:

> It is clear that despite the continuing reality that cyber terror remains a potential threat rather than an ongoing series of events, there has not developed a sense of security, comfort or complaisance in the popular press but rather a fear that this year or next is 'in fact' the year of maximum danger. (Stohl 2007: 223)

This prevalence of fear allows for reactive strategies that promote state meditated control mechanisms as Altheide (1997) puts it this creates a 'risk society'. Extremist groups are now increasingly using cyberspace to create a theatre of psychological fear that they hope will cause pandemonium and instil fear in vulnerable individuals. Grabosky and Stohl (2010) believe that cyber terrorism is a tool for psychological fear which aims to cause fear and provoke public sentiment. Thus Thomas (2003) states the Internet has become the new virtual playground for exacerbating fear: 'the net allows terrorists to amplify the consequences of their activities'(2003:115–116). Stohl (2007) goes further by arguing that the reason the public is fearful is because the word terrorism evokes memories of terrorist atrocities which in turn lead to emotional reactions caused by anger or hatred depending on its significance.

Felson (2002), however, suggests that the fear surrounding cyber crime (not cyber terrorism) is because criminals have become more determined and sophisticated in the level of harm they can inflict. Warr (1984) confirms the findings of Felson (2002) that there is a fear surrounding cyber crime in general. For Warr (1984), however, this is caused by motivated offenders and instead he argues that '*fear*' is measurable by differential age ranges. He argues that a younger individual is likely to be less fearful of cyberspace than an older person who has only used the Internet in limited circumstances. This is perhaps a dated view as the number of older people using Facebook is rapidly increasing after lagging the uptake by younger users (Hall 2011).

Moreover, Kao and Yang (2008) stress that this fear is because of change to peoples activities, as cyberspace has impacted upon everyday life, through telecommunications, entertainment and the media. In his book *Cybercrime: The Transformation of Crime in the Information Age*, David Wall (2007) argues that deviant behaviour can be linked to cyber criminal activity (which the authors argue could include cyber terrorism). In the same way terrorists have begun to use the Internet to create an atmosphere of fear and drama therefore making virtual relationships between vulnerable individuals and extremists.

The Balance between Security and Human Rights

The modern military concern with urban guerrilla action combined with the war on terror catalysed and sustains the growth of globally networked surveillance (Lyon 2007). Many of the creators of the technology and leaders of organisations that enable cyberspace have strong views regarding the use of the Internet and especially the role of the web: they argue that democratic government cannot monitor citizen's online activities as this snooping is against fundamental human rights and human network rights. They call for any legislation, protocols or conventions to respect basic human values and allow unfettered access to the Internet (Berners-Lee 2010). For Arquilla (2001) the balance is to maintain open and free societies and not to develop a society that is so fearful that it allows basic civil liberties to be severely eroded otherwise the terrorists have won.

In reviewing their Anti-Terrorist Act the Canadian Privacy Commissioner stated that the aim was to contain surveillance and increase both oversight and transparency (Stoddart 2005) The British deputy Prime Minister Nick Clegg claimed that the previous government had produced 'the most aggressive period of state interference in this country …' including abuse of surveillance activities and promised reform to get the balance of security and freedom right (Murphy 2011). For Lyon (2007:115) 'Questions of risk and trust, of security and opportunity, are central' and the 'categorical suspicion of today's policing renders everyone if not guilty at least dubious until proven innocent' (Lyon 2007:133). For example, US Senator Edward Kennedy was stopped and investigated while trying to fly within the US because his name appeared on a 'no fly' list (Goo 2004) and so there needs to be global agreement on what data is gathered and with whom and under what situations it is shared not just to fight terror but to protect our personal freedoms and identities. Recent British governments have proposed greater surveillance and disruption of terrorist recruitment campaigns for example on British university campuses – the Education Minister Ruth Kelly in 2005 and the Home Secretary Theresa May in 2011 have used the threat from terrorism to enact unpopular counter-terrorism policies (Lyon 2007 and BBC News 2011b). Furthermore the UK Cabinet Office minister Francis Maude stated that '… the highway needs rules and policing, not so as to restrict its use, but so as to keep it safe, reliable and open for all' (PS 2011c). However, the three cases discussed in Chapter 6 – Samina Malik was convicted under s58 of the Terrorism Act for 'collecting terrorist material' but later acquitted; five young men (R v Zafar 2008) were acquitted of charges of possessing extremist propaganda as they had no intention of using the material; and finally the research student held under the Terrorism Act for downloading terrorist material was researching in the area of 'counter-terrorism' and later released – question how the balance will be maintained under the heightened sense of risk and increased emphasis on fighting cyber threats.

Recent court cases show an increasing interventionist approach to policing cyberspace: Twitter registered in the US was required by the Superior Court of California to reveal the name of a user who posted allegations about fellow councillors of a British local authority in the UK (Dixon 2011). In the first case of its kind in the US, the FBI obtained a High Court order to take control of criminals' servers situated abroad to shut down a botnet that had infected 2 million computers in 2011. However the Dutch police obtained court permission to close down the Russian Bredolab botnet in 2010 (Police professional 2011). Supporting such interventions President Sarkozy spoke against an unregulated Internet and even suggested taxing Internet transactions at the 2011 G8 conference (Hall 2011).The e-crime manager at SOCA called for industry to help in the global fight against all cyber crime and cited problems of working across multiple jurisdictions without any common frameworks or protocols as the main problem in enforcing the law. He also pointed out that the regional Internet registries have little control over who puts material on the web, and SOCA with global partners have submitted proposals to police this aspect to the Internet Corporation for Assigned Names and Numbers (Police Professional 2010a).

Economic Conditions

Recent developments in global economic conditions are impacting security and policing. The UK, for example, has entered a new era of 'austerity policing' (HMIC 2010) and unfolding official policing discourses now refer to a need for organisational redesign, 'achieving more with less', a refocusing on the 'crime' mission and delivering 'value for money' (HMIC 2010, Home Office 2010, May 2010). Cowen (2011) of the independent think tank Civitas sees these developments as an opportunity to re-focus on core priorities based around 'violence and property' crimes. At the same time, he argues for a move away from the previous emphasis on 'hate crimes'. The present pre-occupation with the vague 'Big Society' concept (Home Office 2010) and its purported emphasis on the reassertion of local police professional judgement and increased community participation can also be seen as opening up space for future tensions between previously established victim-centred approaches and police discretion as well as between more and less powerful 'community' interests. It is not clear yet how or whether hate crime, radicalisation and cyber hate, cyber threat and cyber terrorism policing will be affected by this unfolding discourse of austerity policing, but there are certainly early warning signals that there may be new sets of 'winners' and 'losers' in this new policing landscape. An example of limited resources is that only 58 of 385 officers dedicated to online crimes are investigating terrorism, fraud, ID theft and other serious non-personal crimes. The rest are concerned with personal crimes such as child exploitation but all are stretched to the limit: 'all these cases indicate the scale of the challenge facing us. Yet my investigators tell me the expertise available to them is thin compared to that available to the cyber criminals' (Police Professional 2010b:12). However, Nick Harvey (UK, Armed Forces Minister) stated that offensive cyber weapons are to be developed funded from the £650 million allocated to UK cyber security over the next four years. Harvey also stressed that such cyber weapons were considered an essential part of the defence capability and that more cyber experts would be recruited as part of this expanded programme (PS 2011b, PS 2011c). This is contrary to the general thrust of the British Government's Strategic Defence Review requiring annual cuts of 8 per cent to the defence budget over the next four years (BBC News 2010). Elsewhere, Fleming and Grabosky's (2009) study of Australian police services' efforts to manage the public's 'insatiable appetite' for police services also highlights the potential consequences of adopting particular demand reduction strategies in a climate of reduced funding and rising expectations. The consequences of encouraging the public not to report, for example, raise important questions about trust, confidence and partnership working particularly where major social challenges are involved, such as hate crime and extremism.

The UK government's strategy of creating the 'Big Society' is a 'responsibilisation' strategy (Garland 2002) decentralising policing (and other activities) from government to communities and individuals. The coordination and effectiveness of such a process is ill defined. However, one successful example attributed to the Prevent strategy (part of the UK governments counter-terrorism policy) is the conviction of Isa Ibrahim who was reported to the police by members of his own Muslim community (Coliandris et al. 2011). Conversely the Home Secretary Theresa May stated that the reason for the review of the terrorist strategy was the serious failings identified with the existing Prevent policy (BBC 2011a).

Identifying the Cyber Terrorist

Online counter cyber terrorism operations are like finding a virtual needle in a virtual haystack. The monitoring of Internet communications is a monumental task and one that is increasing rapidly given the growth rate of use of the Internet. For example, analysing illegal online money-raising and flows of funds requires identifying relatively small amounts of funds and transactions in amongst billions of such transactions. The terrorists involved in the 9/11 attacks funded their operation using on average only $16,000 each (Levitt and Dubner 2009). Security forces need to be able to identify profiles of potential terrorists based on many real and/or cyber business and lifestyle datasets that will identify them before they strike. Thus knowledge management and intelligence-led policing approaches (Chapters 7 and 8) are paramount. Some specific aspects found to be used by terrorists in the US include opening a bank account with modest amounts of cash in large well-known banks, use of a post office address and frequent changes of address, the arrival of one large amount of funds that is then consumed in small amounts, regular international transactions, the lack of usual regular debits such as rent, utilities, insurance, no associated savings accounts and a high ratio of cash withdrawals.

This profile may be expected to change from country to country, from cult to cult and over time as the way of living changes generally. For example cash withdrawals may well become less useful as a predictor as society and business financial transactions become more automated and virtual. The profile will need to be particularly accurate because of the scarcity of terrorists in the general population. Levitt and Dubner (2009) give the example of an algorithm that is 99 per cent accurate: assuming there are 500 terrorists and 50 million adults in the UK, then 495 of the terrorists would be identified but so would 500,000 innocent individuals so the terrorists would still be in amongst a vast quantity of innocent individuals and police resources would not be available to investigate and eliminate the innocent from this large list of suspects particularly where the radicalisation process is rapid as in the UK with Al-Qaeda terrorists (Manningham-Buller 2007).

Some research in the UK has produced a profile of activities that will tend to identify terrorists, this includes a Muslim name, owing a mobile phone, registered as a student, renting accommodation. Some activities do not seem to discriminate between terrorist and citizen, such as employment status, marital status and living near to a mosque. Activities that suggest being an innocent citizen are having a savings account and buying life insurance (Levitt and Dubner 2009). Furthermore

Levitt and Dubner claim adding other factors will give the accuracy required to produce a set of suspects where one in six is likely to be a terrorist. The specific factors that make this algorithm so accurate cannot be revealed or the terrorist will merely avoid this set of activities. However, this lower ratio is such that police resources could be put into eliminating the innocent suspects from this list. This assertion is supported by the vice president of Google (Mayer cited in Burkeman 2011) who tweeted that credit card companies can predict with 98 per cent accuracy two years in advance that a couple will divorce, based upon changes in their spending patterns.

Policing or Oppression

Burkeman (2011) notes the erosion of privacy regarding the vast amount of information the police can obtain from Facebook and even to infiltrate where criminals might be interacting with each other or the general public. The Sudanese government allegedly used Facebook to catch dissidents by setting up a Facebook site to prompt a protest gathering then arresting all those who assembled to participate. Shirky (in Burkeman 2011) states that those who assembled did not know each other and obviously believed that the Facebook site was authentic. According to Shirky this proves that online social networking sites cannot be revolutionary on their own. Shirky is another advocate of decentralisation of control on the Internet and especially social networking sites and has coined the term 'the dictator's dilemma': the public can use the Internet as equally well as authoritarian leaders can to publish propaganda. The authoritarian response to block off social network sites or more dramatically turns off the whole Internet (as in Bahrain and Egypt in 2011), will anger protestors further. Not only will the act be seen as totalitarian control but also as affecting their lives which are now so dependent on the cyber world. So the dictator is on the horns of a dilemma in deciding whether to turn off the Internet or not. Another example of proactive online policing is that the UK Child Exploitation and Online Protection Centre (CEOPS) have successfully run sting operations to catch paedophiles with officers posing as young children on social networking sites. Private organisations are seen as a threat to liberty and privacy by some: WPP has built individual profiles of 500 million Internet users to aid targeted marketing by pooling data from many companies' databases (Foley 2011) as yet there are no laws to prevent such activities. The spectre of image recognition from public CCTV cameras, passport databases and Facebook pages being linked with personal transactions on the web to produce a total virtual identity tracking system for all looms large in the thoughts of those opposing the increase in cyber surveillance methods.

Policing Effectiveness, Partnerships and Structures

Security services are gathering increasing amounts of intelligence from an ever increasing amount of ICT usage as Intelligence can be said to underpin all aspects of counter terrorism work and is cast as its very lifeblood (Innes and Roberts, 2008). The modus operandi of the modern-day terrorist reveals increasing levels of sophistication which is making terrorists a formidable threat. Knowledge-management could act as the framework to enable the various organisations involved to counter this escalation in cyber threat. It is only by understanding the intelligence cycle, how information is gathered and disseminated, whilst continuing to engage with communities at all levels, that an effective response can be formulated to global problems such as cyber terrorism.

However, for intelligence to be transformed into knowledge and used holistically there needs to be a change in culture of police officers who are seen to be too fixed in their thinking and working practices. This may be especially true of the police service in England and Wales which has not required its officers to have a tertiary education, unlike some international law enforcement agencies, most notably the Federal Bureau of Investigation (FBI 2009).

Moreover the individual organisations within the partnerships need to understand the philosophy of knowledge-management, its purpose and how it supports that organisation's objectives and working practices. Consideration of intelligence and knowledge sharing is paramount as knowledge-management systems need to be coterminous with such partnerships. If international legislation and protocols allow knowledge management could result in a coordinated approach improved decision-making and strategies thus resulting in improved national and international security. The use of shared data is encouraged by the Prum treaty and the police and other organisations have developed new and innovative ways to communicate using large databases (Ratcliffe 2008). The sharing of such data raises human rights and privacy concerns among some which is exacerbated by the realisation that errors in the data may incorrectly incriminate innocent individuals. To make efficient use of this data the national intelligence model should be used as a common model throughout partnership organisations: NIM can be used at all levels of policing from daily tasking of local issues, then at the force level, both from regional and cross-border approaches – involving different organisations up to the final level, which encompasses national tasking and international coordination, all these levels are important in tackling cyber threats, cyber hate and cyber terrorism (Rogers 2006).

Knutson (in Hudson 1999) criticised the government of the US for its reactive and unstructured approaches to dealing with counter-terrorism arguing that it had been security and police centric and that it was not a coherent and holistic policy that had not moved beyond dealing with symptoms rather than attacking causes. Read in Chapter 9 describes the plethora of overlapping agencies and organisations within the UK; the overlap between the European Union agencies and NATO and the general confusion caused by a multiplicity of bodies at all levels. Arquilla (2001) argued that silos are commonplace in the US and suggests that the reason FBI for example, are not good at sharing information with local police forces is due to the vertical hierarchical policing structure. He promotes Interpol and Europol, as good examples of sharing intelligence. Field (2009) attributes fragmented agencies, cultural and institutional problems as the main areas that need improvement in the UK. Sloan (2010) claims that 'bureaucratic factionalism' is still endemic within security services in the US resulting in a failure to capture local intelligence. Various authors report on failings to share intelligence which may have prevented terrorist attacks (Howells et al. 2007, Shipman and Gardner 2010) and the FBI required some of its partner agencies at an information-sharing meeting to leave the room (USDOJ 2011). Arquilla argues that the security services' structures ought to mirror those of the terrorists, that is, having distributed and decentralised structures with many interconnections to gather data, interpret information and effectively use intelligence. This is necessary given the short time available to carry out investigations into cyber crime and to prevent cyber terror and investigations requiring lengthy formal procedures are unlikely to be effective (UN 2010: 4). Arquilla claims that 'What we really need to do is to focus on actually gathering intelligence by means of the Internet and the World Wide Web' and that such organisations 'can do more of this without impinging on civil liberties' (Arquilla 2001). Information Technology has enabled the police to develop new methods of policing across the world. Such styles include problem-orientated policing, intelligence-led policing, zero-tolerance policing and community policing.

Rogers, Gravelle and Brocklebank (2009) described the EU. Hague programme on cross-border information sharing as the way forward and the American president and the UK prime minister support a jointly funded and resourced review of cyber security projects; and to work on expanding the Budapest Convention on Cybercrime, which they regard as crucial in international cooperation to effectively deal with threats that operate across national borders (PS 20011a). Countries have taken the threat of cyber terrorism seriously and invested heavily in their ICT infrastructure. At the present moment there is a need for a more universal approach to develop protocols, strategies and legislation dealing with cyber terrorism related issues and agreed definitions to replace the vague terminology of current European Conventions. However, at present there is no global multilateral agreement for dealing with cyber terrorism (Harley 2010). The Council of Europe's Convention of Cybercrime (2001) has not attracted support from any countries outside Europe and without agreement from Russia and China and the majority of the international community is unlikely to be effective (see Chapter 9).

Terrorism, cyber terrorism, transnational and organised crime all have a community basis and the inability to implement community interaction effectively may well jeopardise outcomes such as policing and tackling cyber terrorist activity (Tilley 2008). This idea of engaging with communities in order to provide information and intelligence for multi-level use has been strongly reinforced by government in the UK (Home Office 2006). This policing style is citizen-focused, which revolves around policing in a manner that meets the needs of the community. Innes et al. (2011) studied the UK's Prevent strategy and found its implementation displayed considerable local variation 'It does not appear that these local variations have been derived from evidence-based assessments' (Innes et al. 2011:3), but that knowledge management and intelligent policing were not being utilised to their full potential. As ICT continues to develop it becomes even more even important that different agencies work together, in a coherent multi-agency partnership using such approaches to reduce cyber hate, cyber threats and cyber terrorism (see Chapters 5, 8 and 9). Arquilla (2001) proposes that the solution requires creating a hybrid of a hierarchy and a network and argues that this that will produce an efficient anti-terrorist measure. Further he stresses the need for intelligence, and law enforcement and military organisations to begin sharing information, to share the right information and to share useful information immediately. As Manningham-Buller (2007) points out each successful prosecution in the courts gives terrorists more understanding of police and security ability, including cyber-intelligence-gathering methods, and the terrorists will adapt their modus operandi to avoid detection driving technological leapfrogging (Chapter 1). She also stresses the importance of a wide network of foreign security and intelligence agencies and improved intelligence at community level in the UK.

> We must also continue to pursue smarter and more efficient ways of working together; this will include better information technology. Manningham-Buller (2007:45)

Knutson (1984 cited in Hudson 1999) also claimed security and police-centric policing advanced radicalisation and caused dissident groups to go underground to avoid police interventions. Hassan (in Dittmann, 2002:30) supports this view:

> We need to apply what we know about destructive mind-control cults, and this should be a priority with the war on terrorism. We need to understand the psychological aspects of how people are recruited and indoctrinated so we can slow down recruitment. We need to help counsel former cult members and possibly use some of them in the war against terrorism.

Hudson (1999) claims that governments rely too much on a 'military' based approach to counter political and religious extremist groups. On the other hand, market forces are not providing sufficient incentives for the general public and the private sector to invest sufficiently cyber security measures. To address this governance problem public–private partnerships would also be desirable on a national and international level; however European PPPs have not materialised so far (Commission of the European Communities 2009: 5–6).

Proactive counterterrorism policy should address root causes of the problem (see below). Counter strategies such as Prevent in the UK attempt to build social cohesion. Innes et al. (2011) found that British Muslims expressed a higher level of both trust and confidence in the police than do the general population. Innes et al. point out that this is so even though British Muslims are subject to more crime and disorder than are the general population. They conclude that Prevent policing does not appear to negatively impact on police and Muslim community relations despite the use of disruptive police interventions which are considered an important element of Prevent policing. Innes et al. (2011) suggest that they may be effective to deter extremists before they commit illegal acts. Unfortunately, they found that this element was the least well-developed part of 'Prevent' policing. However, Innes et al. research did indicate that young British Muslims had a negative perception of the police and indeed Awan (2011a) argues that Prevent policing tactics had led to Muslims feeling victimised and as a result have lost trust in policing. Manningham-Buller (2007) states that community engagement is important and that intelligence led targeting within a community will cause tension and that such tensions will arise will occur many times in the years ahead. She confirms that reducing these tensions and maintaining public support in such communities will require substantial effort and good communication channels and skills. Innes et al. (2011) found that British Muslims prefer informal social control that can be exerted within family and community to deal with issues if this is feasible. Also that the Muslim communities can be categorised into three groups: those who are anti-Prevent and anti-police, those who fully support Prevent and may be involved in or support prevent activities, and those who recognise the problems but have concerns regarding Prevent policing. So that the effort and communications referred to by Manningham-Buller (2007) will need to be customised for these three groups. Pantazis and Pemberton (2009) posit that the combination of recent government and media action in the UK has constructed the Muslim population as a suspect community; this labelling may hinder the social control needed and expected of this community. The arrest of five Bangladeshi tourists near to a nuclear power plant in England, who were later released without charge, is perhaps an illustration of this suspicion (Jeeves and Twomey 2011).

Dawar (2011) notes the reluctance of the British government to become 'subservient' to the European Union by agreeing to be part of a European-wide border guard system (Frontex). In general what is required for effective partnerships between security agencies within and across national boundaries is interagency relations (Crawford 1998) rather than multiagency relations. Crawford differentiates these two forms on whether the internal working of the partners are changed to suit the partnership (interagency) or whether they remain fixed in their old patterns and structures (multiagency) and so are not fit for the wider roles required of the organisation.

Cyber Hate

Hate crime cannot be meaningfully reduced to simple or single explanations or solutions. Attacks on the general public by terrorists or cyber terrorists are not hate crimes although anyone can be a victim. However, there are many similarities with cyber terrorism including:

- a continuum of escalation of activities similar to terrorism;
- the Janus face of the Internet, an aid both the commission of hate crime and the policing of it;
- the Internet amplifies messages and ideologies and creates space for a sense of belonging and identity to emerge that allows otherwise separate interests to unite and to be recruited;
- criticism of contemporary UK government security strategies for their 'bias' and disproportionate targeting of Muslims while neglecting other forms of extremism or terrorism;
- disconnects between high-level policy and frontline police practice and between different organisations that are involved in countering such activities;
- use of intelligence-led policing and community policing is vital common to policing both activities;
- use of less formal social control such as Southern Poverty Law Center and its 'Intelligence Project' for countering cyber hate;
- requirement for multidimensional strategies to operate transnationally as well as accounting for localised conditions and to create improvements at the policy and practice levels among a broad range of services.

Chakraborti and Garland (2009) note evidence for both progress and ongoing concern in the UK policing of hate crime. Examples of progress include the move towards a more victim-centred approach, the establishing of hate crime as a policy priority and the introduction of more sensitive and sophisticated reporting and investigation procedures (see also Hall 2005). However, as Chakraborti and Garland (2009) argue, there is a need for caution when assessing levels of progress in this area in the post-Macpherson era. In his view, there remain major concerns over policing, particularly in respect of responses to the needs of internally heterogeneous communities and in relation to the power of discretion that persists at the level of the individual frontline officer.

Social Control

Civil social control can be a strong factor in countering terrorism: in Peru the government defeated rural terrorists using an armed civilian militia that not only fought the terrorists but also generated reassurance that enabled them to collect the intelligence needed for government action (Hudson 1999). Can this level of involvement be generated online to help counter cyber hate, cyber threat and cyber terrorism activities? British minister Francis Maude recognises the need for such involvement as part of a wide network: 'Making it happen means working together; forging relationships not only between government departments and agencies but between public and private, across borders and with wider society, right down to each individual one of us, sitting at home in the glow of our all-enabling laptops' (PS 2011c). The use of an anonymous referral system for members of the public set up by the Counter Terrorism Internet Referral Unit in March 2011 aims is encourage this form of social control as outlined in Chapter 6. The problem with such cyber terrorism policing is that it allows for state censorship and the individuals fearing openly expressing their views on chat rooms or Internet forums through fear of prosecution. Social coherence is vital hence initiatives such as those within UK Contest, Prevent strategies as Bacon et al. (2006:24) state 'When social cohesion breaks down, one of the losses is communities' capacities to self police ...'. How applicable this argument is to social control on in cyberspace is unknown. Virtual networks can produce social interaction, generate ties and provide support mechanisms in other words become a community with social capital (Wellman and Gulia 1998).However, to understand cyber terrorism governments need to develop effective ways to challenge the role of the Internet as a radicalisation tool. They have developed some interventions which have been addressed at this that seek to change behaviour (that is, disengagement) and others that aim to de-radicalise.

Dealing with Root Causes

As argued in Chapter 3 the only way to manage cyber hate and cyber terrorism psychologically is to focus on the prevention of recruitment of new members. The issues identified in Chapters 3 and 4 such as social identity theory, de-individuation, social categorisation, out group hostility and models of cultic recruitment and thought reform must be harnessed in order to deter others from becoming radicalized and eventually joining a terrorist group.

Within this context it is also crucial to try and understand the link of cyber terrorist activity with individual's actions that is, understanding the process of how people become terrorists and their method of choosing the Internet to promote violence. Personality tests have found that those within a terrorist group tend to have similar results with regard to schizophrenic tendency, psychotic deviation, depression and hypomania (see Chapter 3) how this similarity might drive behaviour is less clear. The social learning theory is a good example (Freiburger and Crane 2008). This theory asserts that individuals learn deviant behaviour from other groups, which then leads to extremist learning that is categorised by association, definitions, differential reinforcement, and imitation processes. Freiburger and Crane (2008) argue that mechanisms of the social learning theory are used by terrorist groups when on the Internet as a tool that helps them to facilitate terror attacks and recruitment. This perspective of deviant behaviour and methods offers a thought provoking insight into the processes that transform naive individuals like David Copeland and Andrew Ibrahim into violent extremists (see Chapters 2 and 3).

Freiburger and Crane refer to a European case study in which Peter Cherif was recruited by Al-Qaeda over the Internet through a similar learning process. They argue that if groups become marginalised they become more susceptible to using the Internet for terrorist purposes. Furthermore, Day (2011) asserts that he became a hacker to belong to the digital community which is supported by Rogers (2003) who noted hackers were loners that had a desire to form groups with others through online chat rooms.

Political and religious discontent, radicalisation, extremism and terrorism may have several specific root causes driving each activist group for example Day (2011) notes terrorist activities including cyber attacks by Team Hell – Palestinian activists who attack Israeli networks and Chinese hackers inspired by anti-American sentiments who target US companies. At some point the government(s) concerned must discuss the root cause with some form of representative body in an open dialogue to find a compromise solution for the majority of those affected in order to defeat the extremists elements within their midst. Faria and Acre (2005, see Chapter 3) stress that openness in discussing and solving differences of political opinion is the most important factor in the prevention of terrorism. This reconciliation process has achieved some success in both South Africa and in Northern Ireland. However, splinter extremist groups may continue even though the majority no longer support them or their actions. Taylor and Quayle (1994 cited in Hudson 1999) note the Provisional IRA in 1994 still mustered electoral support of around 60,000 in Northern Ireland elections. In more recent times sporadic bomb attacks have resumed despite shared government involving the political wing of the original IRA and in a recent British security strategy (A Strong Britain in an Age of Uncertainty), the government included the possibility of an increase in violence from dissident groups in Northern Ireland in future calculations (BBC News 2010).

Amnesty offers and reducing penal sentences can also help to reduce the number of activists Taylor and Quayle (1994 cited in Hudson 1999) suggest that it produced significant long-term reduction in terrorist violence in both Italy and Germany. The terrorists do not have to renounce their ideological convictions, only their violent methods. So that extremist and terrorist activities should be replaced by legal actions of a political party representing the ideals of the former terrorist group.

Conclusion

The need for concerted holistic flexible rapid action both prevention and possible response at all levels from neighbourhood to international has been made but little headway has been made to date. Policing models and analytical models exist and can be effective if used within accepted and agreed frameworks. The balance between human rights and counter-terrorism policing is a sensitive issue and all parties to any changes in legislation and practice need to be involved and supportive of the changes. There also needs to be more accountability when it comes to dealing with Muslim communities in the realms of cyber space by making counter-terrorism legislation proportionate (Awan 2011b). Ultimately the roots causes of cyber hate and cyber terrorism must be resolved to provide a long-term solution.

Further reading

Report on the Operation in 2009 of the Terrorism Act 2000 and Part 1 of the Terrorism Act 2006. Carlile, Lord of Berriew, QC. 2010. [Online]. Available at: http://www.homeoffice.gov.uk/publications/counter-terrorism/independent-reviews/ind-rev-terrorism-annual-rep-09?view=Binary [accessed: 8 July 2011].

References

Altheide, D. 1997. The News Media, the Problem Frame and the Production of Fear. *The Sociological Quarterly*, 38 (4), 647–68.

Arquilla, J. 2001. *Global Q & A: Netwar – Fighting a Global Terrorist Network.* [Online]. Available at: http://www.fpa.org/topics_info2414/topics_info_show.htm?doc_id=85640. [accessed: 3 March 2011].

Awan, I. 2011a. Rebels with a Cause: Terror in the name of Prevent. *Police Professional*. February 24.

Awan, I. 2011b. A Lesson in How Not to Spy upon Your Community, Special Issue, Myths and Criminal justice. *Criminal Justice Matters*, 80, 10–11.

Bacon, N. and James, S. 2006. Working with Communities to Tackle Low Level Disorder and Antisocial Behavior. *Criminal Justice Monthly*, 64, summer edition, 24–5.

BBC News. 2010. Cyber attacks and terrorism head threats facing UK. [Online]. Available at: http://www.bbc.co.uk/news/uk-11562969 [accessed: 30 March 2011].

BBC News. 2011a.Updated anti-extremism strategy published. [Online]. Available at: http://www.bbc.co.uk/news/uk-13679360 [accessed 17 June 2011].

BBC News. 2011b. Loughborough student disputes Islamic extremism claims. [Online]. Available at: http://www.bbc.co.uk/news/uk-england-leicestershire-13681066. [accessed: 1 June 2011].

Berners-Lee, T. 2010. Long Live the Web. *Scientific American*, December, 56–61.

Burkeman, O. 2011. Reality Check, *Guardian*, g2, 15 March, 7–10.

Chakraborti, N. and Garland, J. 2009. *Hate Crime: Impact, Causes and Responses.* London: Sage Publications.

Coliandris, G., Rogers, C. and Gravelle, J. 2011. Smoke and Mirrors, or a Real Attempt at Reform?. *Policing: Journal of Policy and Practice*, 1–1.1.

Collin, B. 1997. The Future of Cyberterrorism: The Physical and Virtual Worlds Converge. *Crime and Justice International*, March.

Commission of the European Communities. 2009. Protecting Europe from large scale cyber-attacks and disruption: enhancing preparedness, security and resilience. [Online]. Available at: http://ec.europa.eu/information_society/policy/nis/docs/comm_ciip/comm_en.pdf [accessed 5 July 2011].

Cowen, N. 2011. These Are the Crimes to Fight, PC Cutback, *Sunday Times*, 13 March, 27.

Crawford, A. 1998. Community Safety and the Quest for Security: Holding Back the Dynamics of Social Exclusion. *Policy Studies*, 19, 237–53.

Dawar, A. 2011. New EU Guards to Police Our Borders, *Daily Express*, 2 May, 30.

Day, C. 2011. Superhackers: Inside the mind of the new cyber vandals threatening global security - by a man who used to be one. *Daily Mail* [Online]. Available at: http://www.dailymail.co.uk/news/article-2008841/Superhackers-Inside-minds-cyber-vandals-threatening-global-security.html. [accessed: 22 February 2012].

Denning, D. 2000. Cyber-terrorism: Testimony before the Special oversight Panel on Terrorism Committee on Armed Services, US House of Representatives, 23 May 2000. [Online]. Available at: www.cs.georgetown.edu/~denning/infosec// cyberterror.html [accessed: 10 March 2011].

Dittmann, M. 2002. Cults of Hatred. *The Monitor*, American Psychological Association. [Online]. 33 (10), 30. Available at: http://research.apa.org/ monitor/nov02/cults.aspx. [accessed: 1 March 2011].

Dixon, S. 2011. Twitter Forced to Hand Court User's Secrets, *Daily Express*, 25 May, 30.

Duaux, K. 1996. Social Identification, in Higgins, E.T. and Kruglanski, A.W. (eds.), *Social Psychology: Handbook of Basic Principles*. New York: Guilford Press, 777–98.

Faria, J. and Arce, D. 2005. Terror Support and Recruitment. *Defence and Peace Economics*, 16 (4), 263–73.

FBI. 2009. *Federal Bureau of Investigation: Career*. [Online]. Available at: http:// www.fbijobs.gov/111.asp [accessed: 9 September 2009].

Felson, M. 2002. *Crime and Everyday Life*. 3rd edn, California: Sage.

Field, A. 2009. Tracking Terrorist Networks: Problems of Intelligence Sharing within the UK Intelligence Community. *Cambridge Journals, Review of International Studies*. (35), 997-1009.

Fleming, J. and Grabosky, P. 2009. Managing the Demand for Police Services, or How to Control an Insatiable Appetite. *Policing: A Journal of Policy and Practice*, 3 (3), 281–91.

Foley, S. 2011. Database Boasts It Will Track Web Behaviour of Everyone in UK, *Independent*, 28 June, 7.

Freiburger, T. and Crane. J. 2008. A Systematic Examination of Terrorist Use of the Internet. *International Journal of Cyber Criminology*, 2 (1), 309-319.

Garland, D. 2002. *The Culture of Control: Crime and Social Order in Contemporary Society*. Oxford: Oxford University Press.

Goo, S.K. 2004. Sen. Kennedy Flagged by No Fly List. *Washington Post*. [Online]. Available at: www.washingtonpost.com/wp-dyn/articles/A17073–2004Aug19.html [accessed 15 April 2011].

Grabosky, P. and *Stohl*, M. 2010. *Crime and Terrorism*. Sage: London.

Hall, M. 2011. Sarkozy Targets Web 'Anarchy', *Daily Express*, 5 May, 27.

Hall, N. 2005. *Hate Crime*. Cullompton: Willan Publishing.

Harley, B. 2010. A global convention on cybercrime? *The Columbia Science and Technology Law Review*. [Online]. Available at:http://www.stlr.org/2010/03/a-global-convention-on-cybercrime/ [accessed 10 June 2011].

Hall, R. 2011. Facebook Flourishes among Over-50s, *Independent*, 28 June, 11.

Her Majesty's Inspectorate of Constabulary (HMIC). 2010. *Valuing the Police: Policing in an Age of Austerity*. London: Home Office.

Home Office. 2006. *From Policing the Local beat to Disrupting Global Crime Networks: Reforming the Structure of Policing in the 21st Century*. London: TSO.

Home Office. 2010. *Cyber Crime Strategy.*Cm. 7842. London: TSO.

Howells, K. and Beckett, M. 2007. Could 7/7 have been prevented? Review of the intelligence on the London terrorist attacks on 7 July 2005. Report presented to Intelligence Security Committee. [Online] .Available at: http://www.fas.org/irp/world/uk/july7review.pdf [accessed 8 July 2011].

Hudson, R.A. 1999. The sociology and psychology of terrorism: who becomes a terrorist and why? Federal Research Division, Library of Congress. [Online]. Available at: http://www.loc.gov/rr/frd/pdffiles/Soc_Psych_of_Terrorism.pdf. [accessed: 28 February 2011].

Innes, M. and Roberts, C. 2008. Reassurance Policing, Community Intelligence and the Co-Production of Neighbourhood Order, in Williamson, T., *The Handbook of Knowledge-Based Policing*. Chichester: Wiley.

Innes, M., Roberts, C. and Innes, H. 2011. Assessing the effects of prevent policing. A report to the Association of Chief Police Officers Cardiff University's Police Science Institute March. [Online]. Available at: www.upsi.org.uk [accessed 31 may 2011].

Jeeves, P. and Twomey, J. 2011. Five Arrested at Nuclear Plant, *Daily Express*, 1 May, 4.

Kao, D. and Yang, S. 2008. The IP Address and Time in Cyber-Crime Investigation. *International Journal of Police Strategies and Management*, 32 (2), 194–208.

Knutson, J.N. 1984. Toward a United States Policy on Terrorism. *Political Psychology*, 5 (2), June, 287–94.

Levitt, S.D. and Dubner, S.J. 2009. *Super Freak-onomics*. London: Penguin.

Lyon, D. 2007. *Surveillance Studies: An Overview*. Cambridge, UK: Polity.

Manningham-Buller, E. 2007. Partnership and Continuous Improvement in Countering Twenty-First Century Terrorism. *Policing: A Journal of Policy and Practice*, 1 (1), 43–5.

May, T. 2010. Theresa May's speech to the National Policing Conference. [Online]. Available at: http://www.homeoffice.gov.uk/media-centre/speeches/ [accessed 05 July 2010].

Murphy, J. 2011. Clegg: Scrap Control Orders and Give People Freedom, *Evening Standard*, 7 January, 8.

National White Collar Crime Center. 2002. *Computer Crime: Computers as the Instrumentality of the Crime*. Washington: US Congress.

Osborne, R. 2002. *Megawords*. London: SAGE Publications.

Pantazis, C. and Pemberton, S. 2009. From the 'Old' to the 'New' Suspect Community. *British Journal of Criminology*, 49 (5), 646–66.

Pilkington, E. 2011. Evgeny Morozov: How Democracy Slipped through the Net. *Guardian*. [Online]. Available at: http://www.guardian.co.uk/technology/2011/jan/13/evgeny-morozov-the-net-delusion [accessed: 14 January 2011].

PS. 2011a. Obama and Cameron take steps on cyber security. [Online]. Available at: http://www.publicservice.co.uk/news_story.asp?id=16411 [accessed 6 June 2011].

PS. 2011b. UK to go on cyber offensive. [Online]. Available at: http://www.publicservice.co.uk/news_story.asp?id=15539 [accessed: 6 June 2011].

PS. 2011c. Maude: cyber highway needs policing. [Online]. Available at: http://www.publicservice.co.uk/news_story.asp?id=16493 [accessed 6 June 2011].

Police professional. 2010a. SOCA emphasises value of collaboration in fight against cyber crime. [Online]. Available at: www.policeprofessional.com [accessed: 13 April 2011].

Police professional. 2010b. E-specialists as important as frontline officers. [Online]. Available at: www.policeprofessional.com [accessed: 13 April 2011].

Police professional. 2011. FBI controls criminal servers to disable international botnet. [Online]. Available at: www.policeprofessional.com [accessed: 5 June 2011].

Ratcliffe, J. 2008. Intelligence-Led Policing, in Worthley, R., Mazerolle, L., Rombouts, S. (eds), *Environmental Criminology and Crime Analysis*. Cullompton, Willan Publishing.

Robinson, D. 2011. Don't get Caught Cold!. *Chemical Engineer*, 22, June.

Rogers, C. 2006. *Crime Reduction Partnerships*. Oxford: Oxford University Press.

Rogers, C., Gravelle, J. and Brocklebank, H. 2009. The Knowledge Cycle and Tackling Terror. *Policing Today*, 15 (4), 21–3.

Rogers, M. 2003. The Nature of Computer Crime: A Social-Psychology Examination, in Turrini, E. (ed.), *Understanding Computer Crime*. New York: Auerbach.Shipman, T. and Gardner, D. 2010. Furious Obama Blasts US Intelligence for Failing to Connect the Dots over Christmas Day Bomber, *Daily Mail*, 6 January, 2.

Sloan, S. 2010. Meeting the Threat: The Localization of Counter Terrorist Intelligence. *Police Practice and Research*, 3 (4), 337–45.

Sommer, P. and Brown, I. (2011) Reducing systemic cybersecurity risk. [Online]. Available at: http://www.oecd.org/dataoecd/3/42/46894657.pdf [accessed 21 June 2011].

Stoddart, J. 2005. Letter to Alberta and BC Privacy Commissioners. [Online]. Available at: www.privcom.gc.ca/legislation/let_040312_e.asp/ [accessed 14 January 2011].

Stohl, M. 2007. Cyber Terrorism: A Clear and Present Danger, the Sum of All Fears. Breaking Point or Patriot Games?. *Crime, Law and Social Change*, 46, 223–38.

Taylor, M. and Quayle, E. 1994. *Terrorist Lives*. London and Washington: Brassey's.

Thomas, T.L. 2003. Al-Qaeda and the Internet: The Danger of 'Cyberplanning.' *Parameters*, 33 (1), 112–23.

Tilley, N. 2008. The Development of Community Policing in England: Networks, Knowledge and Neighbourhoods, in Williamson, T. *The Handbook of Knowledge-Based Policing*. Chichester: Wiley.

Tsfati, Y., and Weimann, G. 2002. www.terrorism.com: Terror on the Internet. *Studies in Conflict & Terrorism*, 25 (5), 317–32.

United Nations. 2010. 'Recent developments in the use of science and technology by offenders and by competent authorities in fighting crime, including the case of cybercrime'. Paper prepared for Twelfth United Nations Congress on Crime Prevention and Criminal Justice. [Online]. Available at: http://www.unodc.org/documents/crime-congress/12th-Crime-Congress/Documents/A_CONF.213_9/V1050382e.pdf [accessed: 5 July 2011].

USDOJ. 2011. The federal bureau of investigation's ability to address the national security cyber intrusion threat. Audit Report 11–12 April. Washington: US Department of Justice.

Verton, D. 2003. *Black Ice: The Invisible Threat of Cyber-Terrorism*. New York: McGraw-Hill Osborne.

Wakefield, A. and Fleming, J. 2009. *The Sage Dictionary of Policing*. London: Sage.

Wall, D. 2001. *Crime and the Internet*. London: Routledge.

Wall, D. 2007. *Cybercrime: The Transformation of Crime in the Information Age*. Cambridge: Polity Press.

Warr, M. 1984. Fear of Victimisation: Why are Women and the Elderly More afraid?. *Social Science Quarterly*, 65 (3), 681–702.

Weimann, G. 2005. Cyber Terrorism: The Sum of All Fears? *Studies in Conflict and Terrorism*, 28, 129–35.

Wellman, B. and Gulia, M. 1998. Net Surfers Don't Ride Alone: Virtual Communities as Communities, in Kollock, P. and Smith, M. (eds), *Communities in Cyberspace*. Berkeley: University of California Press.163–90.

Wilson, C. 2005. *Computer Attack and Cyberterrorism: Vulnerabilities and Policy Issues for Congress*. Congress Research Service , 8–10.

Wykes, M. and Harcus, D. 2010. Cyber-Terror: Construction, Criminalisation and Control, in Yar, M. and Jewekes, Y. (eds), *Handbook of Internet Crime*. Willan: Cullumpton, 214.

Yar, M. 2006. *Cybercrime and Society*. London: Sage Publications, 185.

Index

spectrum 80–1
texts 90
see also cyber crime; cyber hate
Homeland Security Service (US) 10
HTTP 6
Hudson, R.A. 58, 59, 60, 66, 182
human rights, security, balance 106, 175–6
Huntley, Ian 137

'I Love You' virus, cost of damage 26
Ibrahim, Andrew 24, 186
Ibrahim, Isa 178
identity
    in crisis 78
    formation 79
        and CMC 84
    and hate crime 78–9
    and religious affiliation 79
India, cyber attacks on 98
individuation 44
indoctrination, cults 64, 70
information
    nature of 113
    transformation of 114
Information and Communication
        Technology (ICT) 182
    definition 6
    success factors 7
Information Management Systems (IMS)
        123
information technology (IT), definition 138
infrastructures, critical
    and cyber terrorism 33, 95, 100, 102
    definition 161fn1
    'five pillars' 162
    information 161
    protection
        CPNI 23, 150, 168
        EPCIP 161
    vulnerability 5, 22, 23, 26, 149
Intel Centre 30
intelligence cycle 130, 131–3, 144, 180
    collection 133
    direction 132–3
    dissemination 133
    evaluation/analysis 133
    see also National Intelligence Model
        (NIM)

Intelligence Project, Southern Poverty Law
        Center (US) 89, 184
Intelligence Surveillance Systems (ISS)
        124
intelligence-led policing *see under* policing
Internet 6
    and cyber hate 88
    Munchausen by 47
    online killings 32
    and social networks 69–70
    and social progress 84
    as terror tool 32, 69–70, 84
    use statistics 33
    see also ISPs
Iran, nuclear capability, cyber attack on 8,
        102
Irish Republican Army (IRA) 28, 67, 186
Islamophobia, and terrorism 79
ISPs (Internet Service Providers) 10, 155

Jonestown mass suicides 64

Karim, Rajib 9, 26, 61
Kaspersky 8
Kelly, Ruth 176
knowledge
    discovering 118
    evaluating 119
    explicit 116–17
    generating 118
    leveraging 120
    processes 113–14
    sharing 120
    tacit 114, 115
        model 116
    types of 115–16
knowledge continuum model 113
knowledge management
    application problems 120–3
    components 123
    coordination 121
    and cyber terrorism 112, 118, 124–5,
        180
    cycle 118–20
    definition 118
    limitations, overcoming 123–4
    role 117–20
    success factors 122

For Product Safety Concerns and Information please contact our
EU representative GPSR@taylorandfrancis.com Taylor & Francis
Verlag GmbH, Kaufingerstraße 24, 80331 München, Germany